A Site of Struggle

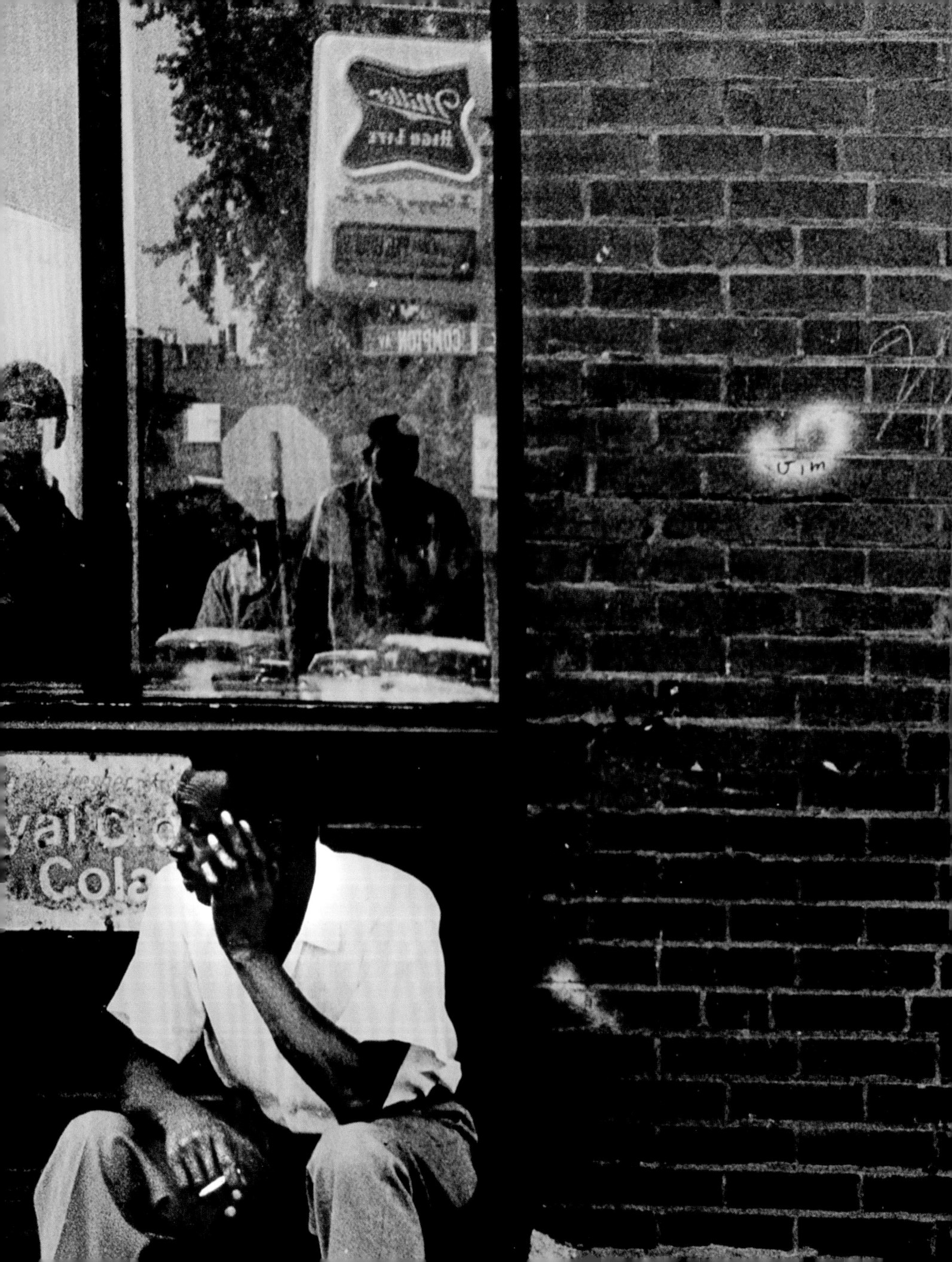

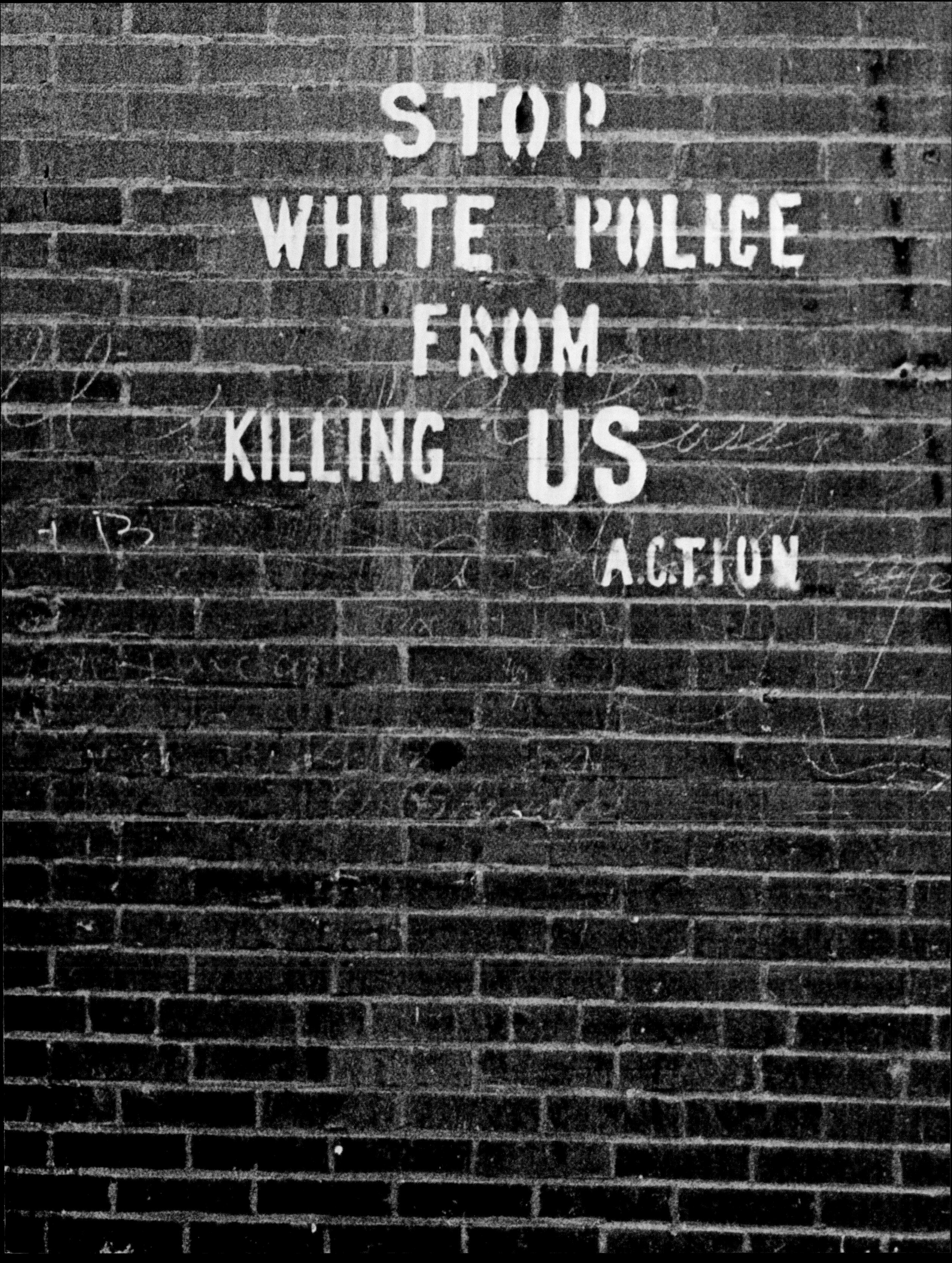
STOP
WHITE POLICE
FROM
KILLING US
A.C.TION

Mary and Leigh Block Museum of Art
Northwestern University, Evanston, Illinois

In association with
Princeton University Press
Princeton and Oxford

A Site of Struggle

American Art against Anti-Black Violence

Edited by Janet Dees

With contributions by
Sampada Aranke
Courtney R. Baker
Huey Copeland
Leslie M. Harris
LaCharles Ward

Contents

Director's Foreword

The Block Museum of Art is committed to scholarship focused on histories that are overlooked, understudied, or suppressed. This commitment acknowledges the imperative for museums to challenge dominant historical narratives. It also centers what works of art do: their particular visual language brings history very close to us by reflecting the perspectives and experiences of others, as well as our own. Works of art are unflinching—they hold our gaze, ask questions of us and our world, and humanize what we learn and unlearn as "history." The Block holds space for visitors to engage in critical acts of looking and meaning making through incandescent encounters with art and with history that illuminate our present. We believe deeply in the powerful capacity of art and exhibitions to awaken empathy and what historian Courtney R. Baker has called "humane insight," and, in so doing, also to awaken a consciousness of our agency in imagining different futures.

When Janet Dees presented the exhibition proposition for *A Site of Struggle: American Art against Anti-Black Violence* in its nascent form in 2017, its significance and connection to the Block's core values were already apparent. The exhibition interrogates the ethical questions surrounding the production and act of looking at images of Black bodies in pain by focusing on some of the artists and activists who shaped this discourse for over one hundred years. With sensitivity and respect for visitors and for the museum staff, and for the Block's frontline workers in particular, Janet and our Block colleagues developed a structure of care—strategies for both display and visitor experience. These efforts, and the essays in this book, bring us into proximity with artists' expressions of mourning, memorializing, and protest, while anticipating the potential for strong emotional responses that may result. In working diligently to balance exhibition content with the responsibility of the Block to that content, *A Site of Struggle* reflects the promise of ethical exhibition making for shaping personally transformative encounters with art and material culture revealing undeniable historical truths.

This exhibition is taking place during a continuing racial reckoning in the United States and across the globe. In this context, it raises critical questions: Who gets to tell this story? Who owns history? Who shapes the future? These questions go to the heart of current cultural debates that are inflected by race and violence, from the teaching of American history to legislation affecting civil liberties, from the electoral process and gun rights to environmental and economic policies. These United States were founded on violence: toward Indigenous populations, toward enslaved Africans, and toward the land itself. The very writing of this history is an ongoing site of struggle. It is unsurprising that artists of diverse identities, attuned to our culture, have taken the many forms of these continuous histories of anti-Black violation and violence in the United States as subjects in their work. The Block honors their work and these histories with *A Site of Struggle*.

At Northwestern University, as at other institutions of higher education in the United States, we continue to reckon with our institutional history of perpetuating injustice and to grapple with what it means to live our stated values. The Block is a unique campus space in which art is a springboard for discussion of current ideas and issues, including racial equity and difficult histories. The Northwestern community embraced the opportunity proffered by *A Site of Struggle* for institutional self-reflection, for teaching, learning, and research, and for strengthening the Block's relationship with the citizens of Evanston, Illinois. I am abundantly grateful to Northwestern University's administration, its faculty and students, the Block's Board of Advisors, and Evanston community advisors for their overwhelming support of the museum's mission and *A Site of Struggle*.

I wish to thank all our funders, lenders, artists, and contributors to this publication for their support. The vision and extraordinary support of the Terra Foundation for American Art has enabled this exhibition to travel to the Montgomery Museum of Fine Arts in Montgomery, Alabama. We thank the museum's director, Angie Dodson; curator, Jennifer Jankauskas; and the city's mayor, Steven L. Reed, for their leadership and for accepting the Block's invitation to share *A Site of Struggle* with their region, a central stopping point on the Civil Rights Trail.

It is humbling to work with my colleagues at the Block, not least of all Janet Dees, who has led this project. It takes extraordinary inner strength to delve so deeply into the subject of anti-Black violence even as Black lives and Black civil rights continue to be violated. Janet and her colleague Alisa Swindell, curatorial research associate, welcomed rigorous discussion and collaboration. Inspired by their scholarship and their generosity, the entire Block team has dedicated itself to realizing the potential for *A Site of Struggle*. Nested within our broader commitment to diversity, equity, access, and inclusion, we are using what we have learned together to continue changing our work and our organizational culture to be true to this commitment. The exhibition and this book are reflections of what the Block aspires to be and how we will use the privileged platform of the academic art museum to have impact in the world.

Lisa Graziose Corrin
Ellen Philips Katz Director

Acknowledgments

A project like *A Site of Struggle* is not possible without the support, participation, critical feedback, and encouragement of numerous individuals and entities.

I would first like to express my deepest appreciation to the artists, both living and deceased, whose work is highlighted in the exhibition. Their vision and willingness to shed light on that which is difficult to look at, but necessary to see, is an inspiration to us all to do the individual and collective work needed to bring us closer to the racial justice we seek. I am particularly appreciative of my conversations with artists Laylah Ali, David Antonio Cruz, Mendi and Keith Obadike, Carl Pope, Paul Rucker, and Molly Jae Vaughan.

I would also like to acknowledge the exhibition funders. The Terra Foundation for American Art's lead support was critical for the exhibition's progress and allowed for its presentation at the Montgomery Museum of Fine Arts. Major support from the Andy Warhol Foundation, first in the form of a Curatorial Research Fellowship, then an exhibition grant, was pivotal. The generous contributions of the National Endowment for the Arts, the Bernstein Family Contemporary Art Fund, the Block DEAI Fund, the Block Board of Advisors, William Spiegel and Lisa Kadin, the Alumnae of Northwestern University, the David C. and Sarajean Ruttenberg Arts Foundation, the Elizabeth F. Cheney Foundation, the Myers Foundations, and Lynne Jacobs have ensured that the exhibition and its attendant programming and engagement work could be realized in their fullest form. In addition, Furthermore: a program of the J. M. Kaplan Fund and the Sandra L. Riggs Publication Fund generously supported the publication.

My gratitude goes to the individual and institutional lenders to the exhibition: Laylah Ali; Ken Gonzales-Day; Hill Harper; Rodney M. Miller; Mendi and Keith Obadike; Carl and Karen Pope; Paul Rucker; Molly Jae Vaughan; Amistad Research Center, Tulane University; the Art Institute of Chicago; Baltimore Museum of Art; Brooklyn Museum of Art; Carolyn Campagna Kleefeld Contemporary Art Museum, California State University, Long Beach; Charles Deering McCormick Library of Special Collections, Northwestern University Libraries; the Isamu Noguchi Foundation and Garden Museum; the Library of Congress; Museum of Contemporary Art Chicago; Museum of Contemporary Photography at Columbia College, Chicago; the National Gallery of Art, Washington, DC; the Newberry Library; Northwestern Pritzker School of Law, Pritzker Legal Research Center; Richard J. Daley Library, Special Collections and University Archives, University of Illinois at Chicago; Smart Museum of Art, University of Chicago; Spelman College Art Museum; Virginia Museum of Fine Arts; Wadsworth Atheneum Museum of Art; the Whitney Museum of American Art; Williams College Art Museum; Alexander Gray Gallery; Garth Greenan Gallery; Jack Shainman Gallery; Kenkeleba Gallery; Luis De Jesus Gallery; Monique Meloche Gallery; Paula Cooper Gallery; and Stephen Friedman Gallery.

I would like to thank our copublisher, Princeton University Press, and particularly Michelle Komie and Kenneth Guay for their support, patience, and management of myriad details, including the peer-review process. I especially want to thank Michelle for her firm interest in and early support of this publication. Without the production team at Lucia|Marquand, this publication would not have been possible. Special thanks are due to Adrian Lucia for his support, Kestrel Rundle and Leah Finger for their deft management of the production process, Tom Eykemans for his thoughtful design, and Meghann Ney for her assistance with image management. Freelance editor Kristin Swan is owed my deep appreciation for her flexibility, patience, and keen eye. I am grateful to Alisa Swindell, Block curatorial research associate, for tirelessly tracking down image permissions, and to Kylie Escudero at the Art Institute of Chicago and Micah Musheno at the Whitney Museum of American for helping with a couple of particularly challenging permissions requests.

I want to express my profound thanks to Sampada Aranke, Courtney R. Baker, Huey Copeland, Leslie M. Harris, and LaCharles Ward for their insightful contributions to this publication. For their early feedback on the exhibition premise, content, and organization during an October 2018 scholarly advisors meeting and continued conversations, thanks are due to La Tanya Autry, Bridget Cooks, Noémi Michel, Shawn Michelle Smith, and Mlondi Zondi, as well as to Sampada, Courtney, Leslie, and LaCharles.

For their insights shared during an April 2019 convening focused on museum practice as it relates to exhibitions engaging with the issue of racial violence, I would like to acknowledge and express my gratitude to Elisabeth Callihan, Ross Jordan, Valerie Cassel Oliver, Kymberly Pinder, Maurita Poole, Risa Puleo, Veronica Roberts,

Nicole Soukup, Lorelei Stewart, and Fred Wilson. Additional conversations with Rocío Aranda Alvarado, Amber Esseiva, Miranda Lash, Meg Onli, Lowery Stokes Sims, and Arielle Weininger and her colleagues at the Illinois Holocaust Museum and Education Center, as well as with Jake Gagne, Liz Harnett, Lisa Hodermarsky, and Molleen Theodore at Yale University Art Gallery, were extremely valuable.

Members of our community advisory committee in Evanston, Illinois, shared profound critical insights and generously lent their support. I thank Melissa Blount, Fran Joy, Rebeca Mendoza, Rev. Michael Nabors, Nathan Norman, Robin Rue Simmons, Angela Williams, and Corey Winchester. Dino Robinson of the Shorefront Legacy Center and Tiffany McDowell and LeAnn Jenkins of YWCA Evanston/Northshore's Equity Institute are owed deep gratitude for their shaping and facilitation of the community advisory committee meetings. I would also like to thank Joshua Bee Alafia for developing a guided meditation to accompany the exhibition.

Northwestern University has provided a rich intellectual environment for the development of *A Site of Struggle*, along with a community of supportive colleagues. Thanks are due to the faculty, undergraduate and graduate students, and staff attendees at my October 2019 Black Arts Initiative lecture for their feedback as potential "first users" of the exhibition, which led to the further refinement of the exhibition's approach and plans for presentation. I wish to recognize the Black Arts Consortium, particularly Director Ivy Wilson, Assistant Director Sheridan Tucker Anderson, former directors Huey Copeland and E. Patrick Johnson, and graduate assistant Chaunesti Webb for their support. For their comments and conversations, I would especially like to thank graduate students Rikki Byrd, Ashley Dennis, Nnaemeka Ekwelum, Candice Merritt, and Angela Tate.

I would also like to thank the members of the 2020–21 Block Undergraduate Student Docent cohort for sharing their perspectives about the exhibition and its intersection with their experiences at Northwestern: Ayinoluwa Abegunde '22, Fiona Asokacitta '21, Claire Corridon '21, Karan Gowda '22, Chayda Harding '22, Brianna Heath '22, Hyohee Kim '22, Mina Malaz '21, Lennart Nielsen '21, Giboom Joyce Park '22, Margeaux Rocco '23, Joely Simon '21, and Rory Kahiya Tsapayi '21.

My gratitude also goes to Heather Basarab, Peter Brace, and their colleagues at the Wirtz Center for Performing Arts for their support of the opening program.

I am indebted to many additional individual conversations with and the support of the following faculty members: Nathalie Bouzaglo, César Braga-Pinto, Joshua Chambers-Letson, Ryan Dohoney, Hannah Feldman, Justin Mann, Susan Manning, Mary Patillo, Miriam Petty, Krista Thompson, Alvin B. Tillery Jr., Natasha Trethewey, Alejandra Uslenghi, and Rebecca Zorach. I extend my thanks as well to those I have not named who will also incorporate the exhibition into their teaching.

Profound gratitude is due to our colleagues in the Social Justice Education program for partnering with us to train our student docents and develop a forum in which they can skillfully facilitate peer-to-peer conversations about the issues raised by the exhibition. Thanks to former director Robert Brown, Assistant Director Chelsea O'Neil Karcher, and especially Graduate Assistant for Sustained Dialogue in Social Justice Education Melina Gooray. Thanks are due as well to colleagues across campus working in student affairs and campus life for their thoughtful contributions and partnership.

Within the university's administration, we would like to acknowledge the support of Vice President and Associate Provost for Institutional Diversity and Inclusion Robin Means Coleman, Provost Kathleen Hagerty, former Provost Jonathan Holloway, Provost Chief of Staff Jake Julia, and President Morton O. Schapiro.

At the Montgomery Museum of Fine Arts (MMFA), I would like to thank Angie Dodson and Jennifer Jankauskas for their early support of *A Site of Struggle* and for seeing how it would be an important exhibition for their institution. Additional thanks go to Sarah Kelly, Cassandra Cavness, and Laura Bocquin for their work on behalf of its presentation at the MMFA.

This exhibition would not have been possible without the unfailing support, tenacity, and hard work of my colleagues at the Block Museum. Much of the final stages of exhibition planning took place during 2020–21 in the midst of a global pandemic. My colleagues handled the unique challenges created by this situation with commitment, creativity, and grace.

My deep appreciation goes to Ellen Philips Katz Director Lisa Graziose Corrin and Associate Director of Curatorial Affairs Kathleen Bickford Berzock for supporting this project when it was just a seed of an idea. Their leadership has a created an environment where a challenging project like *A Site of Struggle* could be effectively realized. For their support of this work, I would also like to thank the Block Board of Advisors and particularly recognize former board chair Chris Robb and current co-chairs Stuart Bohart and Cheryl Johnson-Odim for their leadership.

To Curatorial Research Associate Alisa Swindell, I give my heartfelt thanks and appreciation. Alisa went above and beyond the original scope of her position to become a partner on this exhibition. Her critical insights, attention to detail, and much-needed humor ensured the fullest realization of the project.

For their commitment to the engagement research and work necessary for this exhibition and the development and management of public programs, I would like to thank Erin Northington and América Salomón. Much appreciation goes to Bethany Hill, 2020–21 art history graduate fellow, for her development of a care guide to support Black visitors to the exhibition. Many thanks to Dan Silverstein for his leadership of the exhibitions team, to Kristina Bottomley and Lori Boyer for their expert handling of all things loan related, to Joe Scott for his exhibition design work, and to Mark Leonhart for managing the installation crew. For their work on fundraising and managing fiduciary responsibilities, I am grateful to Kate Hadley Toftness, Elisa Miller Quinlan, Jeff Smith, and Rita Shorts.

My thanks to Malia Haines-Stewart, Rebecca Lyon, and Michael Metzger for their work on the accompanying Block Cinema film program; Lindsay Bosch and Emmanuel Ramos-Barajas for their careful handling of the exhibition's public relations plan in partnership with the team at Blue Water Communications—Amber Hendrickson, Candice Harrison, Stephanie Miller, Sara Stacy, and Lynnette Werning; and to my colleagues in the curatorial department, Corinne Granof, Essi Rönkkö, and Melanie Garcia Sympson, as well as to Jenna Robertson for their ongoing support. I want to particularly recognize the Block's visitor services team led by Aaron Chatman, including Rocío Olasimbo, Jim Stauber, and Vincent Taylor, for their important feedback, for being present with this work in the galleries for six months, and for being the first point of contact for many visitors to the exhibition.

For their ongoing intellectual comradery, I thank Elise Archias, Nicole Awai, Naomi Beckwith, Erin Gilbert, Nikki A. Greene, Kristen Hughes, Carolyn Kastner, Courtney J. Martin, Lee Ann Norman, Geof Oppenheimer, Ryan Rice, Cassandra Smith, J. Michael Terry, Yesomi Umolu, and L. A. Williams. I thank Pamela Ayo Yetunde for her guidance.

Jill Brienza and Lisa M. Gill have my continual gratitude for over two decades of friendship, support, and inspiration, and for helping to keep me sane through the process of bringing this project to fruition. As with all things, my deepest appreciation goes to my family, especially my mother and brother, Dolores Dees and Jason Dees, and to the memories of my father and grandmother, Rev. Lloyd E. Dees and Daisy Mills.

Janet Dees
Steven and Lisa Munster Tananbaum Curator of
Modern and Contemporary Art

Preface

Many of the most vaunted aesthetic achievements of so-called Western civilization would never have materialized without the input and impetus of enslaved labor. Yet the discipline of art history has tended to focus on the formal qualities of isolated masterpieces rather than on the ongoing economies of violence that bring those works into the world and before our eyes. Such a refusal—to see beyond the visual evidence held out by artworks themselves in order to uncover their entanglements with barbarism—holds true even of scholarship focused on societies like the United States, whose history is constitutively marked by racial slavery and its afterlives. As cultural critic Michele Wallace once famously noted, this blindness has resulted in the slighting of cultural practitioners of African descent as well as in artistic discourse's general inability to reckon with the extent to which anti-Blackness structures, haunts, and saturates the modern world.

As an exhibitionary intervention, *A Site of Struggle: American Art against Anti-Black Violence* at once comprehends, responds to, and remedies this predicament, offering a focused consideration of how American artists and activists on all sides of the color line, from the end of Reconstruction (1877) to the launch of Black Lives Matter (2013), have confronted the shifting contours of racial despotism and attempted to make them over into material form. In this sense, *A Site of Struggle* continues and crosswires conversations spurred by similarly pioneering shows undertaken in the last three decades. Think back to *Facing History: The Black Image in American Art, 1710–1940*, mounted in 1990 at the National Gallery of Art in Washington, DC; to *Black Male: Representations of Masculinity in Contemporary American Art*, which opened in 1994 at New York's Whitney Museum of American Art; and to *Without Sanctuary: Lynching Photography in America*, launched in 2000 by Emory University in Atlanta.

While each of these exhibitions aimed for comprehensive surveys of their respective terrains, *A Site of Struggle* learns from rather than reproduces their examples in order to create a vital mix of museum works, popular culture imagery, and activist media not unlike Okwui Enwezor's landmark exhibition *The Short Century: Independence and Liberation Movements in Africa, 1945–1994*, which was on view in Chicago precisely twenty years ago. In mounting *A Site of Struggle*, Janet Dees, Steven and Lisa Munster Tananbaum Curator of Modern and Contemporary Art at Northwestern University's Block Museum of Art, has moved with and beyond such curatorial legacies: the exhibition bears all the marks of her interdisciplinary training and her ethical commitment to Black liberation, whatever guise it

assumes. Cast in this light, *A Site of Struggle* must be seen as unfolding in dialogue with the Black radical re-turn in the humanities and social sciences, which—thanks to the efforts of scholars such as Saidiya Hartman, Fred Moten, Christina Sharpe, and Frank B. Wilderson III—has radically unsettled the operative categories and presumptions of disciplines predicated, whether explicitly or not, on the abnegation of Black being.

In illuminating the varied material forms, regardless of aesthetic hierarchies, that responses to anti-Blackness took and took up, the exhibition provides an important new model that reflects the impact of African American, performative, and material culture studies on cutting-edge art historical praxis. Each of the exhibition's three sections—"A Red Record," focused on depictions of violence; "Abstraction and Affect," which explores non-figurative approaches; and "Written on the Body," which turns us back to the flesh—allows us to consider the longevity and recursiveness of visual tactics for reckoning with the real and symbolic effects of the violence continually enacted upon Black beings. As such, *A Site of Struggle* offers a much-needed intellectual and perceptual framework that enables us both to rethink the art historical past and to rediscover models for cultural transformation in our own highly politicized present.

In this respect, the exhibition could hardly be timelier or better sited. *A Site of Struggle* emerges from Chicagoland, long a center of Black cultural innovation and resistance, in the wake of the summer of 2020, which witnessed unprecedented nationwide protests in response to the often-video-recorded murders of Black men and women at the hands of the state and its agents. The exhibition provides a historical context not only for understanding this movement, but also for grappling with the conscious and unconscious forces that continue to produce Black folks, regardless of gender, as sites of violent fantasy and fungible value. In so thinking with the limits and liabilities of visual representation, Dees's exhibition emphasizes that the twenty-first-century museum cannot be a temple to past masters but must itself become a site of struggle, so that we can truly begin working toward a civilization worthy of the name.

Huey Copeland

Andrew W. Mellon Professor, National Gallery of Art, Washington, DC
BFC Presidential Associate Professor, Department of History of Art, University of Pennsylvania

Kerry James Marshall
(American, b. 1955)
Heirlooms and Accessories
(detail, right panel), 2002

Three inkjet prints on paper in wooden artist's frame with rhinestones
Each: 51 × 46 inches (image); 57 × 53 × 3 inches (frame)
Smart Museum of Art, University of Chicago, Purchase, Smart Family Fund Foundation for Contemporary Art, and Paul and Miriam Kirkley Fund for Acquisitions, 2004.12a-c.

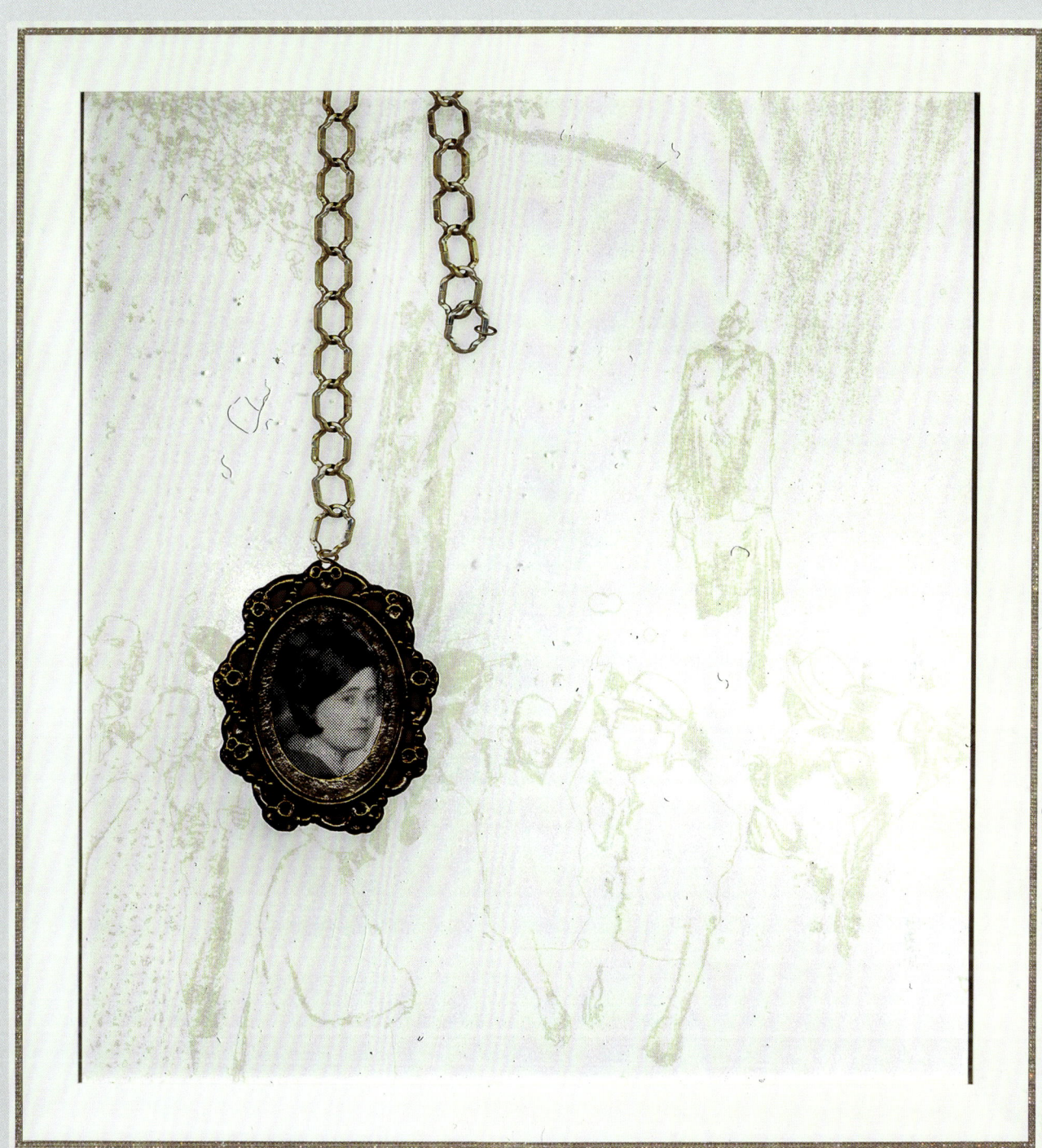

A Site of Struggle

Janet Dees

In a 2020 interview, *New York Times* columnist David Gelles asked Lonnie Bunch, secretary of the Smithsonian Institution and founding director of the National Museum of African American History and Culture, the following question:

In your memoir, you recalled when President Trump visited the National Museum of African American History and Culture. And you shared this detail that the president didn't want to see anything "difficult." I feel like that story is emblematic of this broader tendency in American culture where many people, again, simply don't want to confront the reality of some of the things that have happened in this country. How do we get people to engage with these difficult chapters in our history, especially when the legacy of some of these incidents is still very much with us today?[1]

Bunch responded:

Americans in some ways want to romanticize history. They want selective history. As the great John Hope Franklin used to say, you need to use African American history as a corrective, to help people understand the fullness, the complexity, the nuance of their history. I know that's hard. I remember receiving a letter once that said, "Don't you understand that America's greatest strength is its ability to forget?" . . . But people are now thirsty to understand history. . . . History often teaches us to embrace ambiguity, to understand there aren't simple answers to complex questions. . . . So, the challenge is to use history to help the public feel comfortable with nuance and complexity.[2]

Introduction

A Site of Struggle: American Art against Anti-Black Violence presents a "difficult" art history by engaging with artworks that invoke troubling aspects of US history. Images of African American suffering and death have constituted an enduring part of the nation's cultural landscape, and the development of creative counterpoints to these images has been an ongoing concern for American artists. *A Site of Struggle* explores how artists have engaged with the reality of anti-Black violence and its accompanying challenges of representation in ways that run from the explicit to the resolutely abstract. From the horrors of slavery and lynching, to the violent suppression of civil rights struggles, to contemporary acts of mob violence and police brutality, targeted violence has been an ever-present fact of Black life in the United States.

By investigating the conceptual and aesthetic strategies that American artists have used in works that grapple with anti-Black violence over a 125-year period—from Elizabeth Catlett's direct depictions of lynching to Paul Rucker's abstract memorials for historical incidents of racial violence—*A Site of Struggle* seeks to present a nuanced and complex picture that situates contemporary artistic practice within a longer history of American art. Bracketed by two critical periods of activism, the antilynching campaigns of the post-Reconstruction period and the Black Lives Matter movement, founded in 2013, the exhibition evokes an unbroken history of violence against African Americans in the United States. It includes a focused selection of artworks and ephemera created between the 1890s and 2013, as well as post-2013 works that predominantly take historical events as their subject matter. With an emphasis on how art has been used to protest, process, mourn, and memorialize anti-Black violence, *A Site of Struggle* foregrounds African Americans as active shapers of visual discourse—not merely its victims. It asserts that art's function in relationship to this subject is as much about honoring the dead and metabolizing grief as it is about activism and pedagogy.

This publication represents one facet of the *A Site of Struggle* project. It serves as a companion to the exhibition but departs from the traditional catalogue format to include essays that extend the discussion beyond the artworks included in and the subjects directly addressed by the exhibition. It does not seek to be a comprehensive treatment of the subject but, through selective attention, seeks instead to suggest the depth and breadth of art that has been engaged with and impacted by the continuing legacy of racial violence.

This introductory essay takes a thematic approach to exploring different strategies used by artists to engage with anti-Black violence and employs a structure that mirrors the organizational categories of the exhibition. Whether or not and how artworks that reflect upon anti-Black violence should be exhibited at all and, if so, how to do so responsibly has been the subject of much recent debate. Drawing on extensive research conducted to develop strategies for supporting the presentation of this material within the space of the museum, this essay also offers some reflections on the specific considerations of exhibition making around the subject of anti-Black violence.

Essays from an interdisciplinary group of established and early-career scholars expand the conversation. Some contributions directly engage the exhibition content. In "Functional Abstractions: Sensorial Afterlives of the Black Body," performance scholar Sampada Aranke provides close readings of works by Elizabeth Catlett, Melvin Edwards, and Theaster Gates to explore the ways in which these artists use abstraction to engage with anti-Black violence as part of a Black radical aesthetic tradition that spans more than eight decades. In "Pausing at the Threshold," cultural theorist Courtney R. Baker argues that while the visualization of Black death is a contested practice, when presented with sensitivity, as in the exhibition *A Site of Struggle*, an artist's rendering of violence can contribute to the development of empathy and provide a first step toward meaningful change.

Leslie M. Harris's and LaCharles Ward's essays extend beyond the timeframe of the works featured in the *A Site of Struggle* exhibition to explore varied strategies related to the circulation of images of Black suffering and death in mass media. Harris, a noted historian of slavery in the United States, has participated in crafting public historical exhibitions on the subject. In "Making Racial Violence Visible," she discusses how white and African American activists involved in the nineteenth-century abolitionist movement effectively deployed images of Black suffering to advocate for the end of slavery, making use of a newly robust mass media to disseminate their messages through visual and textual means. At the opposite end of the time spectrum, Ward, an interdisciplinary scholar of visual and cultural studies, considers how artworks created in the wake of police killings of unarmed African Americans since 2013 have critiqued an expansive media field that is saturated with images and narratives of Black death. Through the discussion of works by Alexandra Bell and Titus Kaphar, among others, in "Black Redaction, Black Evidence: Another Testimony of Black Life," Ward argues that these artists employ critical aesthetic practices that disrupt the ways in which anti-Blackness is manifested in journalism, reframing media narratives in order to tell alternative stories of race and violence that center Black life.

This project is in part inspired by the recurrence of the phrase "a site of struggle" in Courtney R. Baker's *Humane Insight: Looking at Images of African American Suffering and Death* (2015) and Leigh Raiford's *Imprisoned in a Luminous Glare: Photography and the African American Freedom Struggle* (2011). In her seminal publication, Baker explores the ways in which African Americans strategically employed images of Black suffering and death in attempts to invoke what she terms *humane insight*, "a kind of looking in which the onlooker's ethics are invoked by the others' embodied suffering."[3] She explores how the possibility that these images could invoke empathy and actions toward justice is weighed against the costs of recirculating traumatic content. Raiford's text considers the visual tactics of Black civil rights organizations from the 1920s to the 1970s. Raiford, in particular, describes her project as engaging in the interrogation of "photography in the service of African American social movements as the site of a threefold struggle through and for the black body, the black eye, and black memory."[4] Baker opens her chapter on photography of the victims of Hurricane Katrina with the pronouncement, "Once again, the image of the black dead was a site of struggle."[5]

For my part, the phrase "a site of struggle" not only references locations of contestation but also implies the importance of the visual by invoking the homophone "sight." The "sites" of struggle grappled with in this context are multiple: the object, the exhibition, the museum, and the wider social context of the present moment and its continuities with the past. The exhibition is concerned with the art object as a site, a location of struggle between artistic intent and audience reception and between visual representation and the "real life" political, physical, and psychological struggles that the artworks invoke.

The Exhibition as a Site

A Site of Struggle has developed in a climate in which images of racial violence proliferate in the media. As art historian Huey Copeland notes in the preface to this volume, the exhibition and publication are coming to fruition in the wake of the summer of 2020, when the murder of George Floyd at the hands of a Minneapolis police officer sparked a national reckoning with the persistence of racialized violence. For many of this generation, the death of Trayvon Martin at the hands of civilian George Zimmerman in 2013 was another such an inflection point, followed by the murders of Michael Brown (2014), Tamir Rice (2014), Eric Garner (2014), Sandra Bland (2015), Freddie Gray (2015), Philando Castille (2016), Ahmaud Arbery (2020), and Breonna Taylor (2020). Indeed, each generation throughout the historical arc of this project has its own memories of anti-Black violence that are points of reference, distilling the constant threat of violence as a reality of Black experience in the United States. Coming of age in New York in the 1980s and 1990s, my experience was marked by several highly visible acts of civilian and state violence against African Americans, including the deaths of Michael Griffith (1986), Yusef Hawkins (1989), James Byrd Jr. (1998), and Amadou Diallo (1999); the beating of Rodney King (1991); and the torture of Abner Louima (1997). For an earlier generation, the murder by lynching of Emmett Till in Mississippi in 1955 was likewise an inflection point. The consistent recurrence of these atrocities has been matched by consistent critical engagement by artists and the development of visual strategies to grapple with the reality of racial violence. This is a history that is important to understanding *American* history, writ large, as well as the singularities of the African American experience.[6]

Public and scholarly discourses have actively engaged with questions about how artists reflect on this violence through their work. Additionally, whether or not art museums should present this material at all and, if so, how to do so responsibly has been a fraught topic of debate. Some argue that making violence visible through art bears necessary witness to ongoing struggles, creating the potential to incite constructive action and creating space for mourning and healing. Others contend that this practice unnecessarily traumatizes those who identify with the victims of violence. Two controversies—over the 2017 Whitney Biennial's inclusion of Dana Schutz's painting *Open Casket*, an abstracted portrait of Emmett Till in his coffin based on a well-known photograph, and the cancellation of Shaun El C. Leonardo's exhibition *The Breath of Empty Space*, consisting of representational drawings of recent victims of police violence, at the Museum of Contemporary Art Cleveland in 2020—highlight many of the relevant issues. The debates around these incidents were multifaceted and complex,[7] prompting a range of questions: Should non-Black (and particularly white) artists engage with the subject of anti-Black violence and, if so, how? Even when the artist is Black, is engaging with this subject matter reproducing and capitalizing on harm in a way similar to the constant recirculation of images of violence in the media, or can art provide a different experience and perspective? Are predominantly white art institutions equipped to provide a supportive context for the presentation of this work, given their own histories of and ongoing problems with institutional racism?

As a Black curator working in a predominantly white institution, I have continually struggled with these issues throughout the process of organizing this exhibition over the last several years. *A Site of Struggle* is not an attempt to close these debates, but to wrestle with their complexities and contradictions. This has resulted in specific curatorial choices. In including art by some white and other non-Black artists in the exhibition, I have focused on works that have been enlisted by Black activists—particularly around the antilynching campaigns in the 1930s—and those where the victimized Black body is not centered. These images provide an opportunity to consider moments of interracial cooperation and empathy, even when they are imperfect. I kept the checklist intentionally concise—suggestive, rather than comprehensive—as a way to mitigate the complete overwhelm that could result from a more exhaustive treatment of the subject.

The many collaborators who have contributed to making this exhibition have grappled with the challenges of developing a project that would do justice to the artists and their works while also creating a space and a structure of care for the exhibition that would center Black experience and support a diverse visitorship. At the Block Museum of Art, I have worked closely with my colleagues in exhibition design, programming, and education/engagement to research and develop a series of best practices that we will apply in the presentation of *A Site of Struggle*.[8] These include opening the exhibition with an invitation to visitors to engage in respectful behavior toward their fellow visitors; the creation of a gallery within the gallery to control sightlines to the more graphic material, so visitors have a choice of whether and/or how to engage with these objects; and a spacious exhibition design with dedicated areas for visitors to rest and take a visual break. Ancillary spaces include a room for quiet reflection and a resource area where visitors can both write comments—encouraging ongoing audience feedback—and access additional resources. These spaces aim to provide support, encourage additional learning, and connect visitors to campus groups and local social justice organizations, facilitating a more active response to the exhibition through opportunities for direct engagement in opposing anti-Black violence in our contemporary moment.

These strategies have been deeply informed by discussions with colleagues in the art museum field as well as conversations with campus and community constituents. Along with feedback from Northwestern University faculty, staff, and undergraduate and graduate students invested in Black arts, the suggestions of a community advisory committee have played a critical role in the development of the strategies outlined above. These conversations have informed the exhibition's design, content, programming, and instruments of support surrounding its presentation. As this book goes to press, these dialogues are ongoing and continue to shape the exhibition's presentation and programming.[9] We have also been inspired by the work of museum colleagues who have sensitively organized earlier exhibitions that engaged with issues of racial violence, particularly *Necessary Force: Art in the Police State* (2015) at the University of New Mexico Art Museum; *Art and Healing: In the Moment* (2018) at the Minneapolis Institute of Arts; *Vincent Valdez: The City* (2018) at the Blanton Museum of Art; *Prisoner of Love* (2019) at the Museum of Contemporary Art Chicago; and the teach-in Art of Collective Care and Responsibility, organized by the Black Liberation Center (2020).

The *A Site of Struggle* exhibition is organized into three thematic sections, grouped around lines of inquiry rather than chronology. This approach emphasizes the use of different visual strategies across time periods. "A Red Record" explores how graphic depictions of violence are enlisted as a form of protest and awareness raising over time. Works in the second section, "Abstraction and Affect," demonstrate how artists employ conceptual strategies and varying degrees of abstraction to avoid literal representations of violence. Works in the third section, "Written on the Body," show artists alluding in more subtle ways to violence and exploring more indirect forms of violence, such as the psychological impacts of racism, through engagement with the body.

Other thematic threads connect works across these three sections and across time periods. For example, Meta Warrick Fuller's *Mary Tuner: A Silent Protest against Mob Violence* (1919, see fig. 1.4), Ernest Crichlow's *Lovers* (1938, see fig. 1.5), Elizabeth Catlett's *. . . And a special fear for my loved ones* (1946, see figs. 3.1, 5.11), and Lorna Simpson's *Untitled (Two Necklines)* (1989, see fig. 1.28) offer different insights into the construction of Black womanhood in relationship to anti-Black violence. In contrast, George Biddle's *Alabama Code: Our Girls Don't Sleep with Niggers* (1933, see fig. 1.6) and Kerry James Marshall's *Heirlooms and Accessories* (2002, see fig. 1.13) highlight the role of white women in instigating and supporting anti-Black violence.[10] Works like Norman Lewis's *Untitled (Police Beating)* (1943, fig. 1.1), Charles White's *The Return of the Soldier* (1946, fig. 1.2), Darryl Cowherd's *Stop White Police from Killing Us—St. Louis, MO* (ca. 1966–67, see fig. 5.2), Howardena Pindell's *Diallo* (2000, see fig. 1.26), and Theaster Gates's *In Case of Race Riot II* (2011, see fig. 3.7) all underscore the ever-present concern of police brutality and use of excessive force over nine decades.[11]

A Red Record
"A Red Record" takes its title from the 1895 antilynching pamphlet *A Red Record: Tabulated Statistics and Alleged Causes of Lynchings in the United States 1892–1893–1894* (fig. 1.3), written and compiled by journalist Ida B. Wells (1862–1931), a founder in 1909 of the National Association for the Advancement of Colored People (NAACP). Wells is widely considered to be the first to appropriate and redeploy lynching photographs in the service of activism.[12] Several of the works in this section, by African American artists and artists of other racial backgrounds, were enlisted by the NAACP in the first half of the twentieth century to build awareness about lynching and garner support for antilynching legislation.[13] For example, *Mary Tuner: A Silent Protest against Mob Violence* (fig. 1.4) was inspired by an article that Massachusetts-based African American sculptor Meta Warrick Fuller read in the September 1918 issue of the NAACP magazine *The Crisis*. Titled "The Work of the Mob," the article gave an account of the brutal lynching of a pregnant Mary Turner, in Georgia. Turner became a target after protesting the murder of her husband, who was also lynched. Her story resonated strongly with Fuller. In this sculpture, Fuller offers an imagined portrait of Turner with the bottom portion of her dress merging with the grasping hands and grotesque faces of an angry, violent mob.[14]

Fuller's work highlights Black women as often-overlooked victims of racial violence, a theme taken up by

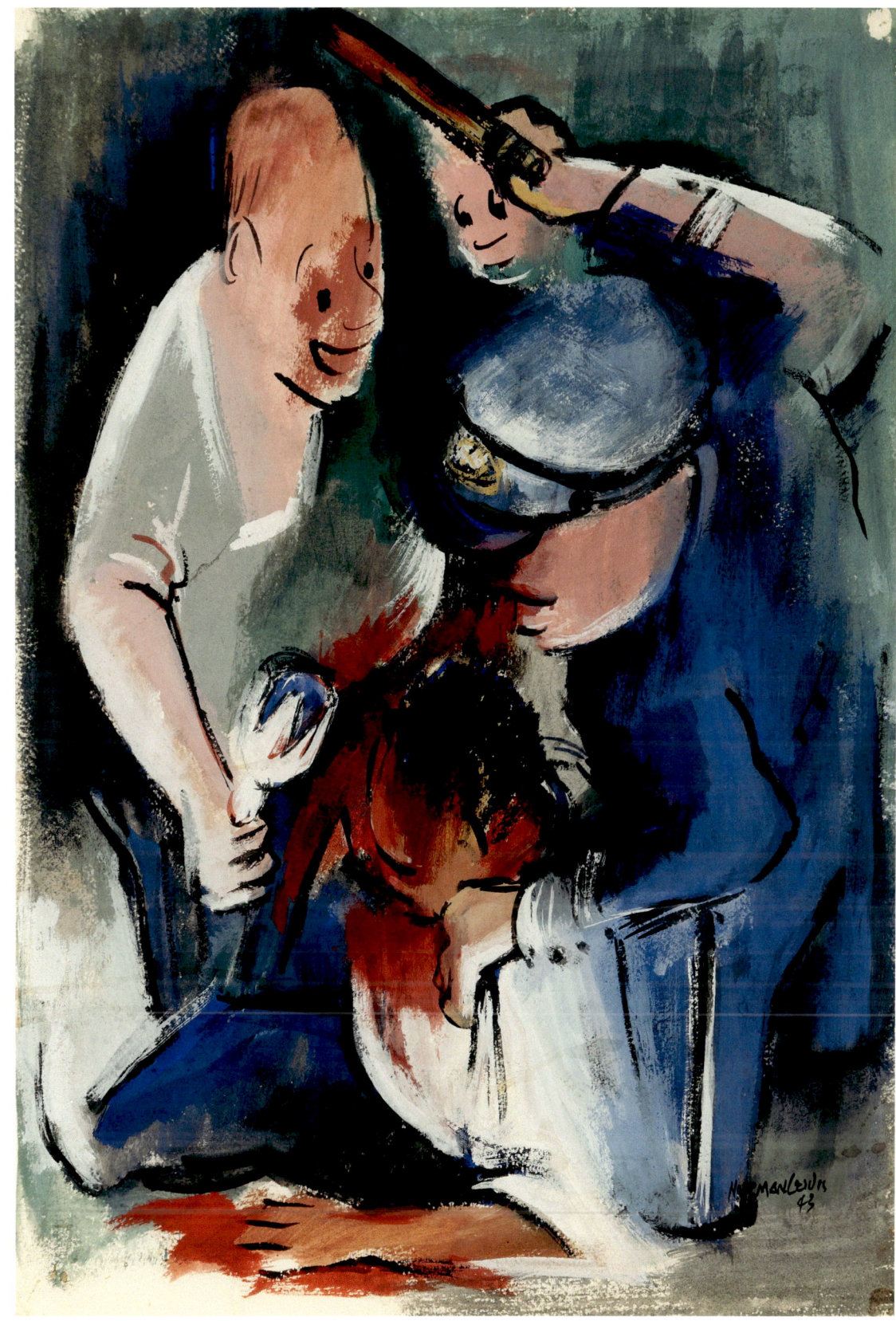

Fig. 1.1 Norman Lewis, *Untitled (Police Beating)*, 1943, watercolor, ink, and graphite on paper, 20 × 13⅞ inches. Rodney M. Miller Collection. © Estate of Norman Lewis; Courtesy of Michael Rosenfeld Gallery LLC, New York, NY.

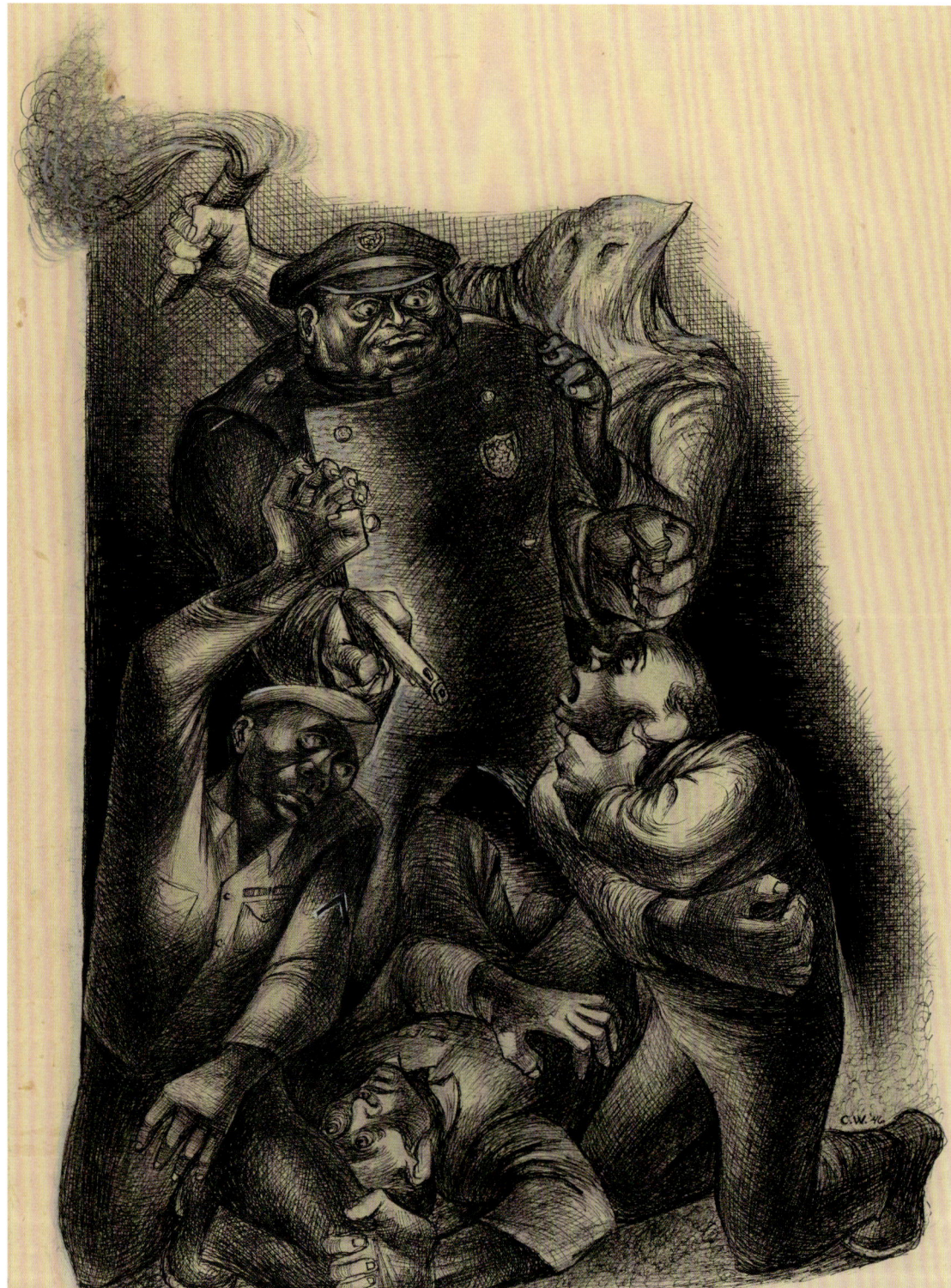

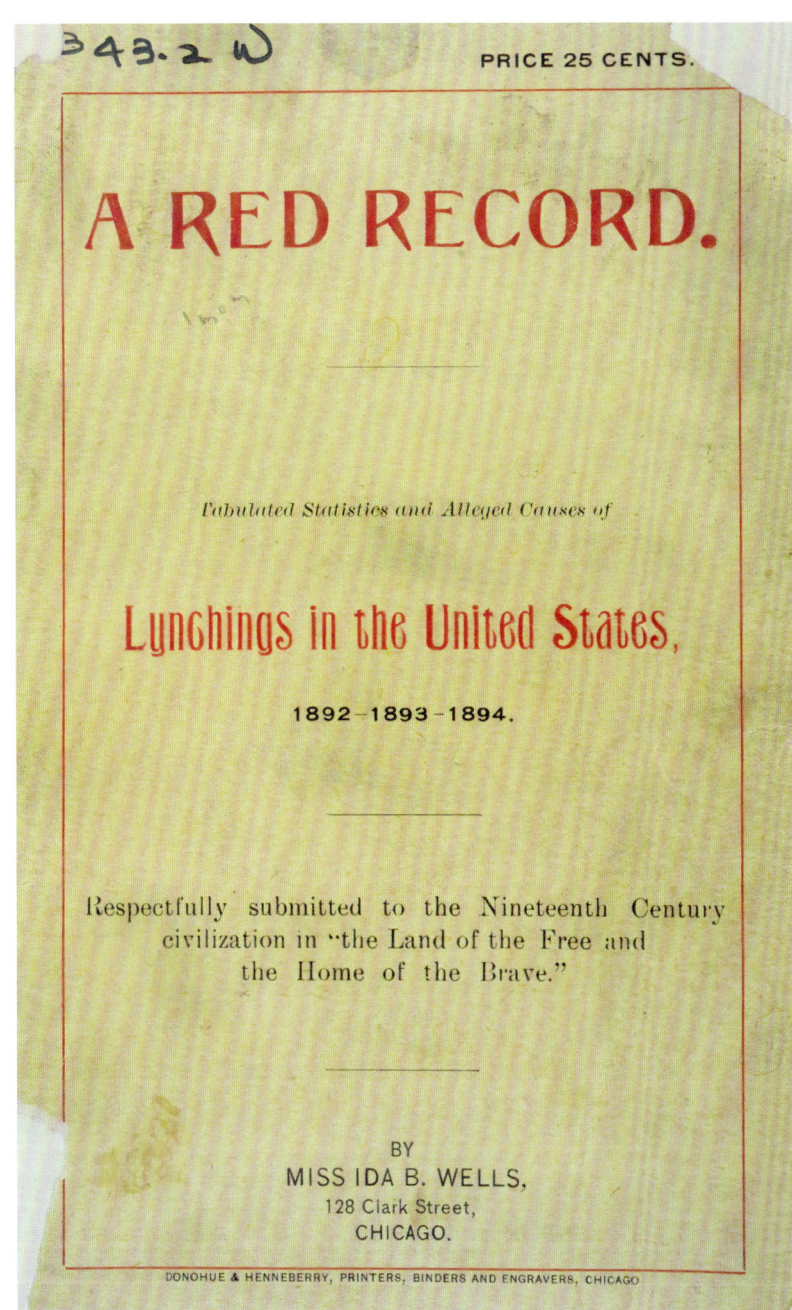

PRICE 25 CENTS.

A RED RECORD.

Tabulated Statistics and Alleged Causes of

Lynchings in the United States,

1892-1893-1894.

Respectfully submitted to the Nineteenth Century
civilization in "the Land of the Free and
the Home of the Brave."

BY
MISS IDA B. WELLS,
128 Clark Street,
CHICAGO.

DONOHUE & HENNEBERRY, PRINTERS, BINDERS AND ENGRAVERS, CHICAGO.

Fig. 1.3 Ida B. Wells, *A Red Record: Tabulated Statistics and Alleged Causes of Lynchings in the United States 1892–1893–1894*, Chicago: Donohue and Henneberry, 1895. Image courtesy of the Schomburg Center for Research in Black Culture, Manuscripts, Archives and Rare Books Division, The New York Public Library Digital Collections.

Ernest Crichlow's ironically titled *Lovers* (1937/1987, fig. 1.5). It shows a figure clad in a Klan robe, holding a Black woman in a menacing embrace. The woman claws at the eyes of her hooded attacker in an ill-fated attempt to stave off sexual assault. In opposition to this, the white artist George Biddle's *Alabama Code: Our Girls Don't Sleep with Niggers* (1933, fig. 1.6) takes on the common use of false allegations of Black men raping white women as the impetus for the formation of lynch mobs. Biddle's work was created in direct response to the trials of the falsely accused Scottsboro defendants in 1931–32. Biddle depicts Victoria Price, one of the accusers in the case. He intended the work to be a protest print to raise awareness about the case and garner support for the young African American men on trial. Yet the focus on white men's policing of white women's sexuality, the darkly ironic title, and the lack of direct representational connection to the facts of the case made the work uncomfortably ambiguous for some Black activists, including Walter White, executive secretary of the NAACP.[15]

The Law Is Too Slow (1923, fig. 1.7), by white artist George Bellows, was originally commissioned to accompany Mary Johnston's antilynching story "Nemesis," which appeared in the May 1923 issue of *The Century* magazine, a publication aimed at a broad American readership. Typical of several works by a variety of artists from this period, the focal point of Bellows's composition is the body of a Black lynching victim. The story, however, also emphasized the psychological effects on the white perpetrators of this violence. Walter White was deeply affected by Johnston's story and specifically requested this work by Bellows for use both on the cover and as the frontispiece of his 1929 book *Rope and Faggot: A Biography of Judge Lynch* (fig. 1.8). White also included the work in the 1935 exhibition *An Art Commentary on Lynching* (fig. 1.9), which he organized to raise awareness about and garner support for antilynching legislation. The exhibition was presented at the Arthur Newton Galleries in New York City and serves as one example of the way African American artists and artists of other races have supported the efforts of activist organizations.[16] The exhibition included works by an interracial group of artists such as Bellows, Julius Bloch, Wilmer Jennings, Reginald Marsh, and Hale Woodruff, among others.[17]

An Art Commentary on Lynching also included work by Isamu Noguchi. His sculpture *Death (Lynched Figure)* (1934, fig. 1.10) was on view in a solo exhibition of his work when he decided to pull it so that it could be included in the NAACP exhibition. The sculpture was influenced by a 1930 photograph of lynching victim George Hughes in Sherman, Texas, which had been circulated widely in

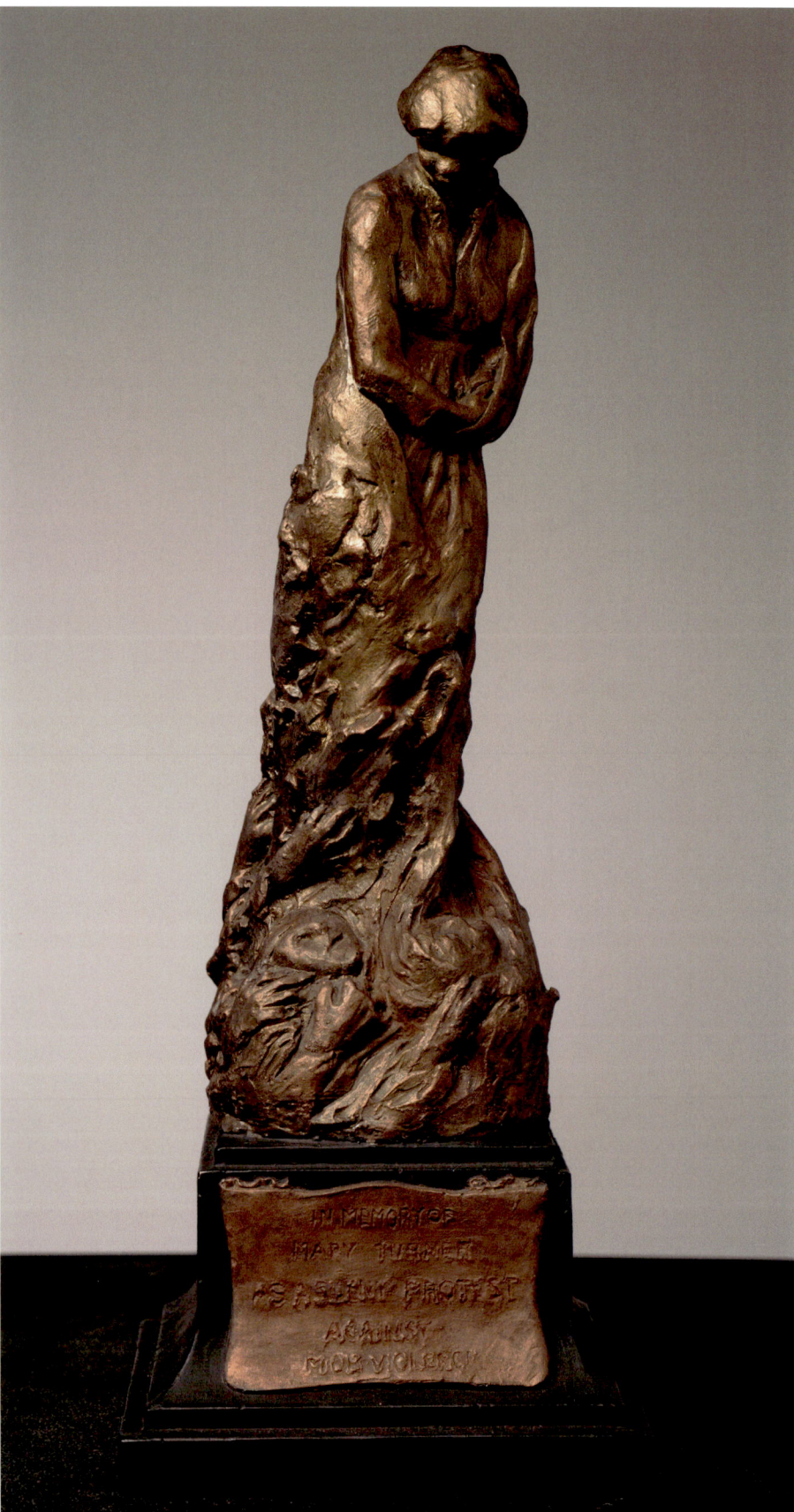

Fig. 1.4 Meta Warrick Fuller, *Mary Tuner: A Silent Protest against Mob Violence*, 1919, painted plaster, 15 × 5¼ × 4½ inches. Museum of African American History, Boston and Nantucket. Image courtesy of the Museum of African American History, Boston and Nantucket.

Fig. 1.5 Ernest Crichlow, *Lovers*, 1938/1987, lithograph on black on wove paper, 14¼ × 11⅝ inches (image); 22 × 15 inches (sheet). National Gallery of Art, Washington, DC, Reba and Dave Williams Collection, Florian Carr Fund and Gift of the Print Research Foundation, 2008.115.45.

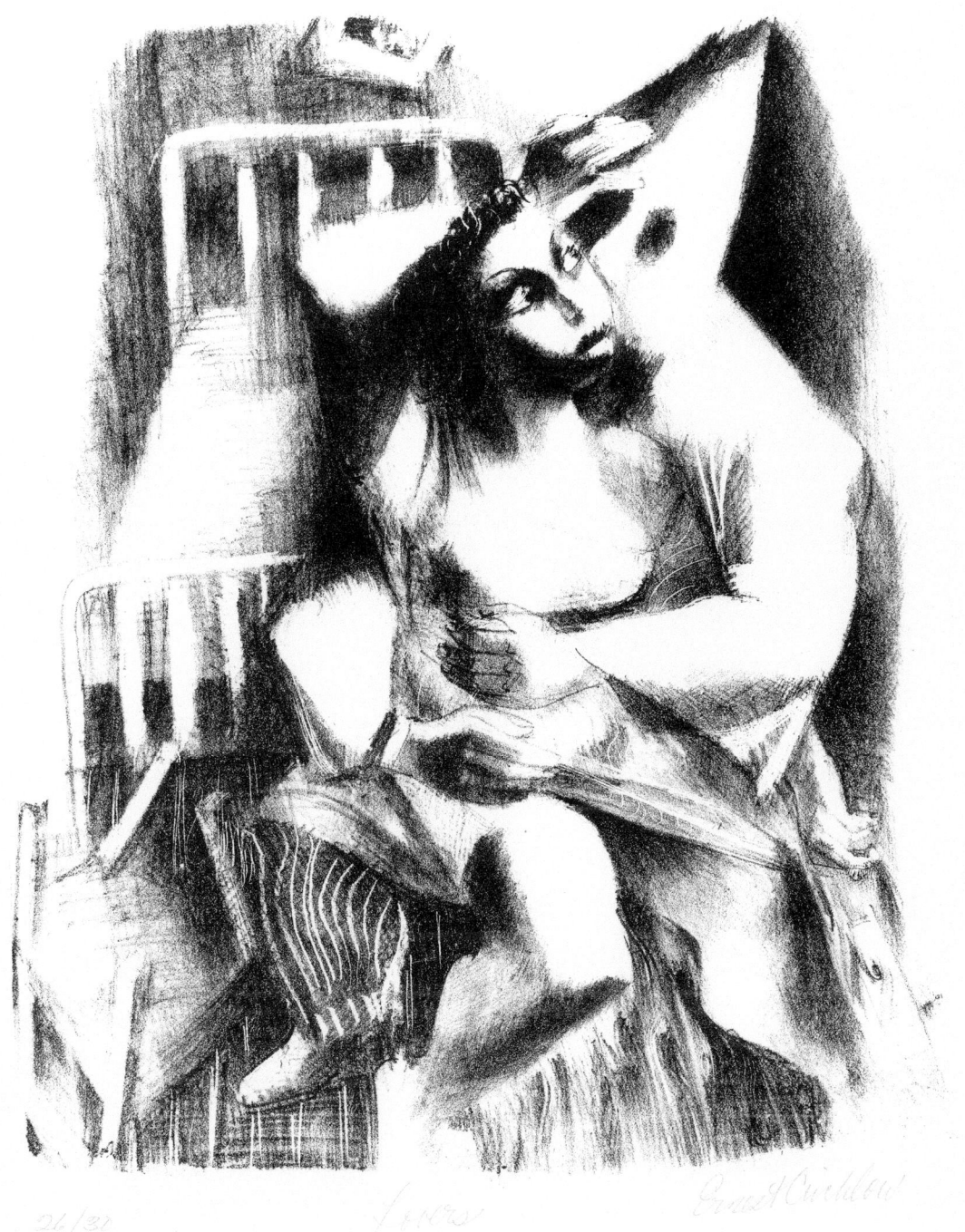

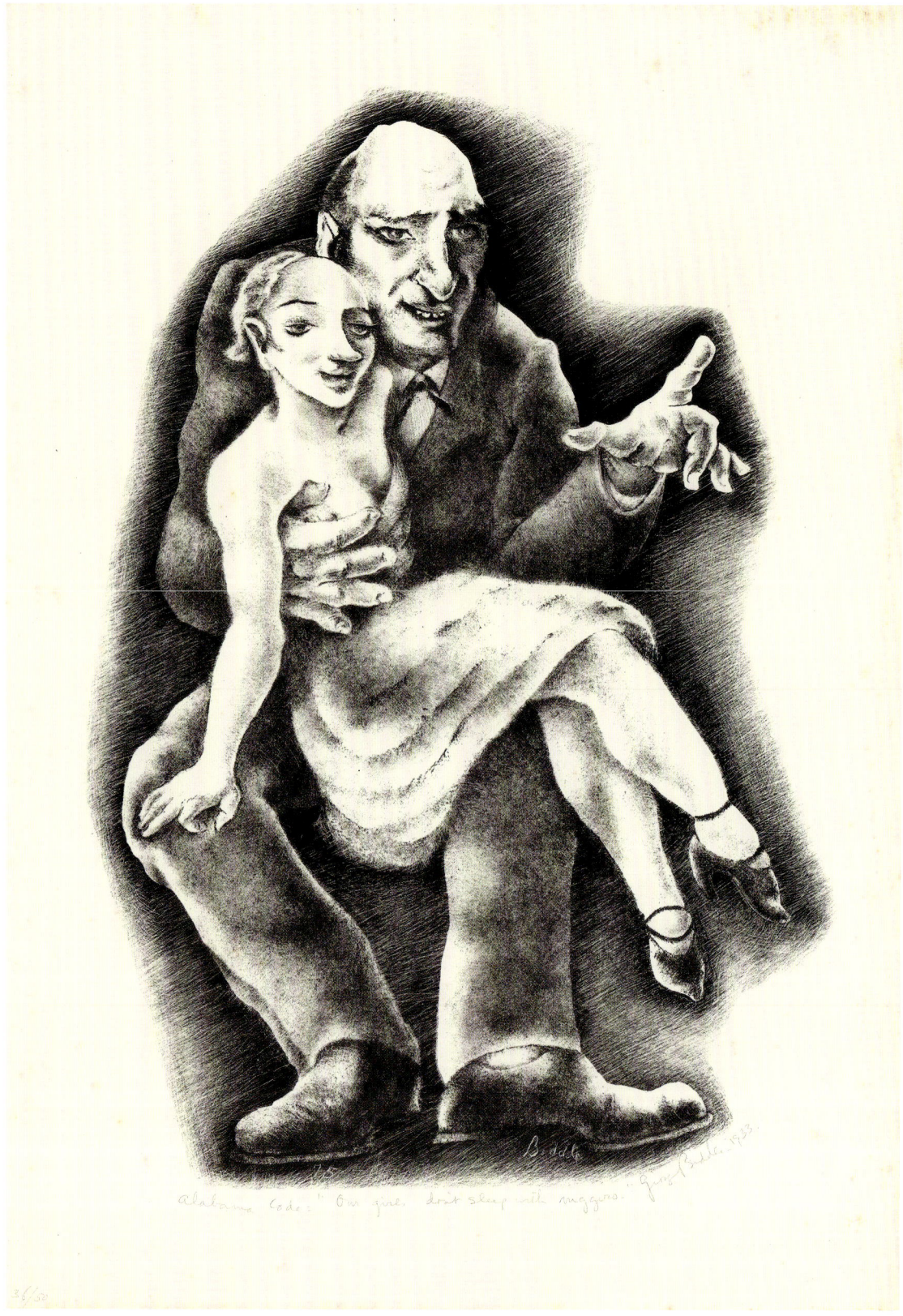

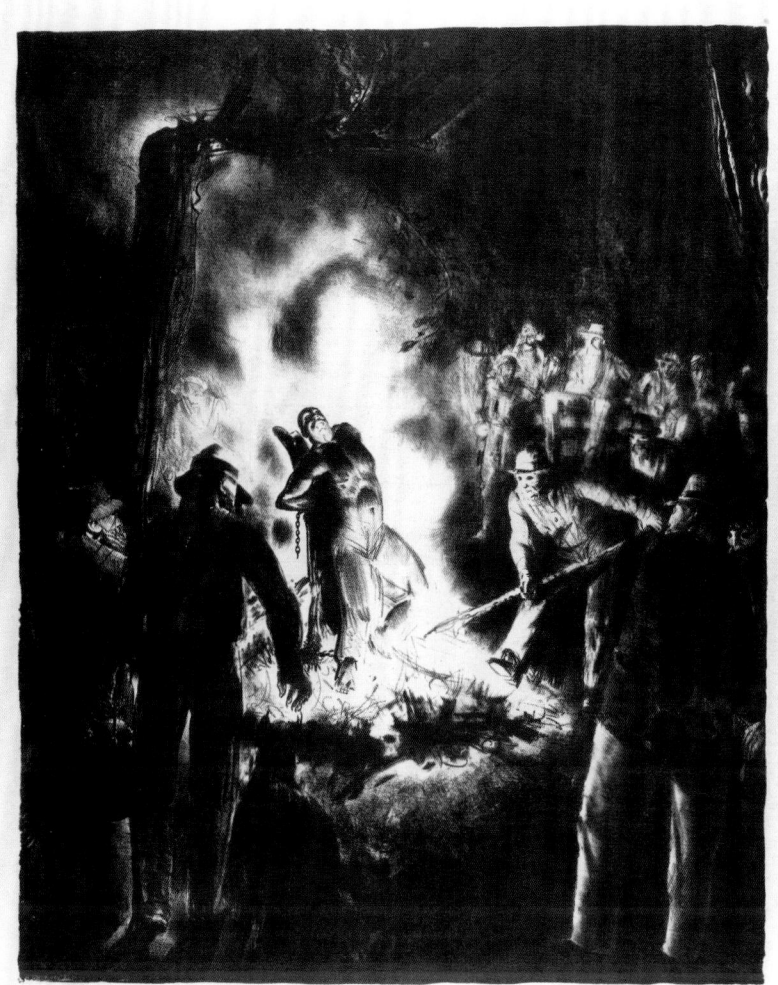

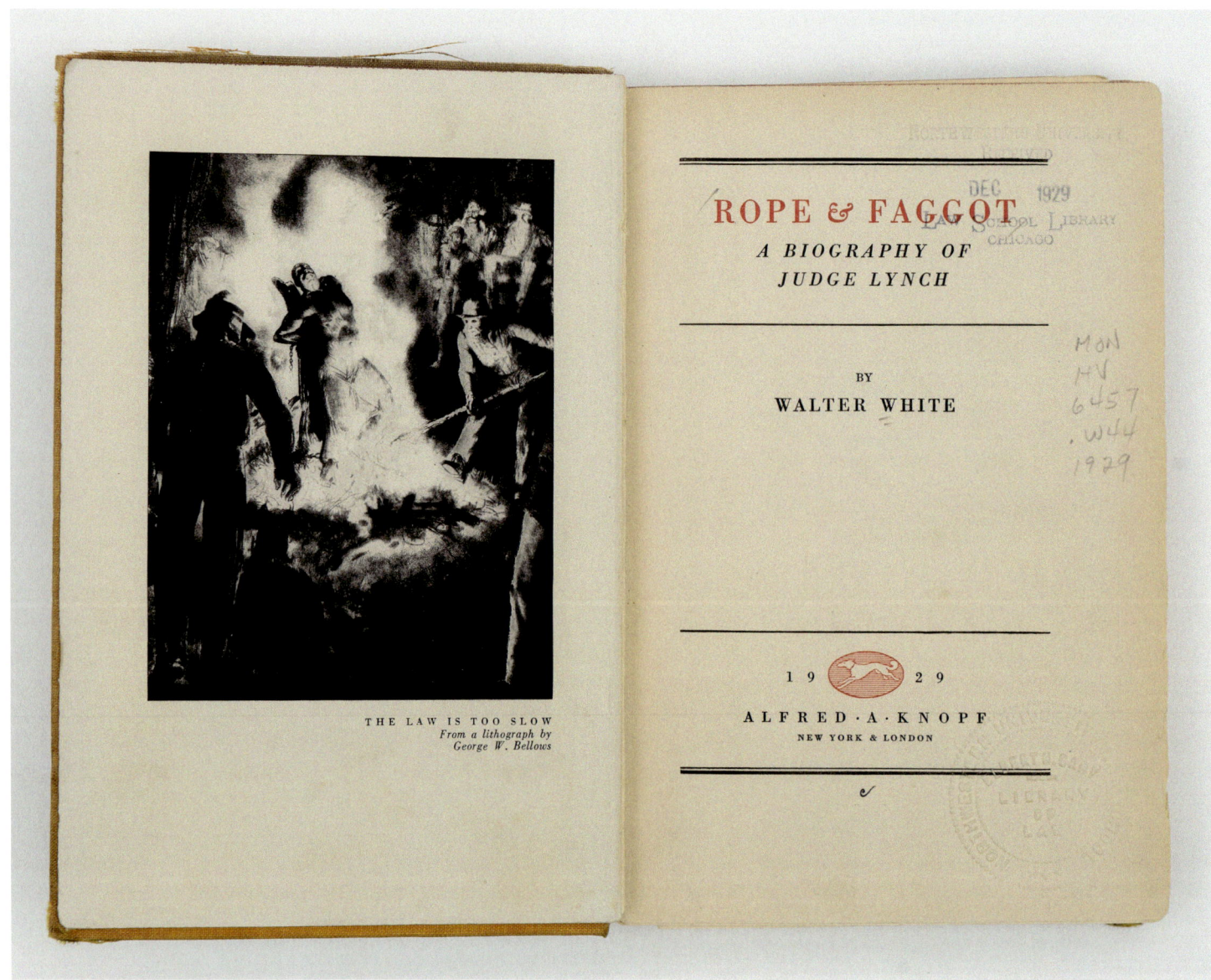

THE LAW IS TOO SLOW
From a lithograph by
George W. Bellows

ROPE & FAGGOT

A BIOGRAPHY OF
JUDGE LYNCH

BY

WALTER WHITE

19 29

ALFRED·A·KNOPF

NEW YORK & LONDON

Fig. 1.8 Walter White, *Rope and Faggot: A Biography of Judge Lynch*, New York: Alfred A. Knopf, 1929. Northwestern University Pritzker School of Law Library. Photograph by Clare Britt.

Fig. 1.9 Arthur U. Newton Galleries, New York, *An Art Commentary on Lynching*, exhibition catalogue, February 15– March 2, 1935. The Newberry Library, Chicago. Image: Hale Woodruff papers, Amistad Research Center, New Orleans, Louisiana.

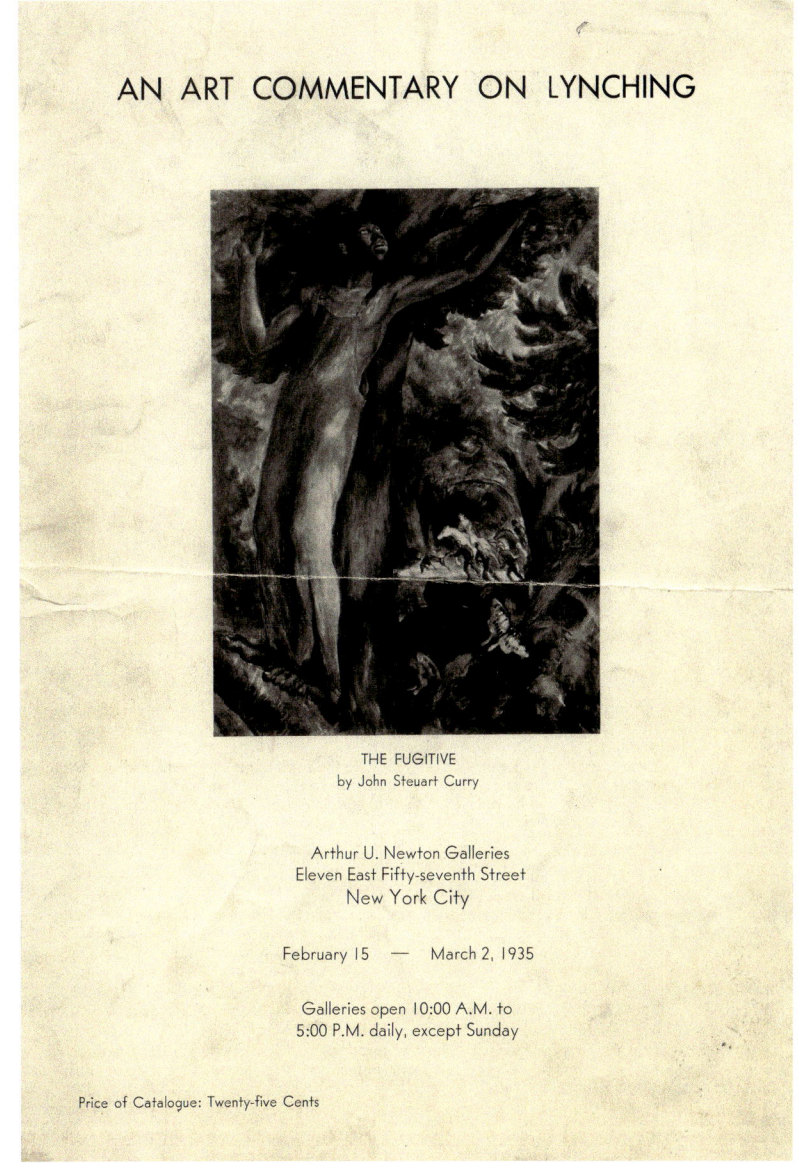

AN ART COMMENTARY ON LYNCHING

THE FUGITIVE
by John Steuart Curry

Arthur U. Newton Galleries
Eleven East Fifty-seventh Street
New York City

February 15 — March 2, 1935

Galleries open 10:00 A.M. to
5:00 P.M. daily, except Sunday

Price of Catalogue: Twenty-five Cents

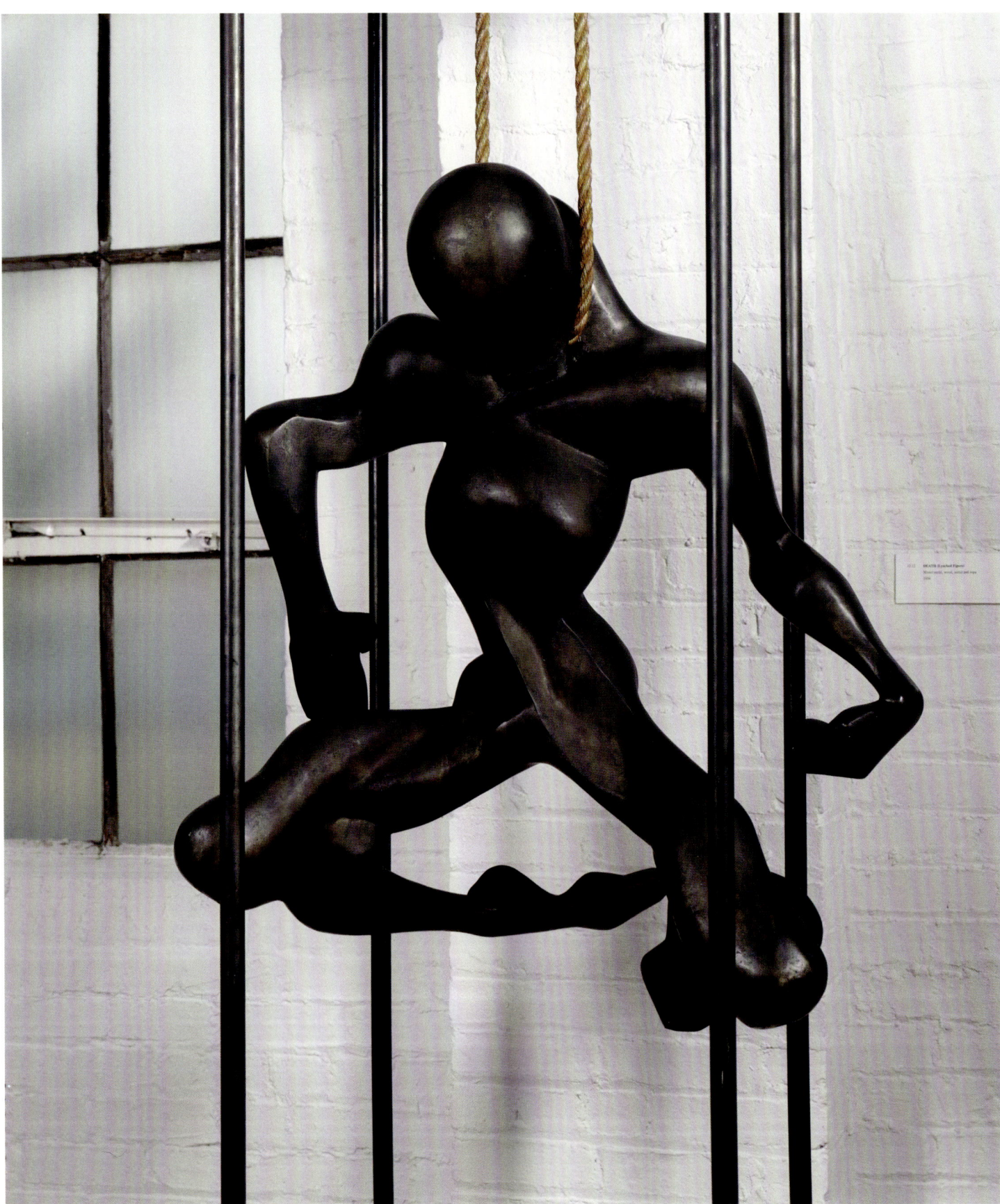

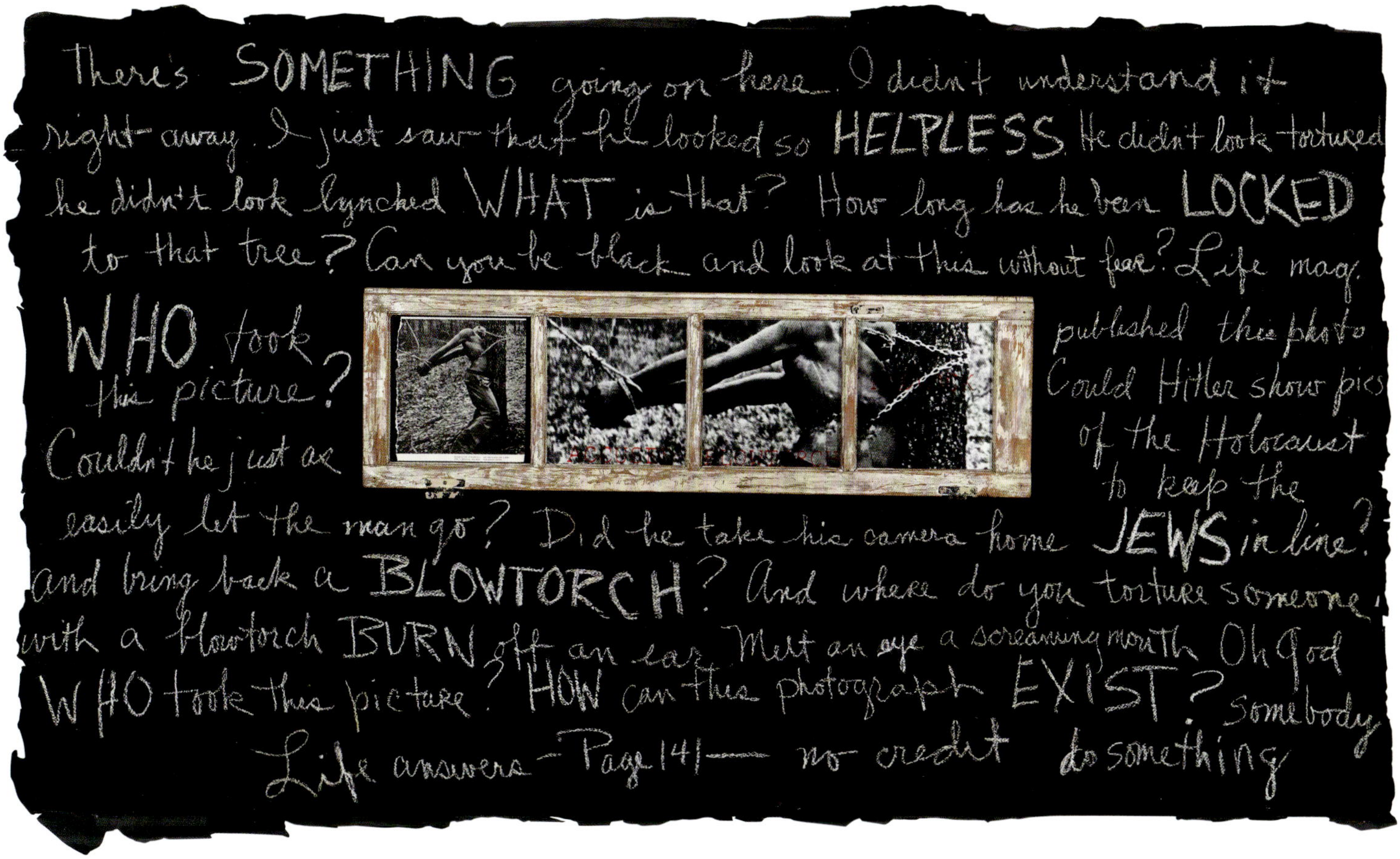

There's SOMETHING going on here. I didn't understand it right away. I just saw that he looked so HELPLESS. He didn't look tortured he didn't look lynched WHAT is that? How long has he been LOCKED to that tree? Can you be black and look at this without fear? Life mag. WHO took this picture? Couldn't he just as easily let the man go? Did he take his camera home and bring back a BLOWTORCH? And where do you torture someone. with a blowtorch BURN off an ear Melt an eye a screaming mouth Oh God WHO took this picture? HOW can this photograph EXIST? somebody Life answers—Page 141—— no credit do something published this photo Could Hitler show pics of the Holocaust to keep the JEWS in line?

Fig. 1.10 Isamu Noguchi, *Death (Lynched Figure)*, 1934, Monel metal, rope, 39 × 29¼ × 21 inches. Isamu Noguchi Foundation, New York. Photo by Sara Wells, © 2021 The Isamu Noguchi Foundation and Garden Museum, New York / Artists Rights Society (ARS), New York.

Fig. 1.11 Pat Ward Williams, *Accused/Blowtorch/Padlock*, 1986, collaged tar paper, oil pastel, found painted wood, found magazine, three gelatin silver prints with printed text on Mylar overlay, and nails and staples, mounted on wood panel, 61¹³⁄₁₆ × 108¼ × 3 inches. Whitney Museum of American Art, New York, Purchase, with funds from the Audrey and Sydney Irmas Charitable Foundation, 93.64. Courtesy of the artist. Digital image © Whitney Museum of American Art / Licensed by Scala / Art Resource, NY.

activist print-media outlets including *Labor Defender* magazine.[18] After his lynching, Hughes's suspended body was set on fire, causing it to shrivel and contort—horrifying physical details that Noguchi rendered faithfully and unflinchingly. Photographs often served as a reference for artists working in other media who wanted to convey the brutality of lynching. In *Accused/Blowtorch/Padlock* (1986, fig. 1.11), African American artist Pat Ward Williams questions how photographs of racial violence are produced and their effects on Black spectators. She reproduces and surrounds a historic lynching photograph from a 1937 issue of *Life* magazine with handwritten questions and statements that take up these issues: "Who took this photo? Couldn't he just as easily let the man go? Did he take his camera home and then come back with a blowtorch? Can you be BLACK and look at this?"[19]

Looking at the Crowd

Picking up the critique implicit in Williams's work, a subset of works in the "Red Record" section draw attention away from the victims of violence by focusing on the everyday perpetrators of and spectators to these acts, highlighting racial violence as a form of white socialization. *This Is Her First Lynching* (1934, fig. 1.12) by Reginald Marsh was first published in the *New Yorker* (September 8, 1934). Marsh donated the original drawing to the NAACP national office in New York, and it was employed as part of the visual arsenal used in the NAACP's antilynching campaigns. The work appeared within the pages of *The Crisis* and on flyers for informational meetings held by affiliated groups.[20]

Kerry James Marshall's triptych *Heirlooms and Accessories* (2002, fig. 1.13; see page 17) similarly focuses on the crowd at a lynching, rather than on the victims' bodies. For this work, Marshall appropriates a well-known 1930 photograph of a lynching in Marion, Indiana. He employs a "ghosting" effect rendering the majority of the image, including the bodies of the lynching victims, only slightly visible. Within the crowd, Marshall isolates and highlights three female spectators who turned to face the camera as the photograph was taken. Marshall has encircled their faces in cameos that appear to dangle from chains. The title of the work plays on a double reading of "accessories." As jewelry, cameos are accessories that carry the image of someone beloved. But here the women are also accessories—accomplices—to murder, as are all of the people who have assembled to participate in the lynching. The cameos, as well as the legacy of violence, can be understood as heirlooms, each of which is passed down to and through these women.

Also begun in 2002, Ken Gonzales-Day's *Erased Lynching* series (figs. 1.14–16) employs a similar strategy. Working with historical lynching photographs, Gonzales-Day digitally erases the bodies of lynching victims from the photographs, putting the focus squarely on the perpetrators of these acts of violence, the crowds assembled to view them, and the landscapes in which they took place. This body of work developed in concert with Gonzales-Day's scholarly research on the history of lynching in the West and Southwest of the United States. While African Americans constituted the majority of lynching victims overall, in the context of the West, Native Americans, Latinos, and Asian Americans were the primary targets of this violence[21]— a history Gonzales-Day seeks to make more visible through his work. Lynchings where African Americans were the victims are sometimes the focus in his work, too, as in *Lynching of Jesse Washington, Waco TX, 1916* (2019, fig. 1.14), which evokes an incident, well-publicized at the time, that was investigated by the NAACP.[22]

Abstraction and Affect

Ambiguity is both an asset and a challenge of works that engage with racial violence through varying degrees of abstraction. In the late 1990s and early 2000s, Laylah Ali became well known for her *Greenheads* series (fig. 1.17), which often employed comic-like characters engaged in acts of choreographed violence, depicted against solid blue fields of color. Though influenced by contemporaneous and historical representations of trauma visited against Black and Brown peoples, as described by Deborah Rothschild these scenarios were "deliberately non-specific." According to the artist, this was done in order to "evoke the viewer's own references," walking a line between abstraction and representation.[23] Ali's later *Note drawings* (2008, figs. 1.18–21) explore some of the same conceptual ground as the *Greenheads* while taking a radically different form and a less-explicit approach. In these works, the artist inscribed her characteristic figural drawings over numbered text fragments derived from snippets she collected from a

Fig. 1.12　Reginald Marsh, *This Is Her First Lynching*, 1934, original drawing in black ink and Conté crayon, 13 × 12⅝ inches (image); 15⅝ × 22³⁄₁₆ inches (sheet); now lost. Reproduced in *The Crisis* 42, no. 1 (January 1935). Charles Deering McCormick Library of Special Collections, Northwestern University Libraries. Image © 2021 Estate of Reginald Marsh / Art Students League, New York / Artists Rights Society (ARS), New York.

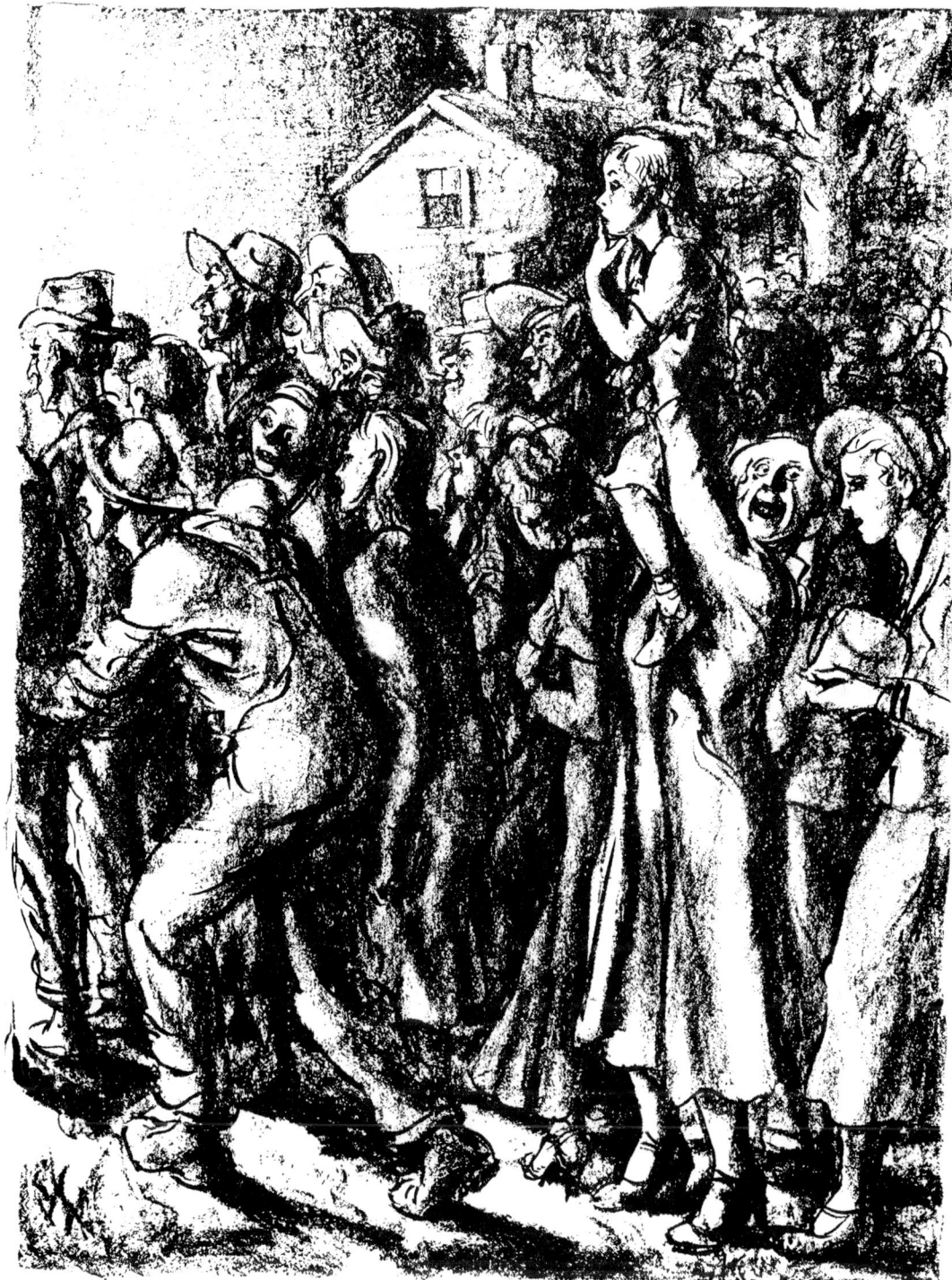

"*This is her first lynching.*"

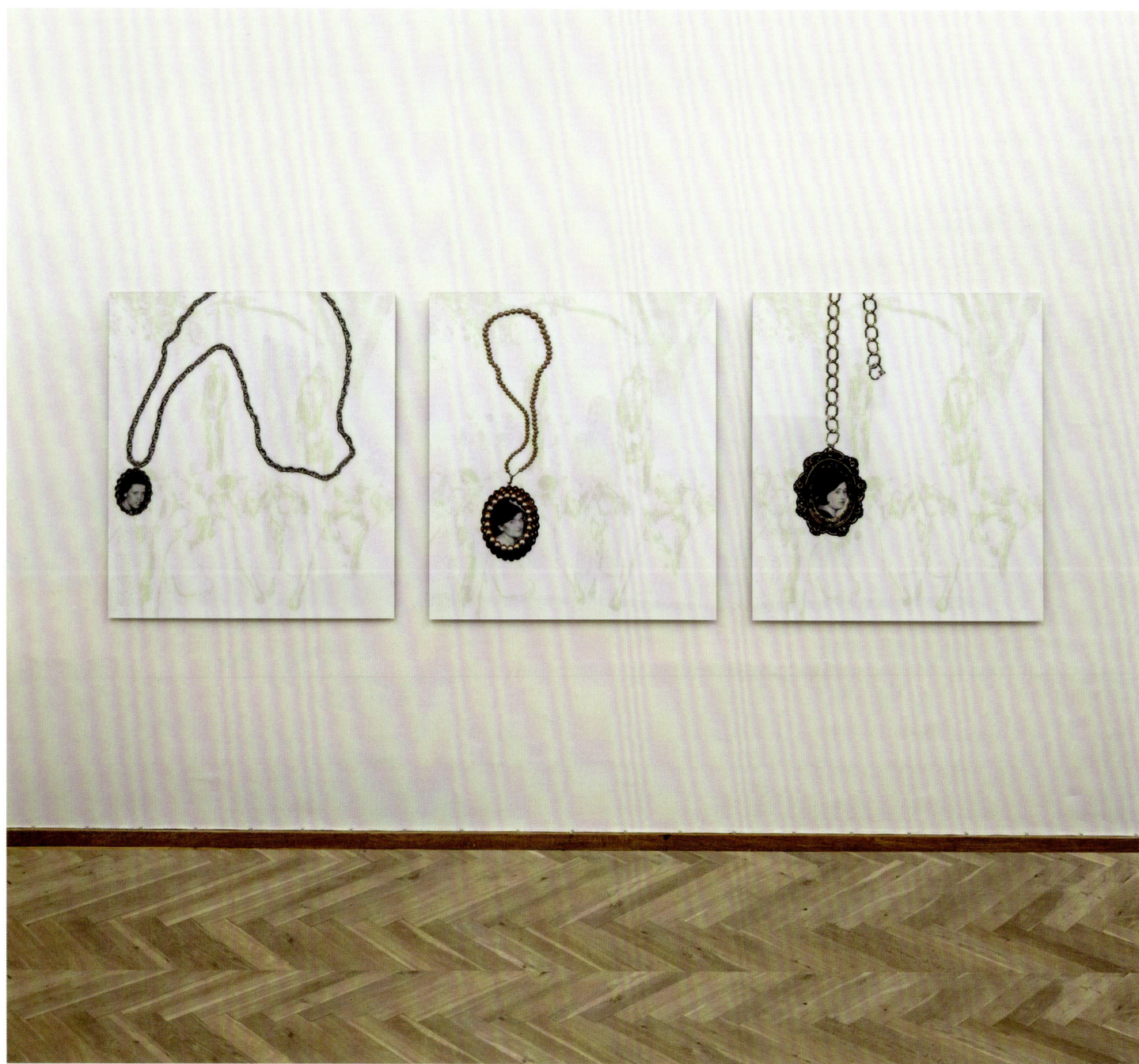

Fig. 1.13   Kerry James Marshall,
Heirlooms and Accessories, 2002,
three inkjet prints on paper in
wooden artist's frame with
rhinestones, each: 51 × 46 inches
(image); 57 × 53 × 3 inches (frame).
Smart Museum of Art, University of
Chicago, Purchase, Smart Family
Fund Foundation for Contemporary Art, and Paul and Miriam
Kirkley Fund for Acquisitions,
2004.12a-c. © Kerry James
Marshall. Courtesy of the artist
and Jack Shainman Gallery,
New York.

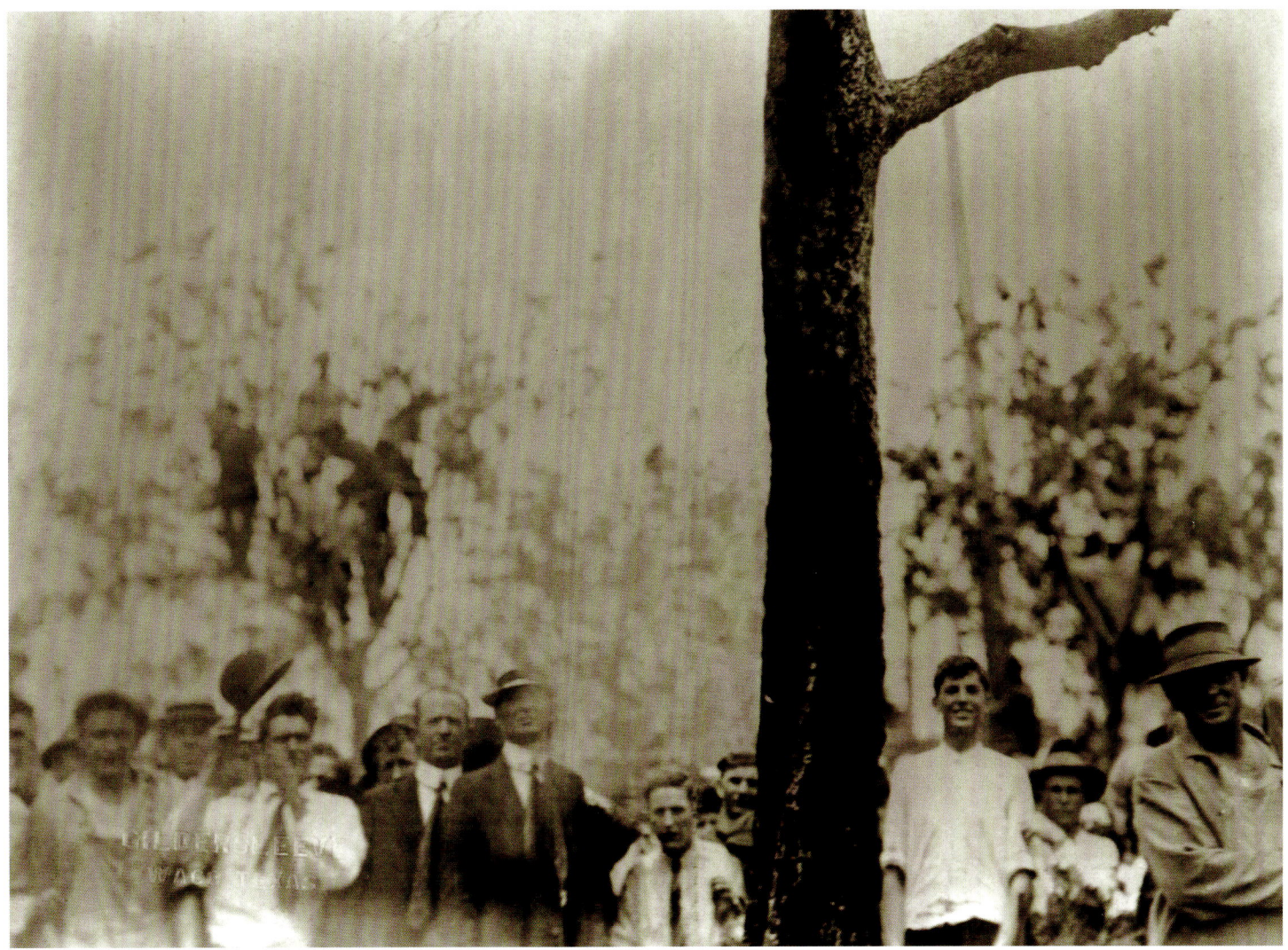

Fig. 1.14 Ken Gonzales-Day,
Lynching of Jesse Washington,
Waco, TX, 1916, 2019, from *Erased*
Lynching Series II, 2006–20,
inkjet on rag paper mounted on
cardstock, 6¼ × 3⅞ inches.
Courtesy of the artist and Luis
De Jesus, Los Angeles.

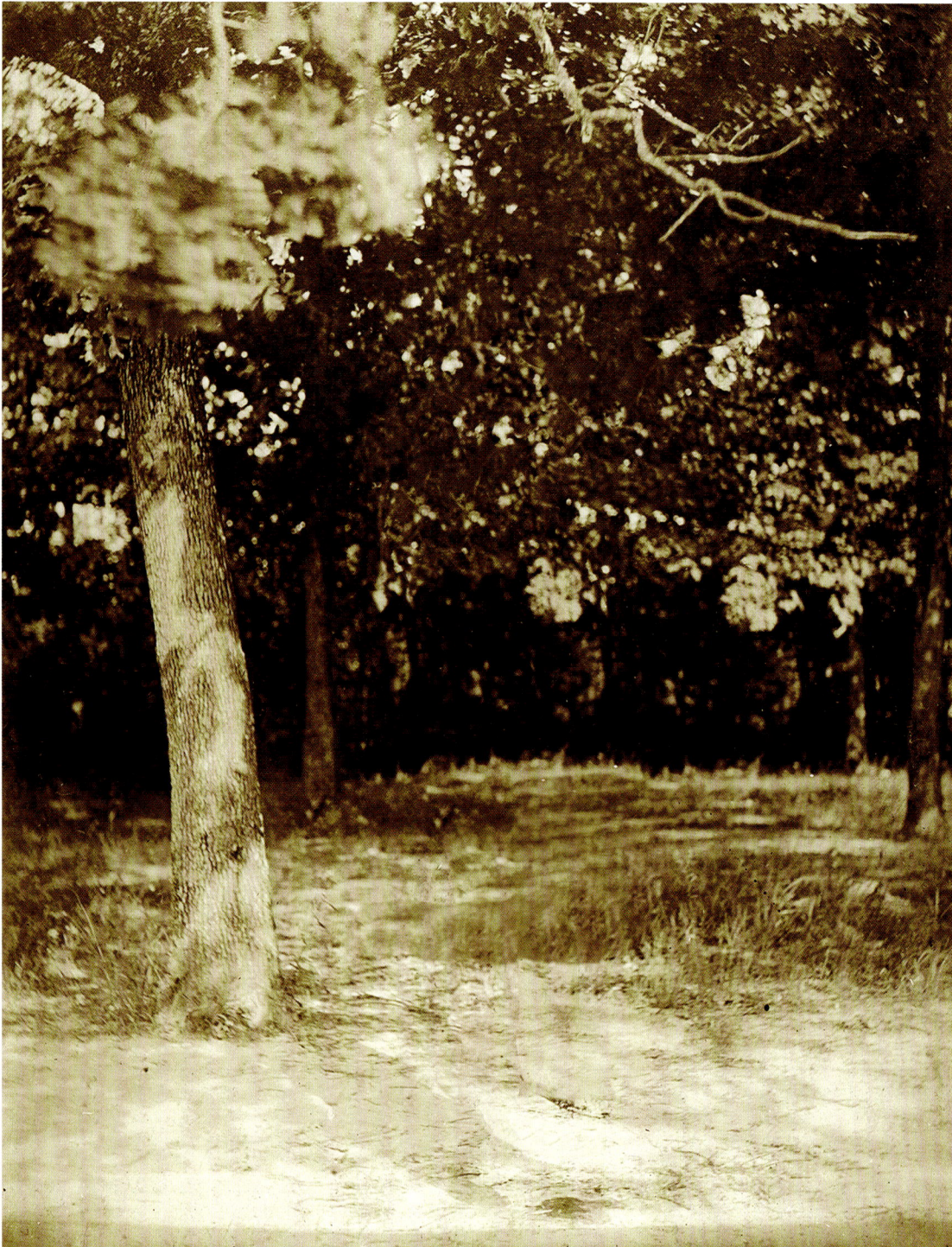

Fig. 1.15 Ken Gonzales-Day, *Lynching of Unidentified African American, c. 1925*, 2017, from *Erased Lynching Series II*, 2006–20, inkjet on rag paper mounted on cardstock, 6 × 4½ inches. Courtesy of the artist and Luis De Jesus, Los Angeles.

Fig. 1.16 Ken Gonzales-Day, *East First Street (St. James Park)*, from *Erased Lynching Series I*, 2000–2013, archival inkjet on rag paper mounted on cardstock, 5 × 3¹³⁄₁₆ inches. Courtesy of the artist and Luis De Jesus, Los Angeles.

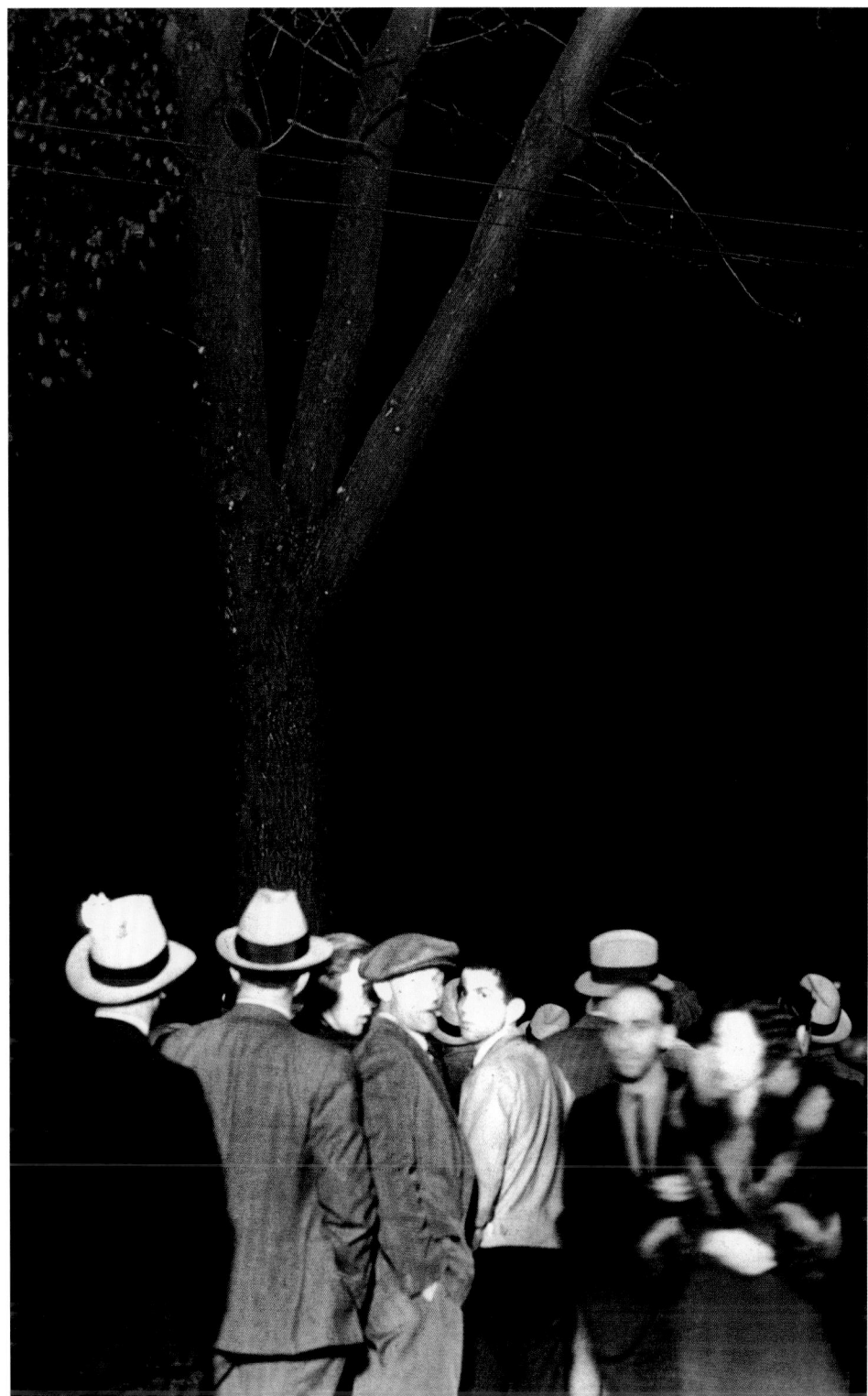

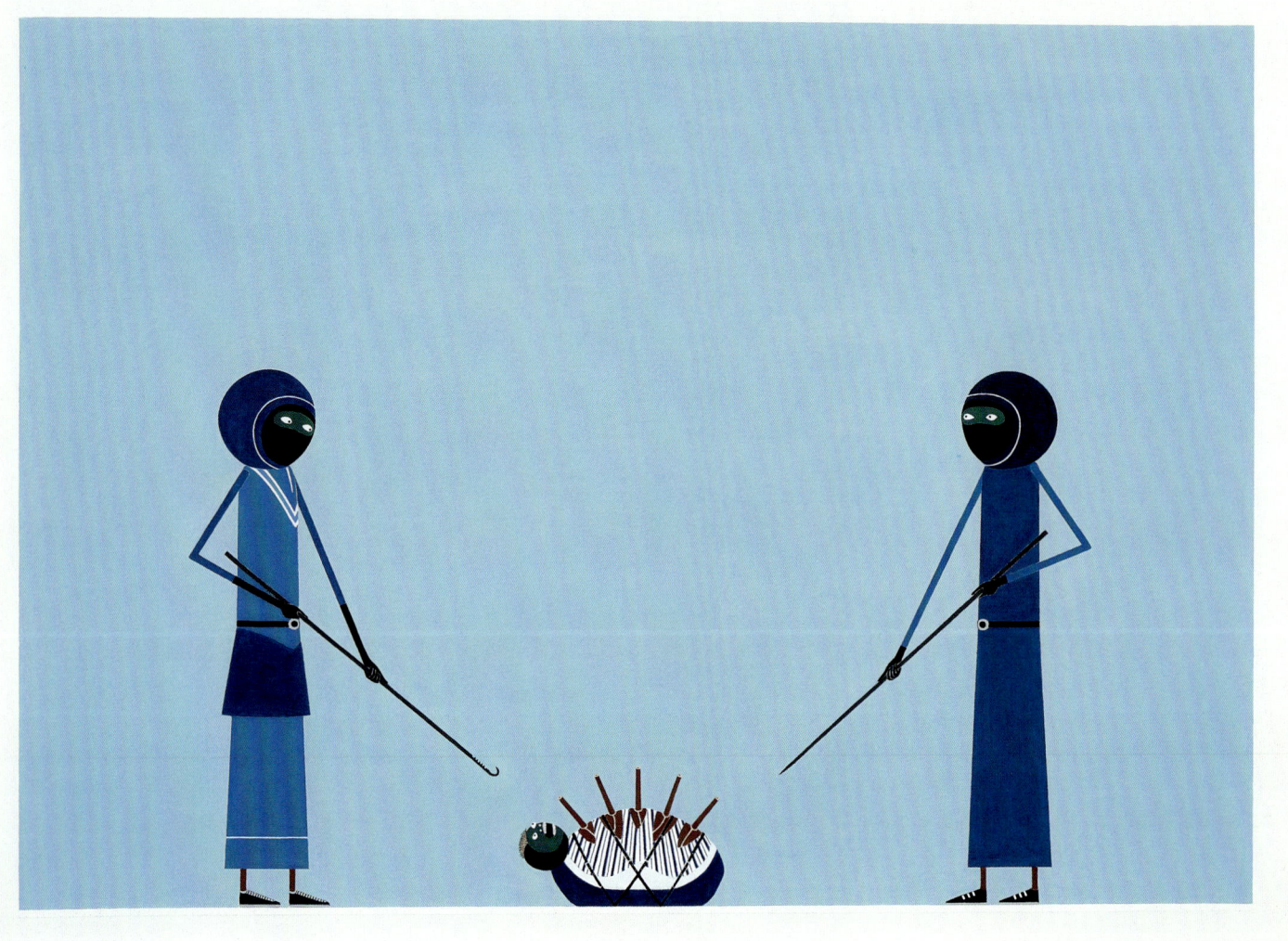

Fig. 1.17 Laylah Ali, *Untitled*, 2004, gouache and pencil on paper, 19½ × 28 inches (sight). Williams College Museum of Art, Museum purchase, Kathryn Hurd Fund, in honor of Linda Shearer, Director 1989–2004, M.2005.1. Image courtesy of the artist.

Figs. 1.18–21 Laylah Ali, *Note drawings*, 2008; all: ink, colored pencil, ballpoint, and gouache on paper; each: 11 × 8½ inches. Courtesy of the artist.

85. What he/she thought after being thrown / jumping.
86. Three notes, one confession.
87. Six fingers, one cut off; twelve fingers, two cut off.
88. "The objective is success."
89. The wood cabin burned down.
90. The school also burned down.
91. Mutualist, mutualism.
92. Narcissism versus solipsism.
93. "I will make you proud."

225. Blood pouring into (your) boots.
226. Lt. brown, prone.
227. Henry O. Flipper (cadet).
228. An aggrieved man who slowly poisons a righteous woman.
229. "Come with us."
230. Public apology: 11am this Wednesday.
231. Please come.
232. Regarding #228, the woman knows and documents each step. (~~----~~!)
233. "Idiot, leave it There."
234. Getting nothing back whatsoever.
235. (leave by roadside.)

256. 100 of the malcontents.
257. Is anything the matter?
258. A young hothead.
259. Beware "the shipload of women."
260. Apology rescheduled to the following morning.
261. The malcontents complain they are suffering from festering bullet wounds.
262. The prison administrator reads the list of demands (flanked by various wives).
263. Killed a man but not "a killer."

284. Pound, pound, pound.
285. Essentially: we don't want him in our hospital.
286. Erratic after going off of his medication.
287. Variety of injuries from the front + from the back.
288. "Severe weather, bomb threats, & other disasters."
289. ... has already ...

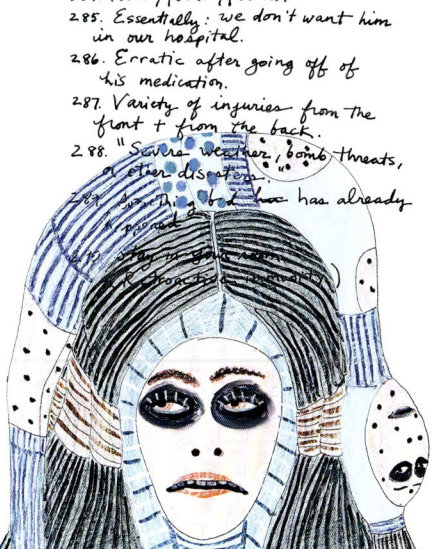

variety of sources, including media reports and conversations, and poetically arranged them on the page.[24] Violence in these works is insidious rather than direct, made palpable through cumulative effect, both within each work and across the series as a whole.

The 1998 dragging death of James Byrd Jr. by a group of white supremacists in Jasper, Texas, informed Christian Marclay's video work *Guitar Drag* (2000, fig. 1.22). Marclay read about the racially motivated murder in *Time* magazine and was struck by the photograph that was used to illustrate the story, which focused on the truck. The work employs a guitar as a substitute for Byrd's body and sound as a metaphor for his suffering and death. Marclay's video shows a guitar that is tied to the back of truck's tailgate and plugged into an amplifier that sits in the truck's bed. As the truck, which has a Texas license plate, takes off down a dirt road, the amplification of the sound of the guitar breaking apart becomes the soundtrack to the work.[25]

Works by Paul Rucker can be seen as silent counterpoints to *Guitar Drag*. Rucker's *Soundless* series memorializes incidents of racial violence from 1893 to 2014. In the series, the artist, who is a trained cellist, creates sculpted wood forms that evoke the portions of stringed instruments known as "the body," deploying them as stand-ins for the human body. Each work's title references the date and location of an incident of racial violence. *June 7, 1998, Jasper, Texas* (2015, fig. 1.23) references the murder of James Byrd Jr., while *September 15, 1963, Birmingham, Alabama* (2015, fig. 1.24) references the bombing by white supremacists of the Sixteenth Street Baptist Church, killing four girls between the ages of 11 and 14.

Melvin Edwards began his ongoing series *Lynch Fragments* in 1963 (fig. 1.25; see figs. 3.4–6), using cast-off industrial materials to create abstract welded compositions. Edwards first developed these sculptures in response to heightened racial violence in the midst of civil rights protests during the 1960s and his reading about the history of related violence in Ralph Ginzburg's 1962 book *100 Years of Lynchings*. Edwards's work is evocative rather than didactic, relying on the power of suggestion and association. Employing a similar strategy in works like *Minority Majority* (2012, see fig. 3.8), Theaster Gates makes abstract two- and three-dimensional works using decommissioned fire hoses to evoke attacks on civil rights protesters. These works convey anti-Black violence without including overt images of the suffering Black body.

Howardena Pindell's *Diallo* (2000, fig. 1.26) is a memorial to Amadou Diallo and Patrick Dorismond, who died as the result of police-involved shootings in New York City in 1999 and 2000, respectively. Words and figurative elements in the composition evoke points in the narrative of the deaths of these two unarmed Black men. For example, the phrase "a wallet" refers to the fact that Diallo was reaching for his wallet to show his identification to police when the officers shot him forty-one times in the doorway of his apartment building. The officers were charged with second-degree murder but were acquitted.[26]

Written on the Body

The spectacular nature of certain forms of anti-Black violence, including lynching, assault against nonviolent protesters, police brutality, and police action killings, has made them obvious focal points for artistic engagement, and the representation of the body is often central to these engagements. However, artists have also directly engaged bodies in order to consider the lasting implications of physical harm from violence, as well as to make visible forms of everyday violence and the psychological impact of long-term racism in its many manifestations within society.

An anchor in this section of the exhibition is Carl and Karen Pope's body art video work *Palimpsest* (1998–99, fig. 1.27). The video consists of edited footage of three permanent modifications that the artist Carl Pope made to his body—a brand of the Asante *adinkra* symbol *Aya* ("I am not afraid of you");[27] a small surgical incision; and a tattoo of poetic text by Karen Pope that invokes W. E. B. Du Bois's "double-consciousness" across the length of the artist's back.[28] Through these physical acts, the artists make an intentional stand against acts of racial violence from slavery to the present day. While the enslaved body was branded without choice, as punishment and to denote ownership, here the Popes have appropriated forms of permanent body modifications, and Carl Pope has asserted agency over his own body by choosing to have these marks inscribed on his skin. In this way, the artists create a protective shield against acts of racial violence.[29]

In *Untitled (Two Necklines)* (1989, fig. 1.28), Lorna Simpson juxtaposes texts and photographs in an evocative combination of words and images that are linked by the concept of circularity. Identical circular photographs of a Black woman's neck are installed on either side of a list of words referencing objects that have circular shapes. Some of the words—"ring," for instance—have multiple associations and can be interpreted as either benign or malevolent. Others, like "noose," are more pointedly sinister. The list culminates with the phrase "feel the

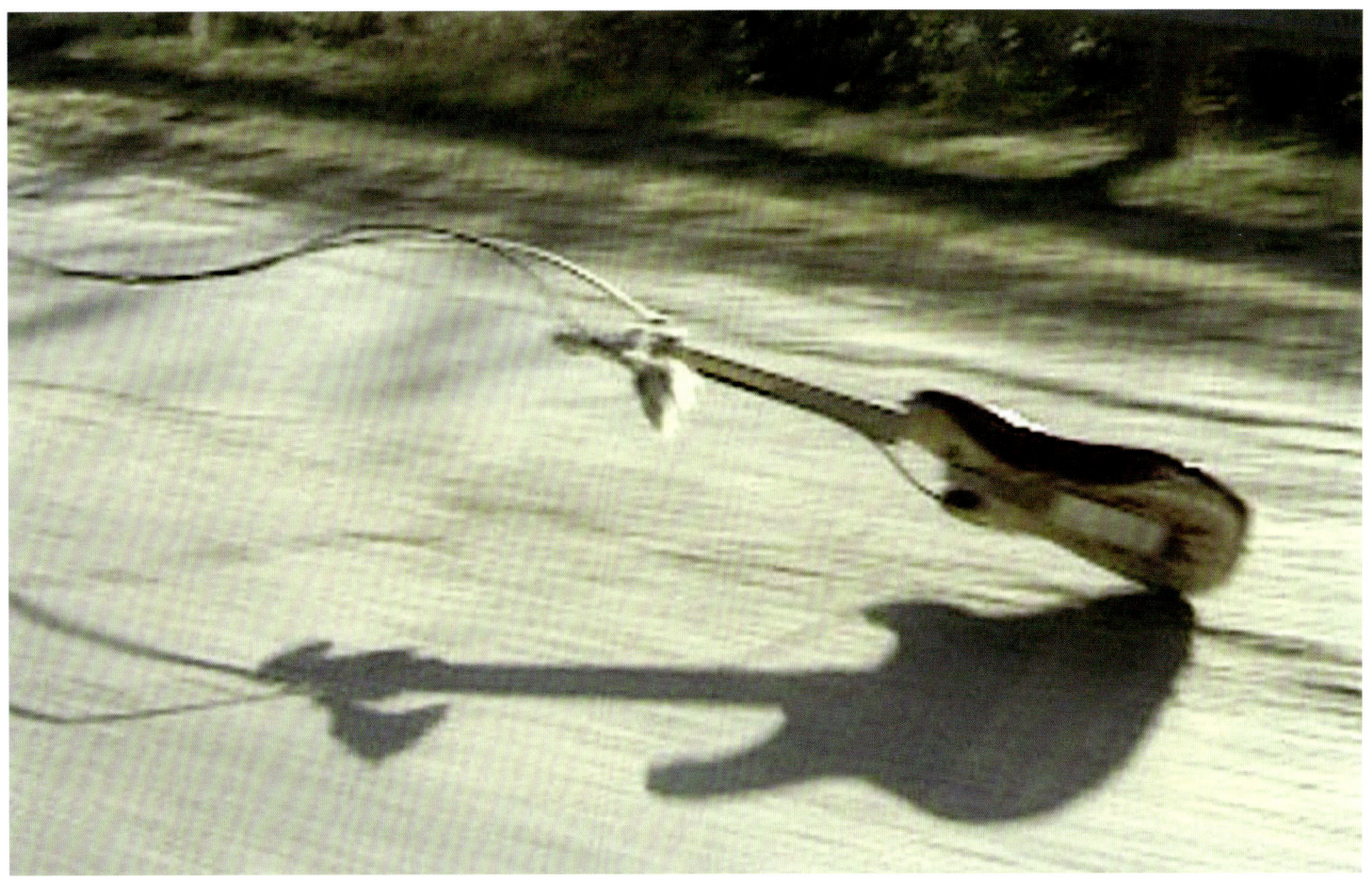

Fig. 1.22   Christian Marclay,
Guitar Drag (still) , 2000, video
projection, 14 minutes. © Christian
Marclay. Courtesy of Paula Cooper
Gallery, New York.

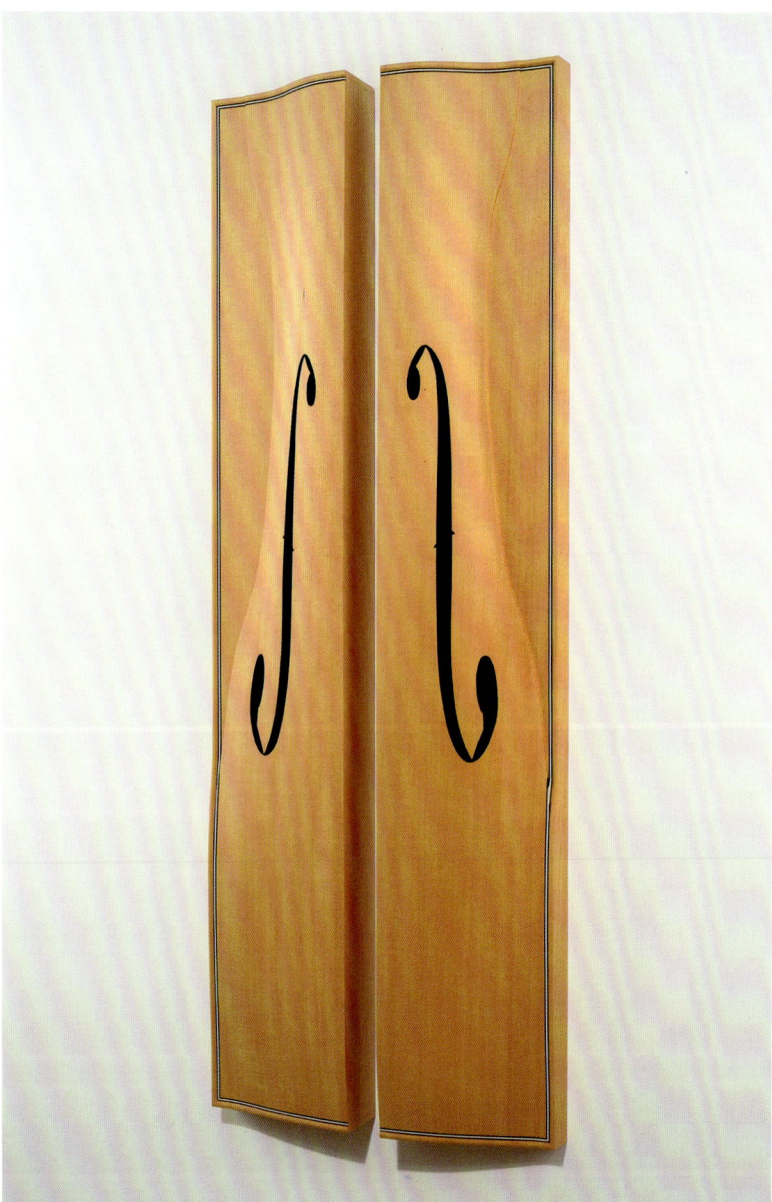

Fig. 1.23 Paul Rucker, *June 7, 1998, Jasper, Texas*, from the series *Soundless*, 2015, spruce, purfling, acrylic, 48 × 16 × 4 inches. Courtesy of the artist.

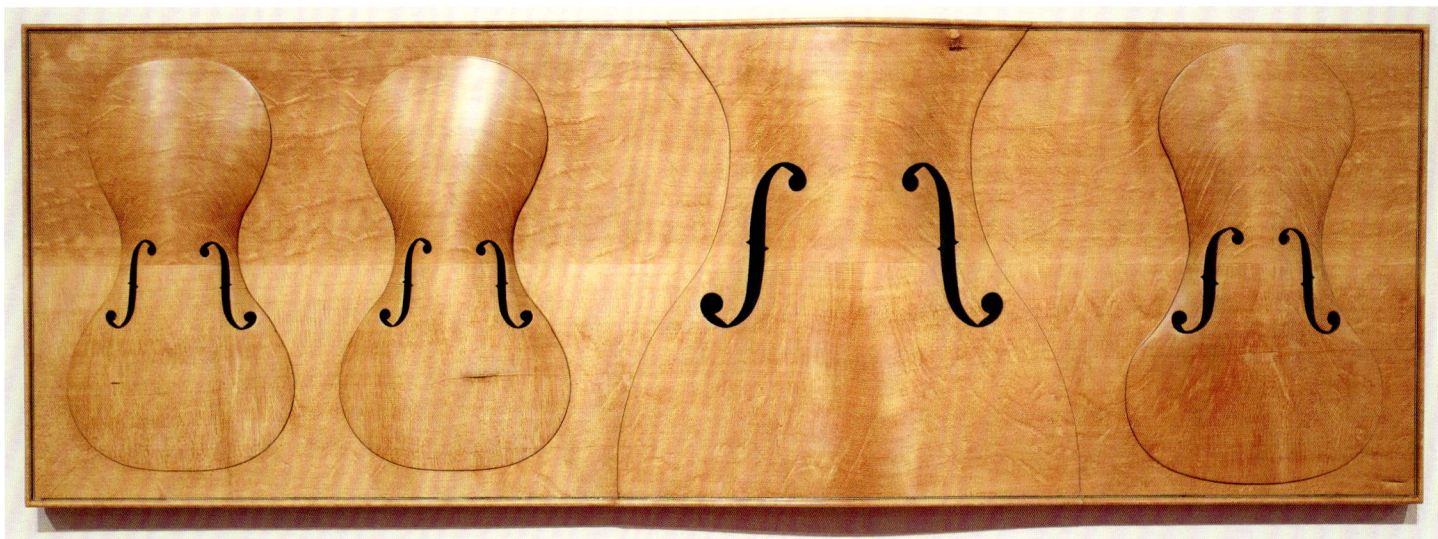

Fig. 1.24   Paul Rucker, *September 15, 1963, Birmingham, Alabama,* from the series *Soundless*, 2015, spruce, purfling, acrylic, 16 × 42 × 2 inches. Courtesy of the artist.

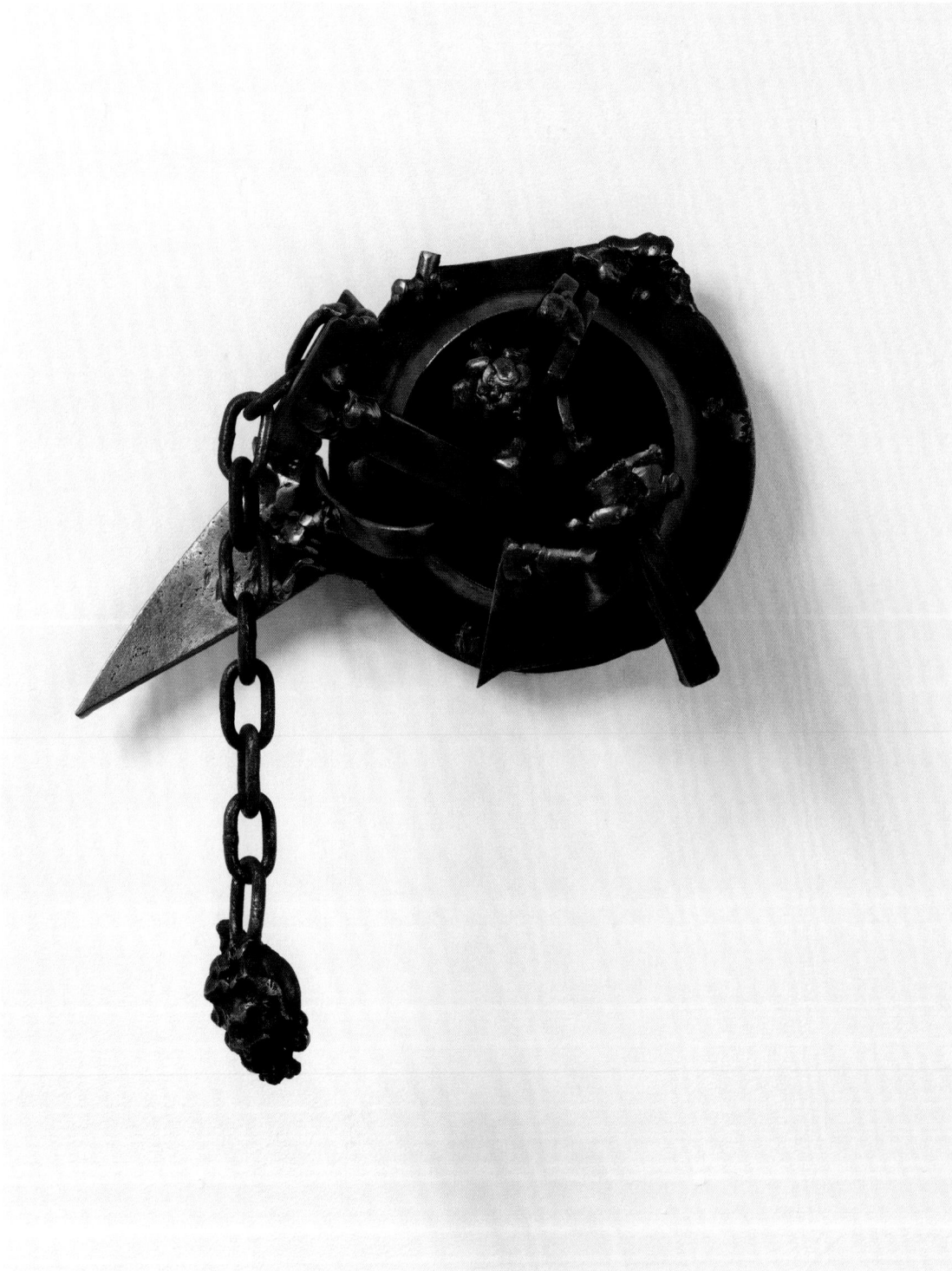

Fig. 1.25 Melvin Edwards, *Some Bright Morning*, 1963, from the *Lynch Fragments* series, welded steel, 14¼ × 9¼ × 5 inches. Courtesy of the artist and Alexander Gray Associates, New York. © 2021 Melvin Edwards / Artists Rights Society (ARS), New York.

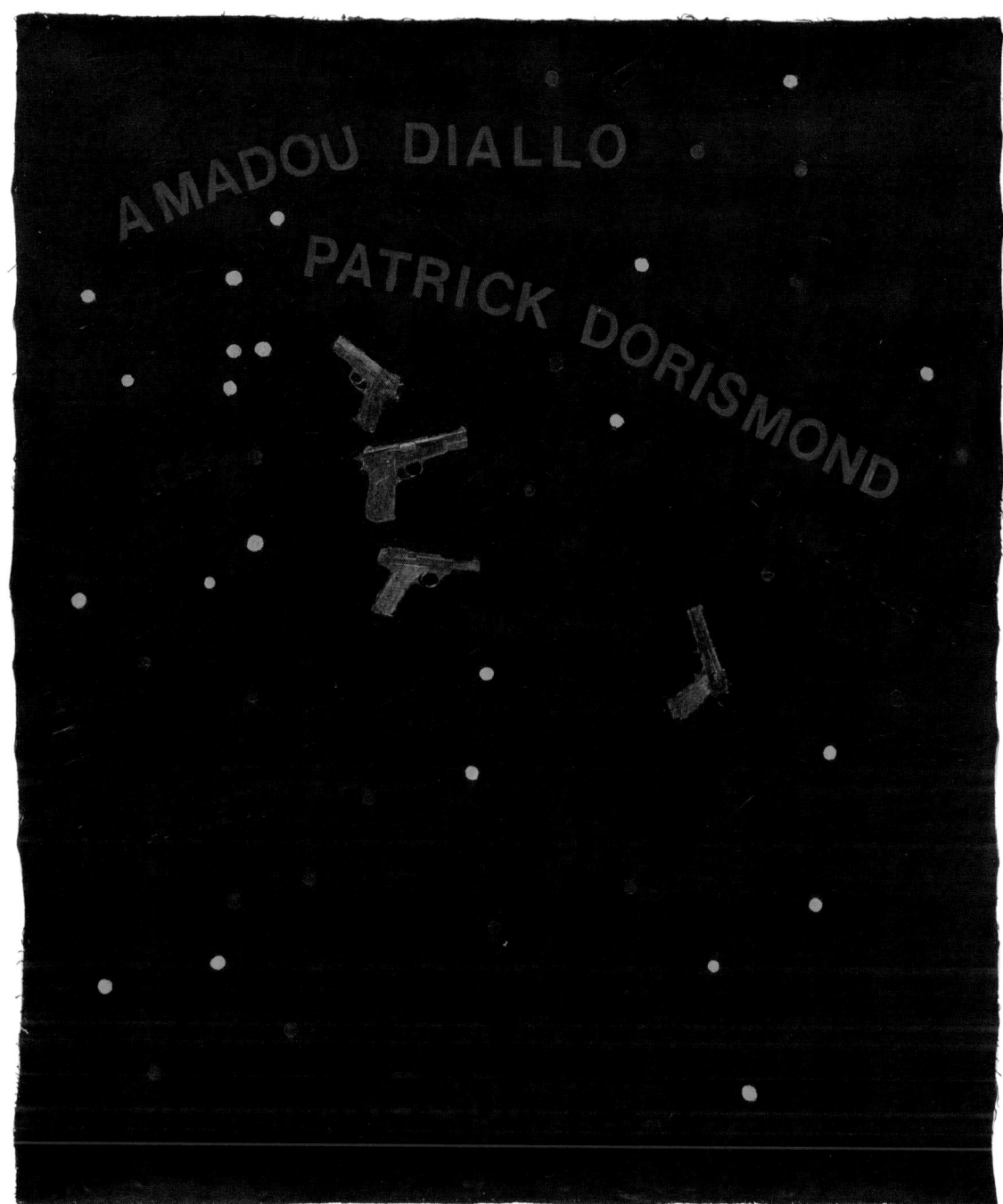

Fig. 1.26 Howardena Pindell, *Diallo*, 2000, mixed media on canvas, 46 × 40 inches. Courtesy of the artist and Garth Greenan Gallery.

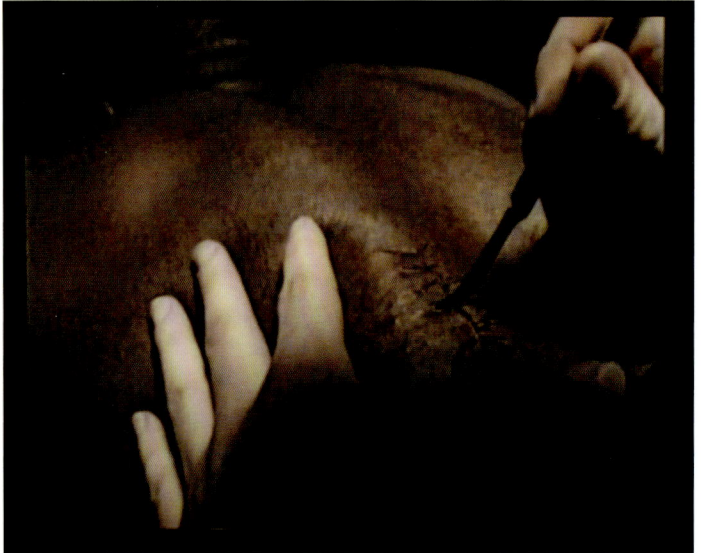
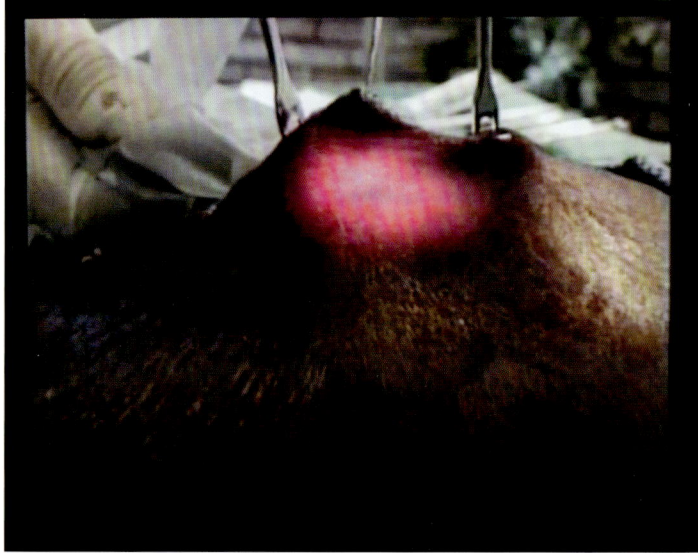
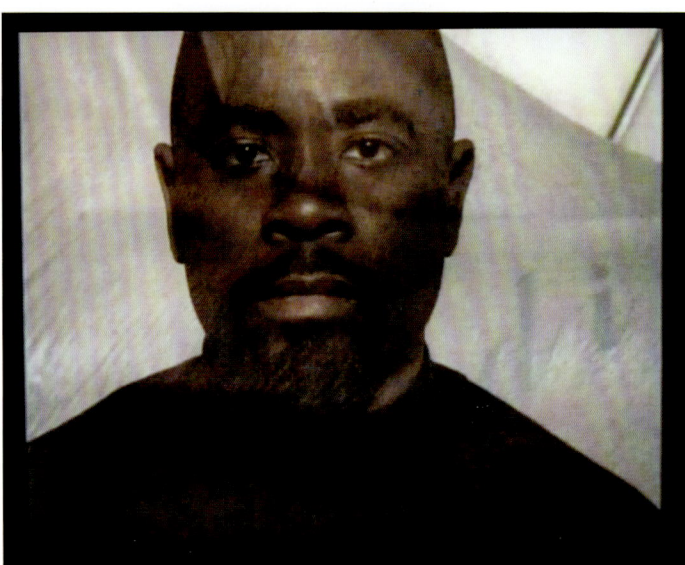
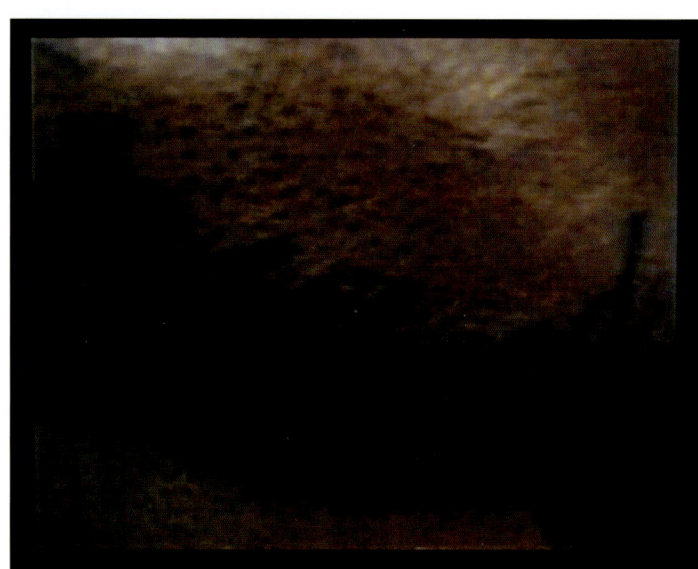

Fig. 1.27 Carl and Karen Pope,
Palimpsest, 1998–99, stills from
single-channel video, color with
sound, 6:37 minutes. Courtesy of
Carl and Karen Pope. Photograph
by Clare Britt.

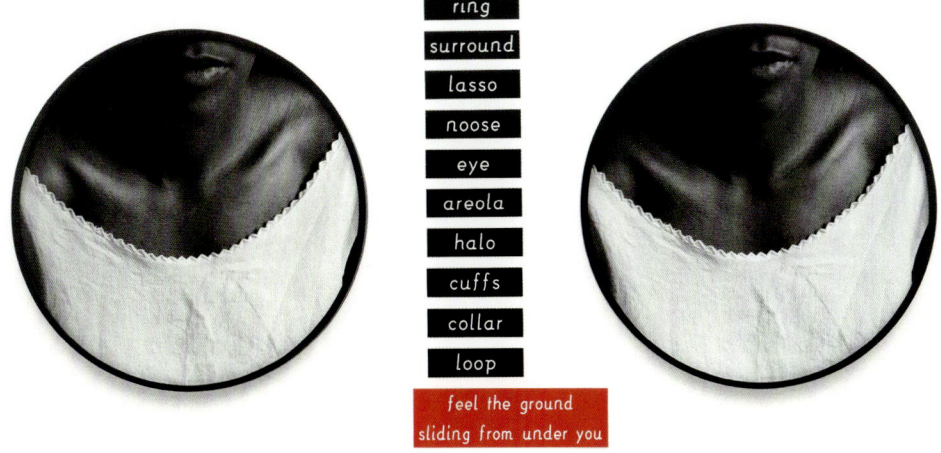

ring
surround
lasso
noose
eye
areola
halo
cuffs
collar
loop

feel the ground
sliding from under you

Fig. 1.28 Lorna Simpson, *Untitled (Two Necklines)*, 1989, two gelatin silver prints on paper and eleven plastic plaques; 36 inches (diameter, each print); dimensions variable (plastic plaques). Collection of Carolyn Campagna Kleefeld Contemporary Art Museum of California State University, Long Beach, Purchased with funds from the National Endowment for the Arts, 1990.6a–m. Image © Lorna Simpson. courtesy of the artist and Hauser & Wirth.

ground sliding from under you," which is engraved on a red plaque. It punctuates the violence that mounts from implicit to explicit as the viewer makes their way down the list, in a way that mirrors the move from explicit to implicit violence in the exhibition.

Conclusion

By drawing upon objects from over a hundred-year period within the space of one exhibition, *A Site of Struggle* addresses the persistence of racial violence in the United States and, through the lens of artistic expression, contextualizes contemporary struggles with racial violence within a wider and deeper history. An understanding of this continuity must be brought to bear on any discussions of anti-Black violence today if they are to lead to meaningful change. By focusing on a selection of works that engage particular strategies rather than seeking to be comprehensive, *A Site of Struggle* offers a contribution to understanding this history with—as Lonnie Bunch urged at the opening of this essay—"nuance and complexity."

During the process of developing *A Site of Struggle*, I have consistently been reminded that struggle connotes not only conflict, but also a sustained and determined effort under great difficulty. Many of the artists discussed above have struggled with the history of racial violence in this country, and their artworks are an invitation for us to do the same. Art can provide a moment of pause, an opportunity for us to sit with the complex and deep-rooted nature of anti-Black violence and contemplate how it impacts us individually and as a society. In these works, we may find recognition of our own suffering—which is important in and of itself—as well as a provocation to continue, or begin for the first time, striving to eliminate this suffering through concrete actions appropriate to our positionality. By highlighting the ways in which American artists have wrestled with the challenges posed by representation in order to protest, process, mourn, and memorialize anti-Black violence, *A Site of Struggle* is a modest offering in the ongoing struggle for the preservation and flourishing of Black life.

Notes

1 David Gelles, "Smithsonian's Leader Says 'Museums Have a Social Justice Role to Play,'" *New York Times*, July 2, 2020, http://www.nytimes.com /2020/07/02/business/smithsonian-lonnie-bunch -corner-office.html. See also Lonnie G. Bunch III, "Chapter 7: Befriending Presidents and Managing Congress," in *A Fool's Errand: Creating the National Museum of African American History and Culture in the Age of Bush, Obama, and Trump* (Washington, DC: Smithsonian Books, 2019), Kindle edition.

2 Lonnie Bunch, quoted in Gelles, "Smithsonian's Leader."

3 See Courtney R. Baker, *Humane Insight: Looking at Images of African American Suffering and Death* (Urbana: University of Illinois Press, 2015), 4.

4 See Leigh Raiford, *Imprisoned in a Luminous Glare: Photography and the African American Freedom Struggle* (Chapel Hill: University of North Carolina Press, 2011), 9.

5 See Baker, *Humane Insight*, 109.

6 On this point, see, for example, Allison Dorsey, "Black History Is American History: Teaching African American History in the Twenty-First Century," *Journal of American History* 93, no. 4 (March 2007): 1,171–77.

7 For insight into some different perspectives on these debates, see, for example, Alex Greenberger, "'The Painting Must Go': Hannah Black Pens Open Letter to the Whitney about Controversial Biennial Artwork," *Art News*, March 21, 2017, http://www .artnews.com/artnews/news/the-painting-must-go -hannah-black-pens-open-letter-to-the-whitney -about-controversial-biennial-work-7992/; Coco Fusco, "Censorship, Not the Painting, Must Go: On Dana Schutz's Image of Emmett Till," *Hyperallergic*, March 27, 2017, http://hyperallergic.com/368290 /censorship-not-the-painting-must-go-on-dana -schutzs-image-of-emmett-till/; Aruna D'Souza, "Act I: Open Casket, Whitney Biennial, 2017," in *Whitewalling: Art, Race and Protest in 3 Acts* (New York: Badlands Unlimited, 2018), 16–53; William C. Anderson, "Against Consuming Images of the Brutalized, Dead and Dying," *Hyperallergic*, June 1, 2018, http://hyperallergic .com/445105/against-consuming-images-of-the -brutalized-dead-and-dying; Sarah Cascone, "'We Failed': A Cleveland Museum Apologizes for Cancelling an Exhibition on Police Brutality without Consulting the Artist," *Artnet.com*, June 9, 2020, http://news .artnet.com/exhibitions/moca-cleveland-apologizes -cancelling-shaun-leonardo-exhibition-1882671; Brian Boucher, "A Museum Canceled a Show about Police Brutality. Here's the Art," *New York Times*, June 9, 2020, http://www.nytimes.com/2020/06/09 /arts/design/moca-cleveland-shaun-leonardo.html.

8 At the Block, I would like to acknowledge Joe Scott and Dan Silverstein for their research and discussions related to exhibition design; as well as Bethany Hill, Erin Northington, and América Salomón for their research and discussions related to visitor support; and Alisa Swindell for working on both sets of issues.

9 I would like to acknowledge Elizabeth Callihan, Ross Jordan, Valerie Cassel Oliver, Kymberly Pinder, Maurita Poole, Risa Puleo, Veronica Roberts, Nicole Soukup, Lorelei Stewart, and Fred Wilson for their insights shared during an April 2019 convening of museum colleagues. Additional conversations with curators La Tanya Autry, Amber Esseiva, Miranda Lash, Meg Onli, and Lowery Stokes Sims were influential on my thinking. Thanks are due to the faculty, undergradu- ate and graduate students, and staff attendees at Northwestern University's October 2019 Black Arts Initiative lecture/forum for feedback, as potential "first users" of the exhibition, which led to the further refinement of the exhibition's approach and plans for presentation. Thanks are due to the members of the community advisory committee: Melissa Blount, Fran Joy, Rebeca Mendoza, Rev. Michael Nabors, Nathan Norman, Robin Rue Simmons, Angela Williams, and Corey Winchester; and to Dino Robinson of the Shorefront Legacy Center and Tiffany McDowell and LeAnn Jenkins of YWCA Evanston/Northshore's Equity Institute for their facilitation of the community advisory committee meetings.

10 For more on this topic, see Dora Apel, *Imagery of Lynching: Black Men, White Women, and the Mob* (New Brunswick, NJ: Rutgers University Press, 2004).

11 For their early feedback on the exhibition premise, content, and organization during an October 2018 scholars meeting and in continued conversations, I would like to thank Sampada Aranke, La Tanya Autry, Courtney Baker, Bridget Cooks, Leslie M. Harris, Noémi Michel, Shawn Michelle Smith, LaCharles Ward, and Mlondi Zondi. Thanks to Sarah Estrela for her meticulous note taking.

12 For more on Wells's activism and the context and text of *A Red Record*, see Jacqueline Jones Royster, ed., *Southern Horrors and Other Writings: The Anti-Lynching Campaign of Ida B. Wells, 1892–1900* (New York: Bedford Books, 1997).

13 For more on the role art played in the NAACP's strategy, see Amy Kirschke, "The 'Crime' of Blackness: Lynching Imagery in *The Crisis*," in *Art in Crisis: W. E. B. Du Bois and the Struggle for African American Identity and Memory* (Bloomington: Indiana University Press, 2007), 48–114.

14 For more on this sculpture, see Caitlin Beach, "Meta Warrick Fuller's Mary Turner and the Memory of Mob Violence," *NKA: Journal of Contemporary African Art* 36 (May 2015): 16–27; Huey Copeland, "Making Black Feminist Art Histories," *American Art* 31, no. 2 (Summer 2017): 27–29; Renée Ater, "Race, Gender, and Nation: Rethinking the Sculpture of Meta Warrick Fuller" (PhD diss., Univ. of Maryland, 2000), 125–55; Walter F. White, "The Work of the Mob," *The Crisis* (September 1918): 221–23.

15 Lisa Gail Collins, Lisa Mintz Messinger, and Rachel Mustalish, *African American Artists, 1929–1945, Prints, Drawings, and Paintings in the Metropolitan Museum of Art* (New York and New Haven, CT: Metropolitan Museum of Art and Yale University Press, 2003), 40. Apel, *Imagery of Lynching*, 116–18.

16 For more about the NAACP's use of visual arts, see Kirschke, *Art in Crisis*.

17 A second exhibition was organized by the Communist Party USA. For more on these exhibitions, see Helen Langa, "Two Antilynching Exhibitions: Politicized Viewpoints, Racial Perspectives, Gendered Constraints," *American Art* 13, no. 1 (Spring 1999): 10–39; and Apel, "The Antilynching Exhibition of 1935: Strategies and Constraints," in *Imagery of Lynching*, 83–131. For the NAACP's exhibition, see also Marlene Park, "Lynching and Anti-lynching: Art and Politics in the 1930s," *Prospects: Annual of American Cultural Studies* 18 (1993): 311–65; and Margaret Rose Vendryes, "Hanging on These Walls: An Art Commen- tary on Lynching, the Forgotten 1935 Art Exhibition," in *Race Consciousness: African-American Studies for the New Century*, ed. Judith Fossett and Jeffrey Tucker (New York: New York University Press, 1997), 153–76.

18 Isamu Noguchi Catalogue Raisonné, entry 131, Archives of the Isamu Noguchi Foundation and Garden Museum, http://archive.noguchi.org/Detail /artwork/165.

19 On Williams's work, see Elizabeth Alexander, "'Can You Be BLACK and Look at This?': Reading the Rodney King Video(s)," in *Black Male: Representations of Masculinity in Contemporary American Art*, ed. Thelma Golden (New York: Whitney Museum of American Art, 1994), 108–10.

20 Thank you to Carmenita Higginbotham for her discussion of this work with me. See also Carmenita Higginbotham, *The Urban Scene: Race, Reginald Marsh and American Art* (University Park: Pennsylvania State University Press, 2015), 1–3.

21 See Ken Gonzales-Day, *Lynching in the West, 1830–1935* (Durham, NC: Duke University Press, 2006).

22 "The Waco Horror," supplement to *The Crisis* 12, no. 3 (July 1916): 8-page insert.

23 Deborah Rothschild, "A Conversation with Laylah Ali," in *Laylah Ali: The Greenheads Series* (Williams- town, MA: Williams College Museum of Art, 2012), 8.

24 Dina Deitsch, "Notes on Drawings: Laylah Ali's Textual Turn," in *Laylah Ali: Note Drawings* (Lincoln, MA: deCordova Sculpture Park and Museum, 2008), 3.

25 See Carlos Kase, "'This Guitar Has Seconds to Live': *Guitar Drag*'s Archaeology of Indeterminacy and Violence," *Discourse* 30, no. 3 (Fall 2008): 419–42; Greil Marcus, "Guitar Drag: 2006/2000," in *The History of Rock 'n' Roll in Ten Songs* (New Haven, CT: Yale University Press, 2014), 215–35.

26 See Naomi Beckwith and Valerie Cassel Oliver, eds., *Howardena Pindell: What Remains to Be Seen* (Chicago: Museum of Contemporary Art, 2018), 49–50.

27 Literally meaning "to employ a message," *adinkra* symbols traditionally represent proverbs and are printed on cloth. For more on adinkra symbols, see W. Bruce Willis, *The Adinkra Dictionary: A Visual Primer on the Language of Adinkra* (Washington, DC: Pyramid Complex, 1998); and "Adinkra," *Inscribing Meaning: Writing and Graphic Systems in African Art*, exhibition website, Smithsonian Institution, accessed February 17, 2021, http://africa.si.edu/exhibits/inscribing/adinkra .html.

28 See W. E. B. Du Bois, *The Souls of Black Folk*, in John Hope Franklin, *Three Negro Classics* (New York: Avon Books, 1965).

29 See Janet Dees, "Rewriting the Body: Carl and Karen Pope's 'Palimpsest'" (MA thesis, University of Delaware, 2005).

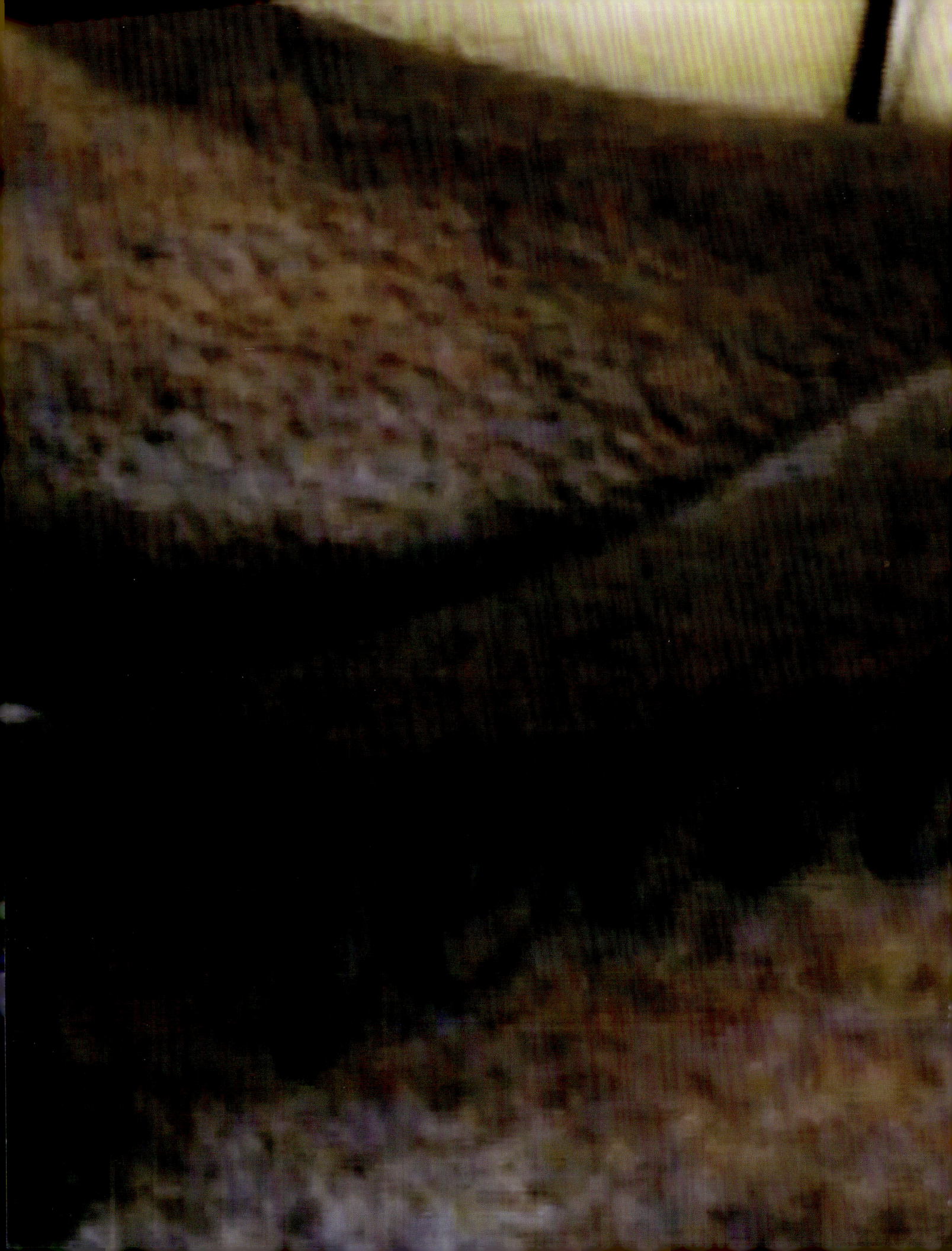

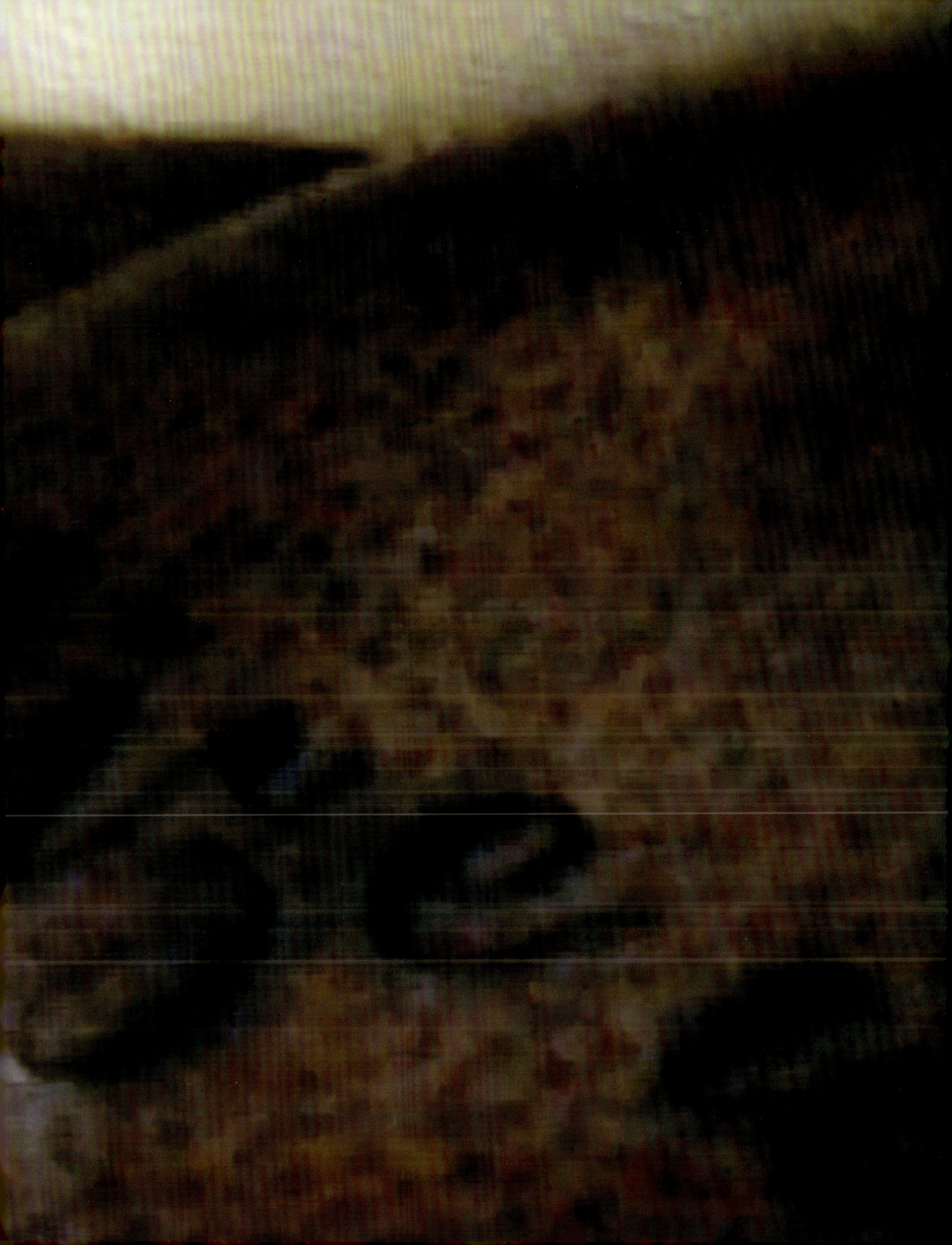

Making Racial Violence Visible

Leslie M. Harris

We are saturated with and have unending access to images of racial violence. Today, photographs and videos of police brutality, the bodies of refugees, separated families, genocidal concentration camps, lynchings, and colonial-era violence, as well as photographs and drawings from the era of slavery are all widely available via a range of digital devices—most intimately, our phones, or at the click of a computer keyboard. We worry that repeated engagement with such images reinforces rather than works against societal beliefs that nonwhite people should be subject to such violence, and that the display of brutalized non-white bodies dehumanizes the victims rather than indicts those responsible for violence. This essay explores one source for the development of the strategy of exposure: the eighteenth- and nineteenth-century anti-slavery movements. At that time, the kind of visual saturation we live amid was almost unimaginable. Yet, some of the fault lines we struggle with—balancing the need to expose the injustice of violence with the need to assert the humanity of those victimized—were there at the inception.

By the early nineteenth century, two kinds of images were poised to become central to the struggle against the enslavement of people of African descent in the Atlantic World. One set of images sought to impress the urgency of slavery's wrongs through depictions of the physical violence enslavers inflicted. Another set of images sought to depict people of African descent as equal to those of European descent. We can think of these sets of images as opposite sides of the same coin. The moral urgency of the campaign for which anti-slavery activists produced them meant that they shadowed each other: by the end of slavery in the United States in 1865, one could hardly look at people of African descent without summoning up an idea of the brutal system of coerced labor from which they were in the process of escaping. This indicated the success of the anti-slavery movement in creating a widespread understanding of the harms of slavery to people of African descent. Indeed, by the time of the Civil War, pro-slavery activists were losing the battle to justify racial violence as a demonstration of the morality of their cause. The creation of the ideology of paternalism—the belief that enslavers were kindly, often male, parental figures to the enslaved—was a means to explain away the violence of slavery that anti-slavery activists had successfully publicized. But these images of violence could also reduce people of African descent to their degradation in a mainstream white society already poised to see them that way.

Images depicting the violence of slavery did not appear sui generis in the late eighteenth century. From the time of contact between Europeans and Africans, artists based in Europe created depictions of people of African descent as well as representations of the variety of contact between Africans and Europeans. Europeans who traveled to Africa as the slave trade developed created drawings of high-level diplomatic exchanges between African rulers and European rulers' envoys, fantastical and exaggerated as well as realistic depictions of the variety of people in Africa, and depictions of the violence rooted in war that accompanied and accelerated enslavement. These images circulated among the small groups of literate people in Europe as parts of books, were held in private hands in journals and diaries written by those who accompanied voyages to Africa, and were part of the output of professional artists.[1]

As the slave trade and slavery developed in the Atlantic World, the catalogue of images produced by white Europeans grew as well. But images from the period before the late eighteenth century are less well known because of their creation before mass production, mass culture, and rising literacy rates. When late eighteenth-century British anti-slavery activists created their first anti-slavery images, their melding of political energy and artistry was part of a new era of visual culture.[2] At the same time that this mass literary and visual culture created the possibility for a common world of ideas, it also had the potential for flattening out individuality. Two sets of images from the early anti-slavery movement present the possibilities and limits of this tension. One is the cutaway image of the slave ship. As art historian Cheryl Finley has recovered, that imagery was inaugurated in 1788 by the Plymouth Committee of the Society for Effecting the Abolition of the Slave Trade in England.[3] One of the most popular versions was that of the ship *Brookes* developed in 1789 by the British Society for Effecting the Abolition of the Slave Trade (fig. 2.1). Anti-slavery societies sought to depict the horrific conditions in which slave traders transported people of African descent to the Americas—conditions much worse than those experienced by whites who made the treacherous journey from Europe to the Americas. Each ship held several hundred enslaved people as the trade reached its peak numbers in the late eighteenth century. The enslaved, depicted as tiny silhouetted bodies transfixed in their positions as cargo, lost all individuality as they were summoned to demonstrate for European audiences the brutality of the crowded conditions. Indeed, these images also erased the array of violent tactics used by slave ship crews to enforce order on these ships. Moreover, they removed all sense of agency from the enslaved, despite the fact that historians now estimate that at least ten percent of all slave ships during the trade experienced slave rebellions. The *Brookes* image was reprinted by the thousands in Great Britain and then in revised versions in France and the United States. Combined with an effective campaign of texts and court cases in Great Britain and the United States that emphasized the physical brutality of the trade, the image was a central tactic in ending the slave trade.[4]

Around the same time, Josiah Wedgewood created the similarly iconic image of a kneeling, partially clothed enslaved man of African descent with broken chains on his wrists, encircled by the caption "Am I Not a Man and a Brother?" The image of the half-clothed man was soon joined by one of a half-clothed woman with the caption "Am I Not a Woman and a Sister?" Although the captions proclaimed that people of African descent were part of the family of man, the kneeling, partially clad figures positioned them as figuratively and culturally below white Europeans. By the third decade of the nineteenth century, these images had become ubiquitous among white anti-slavery activists in England and the United States. Although the activists proclaimed their commitment to ending slavery and racial inequality, such images also revealed that they could not completely escape the limits of their own hierarchical thinking. The fact that these Black figures, whether kneeling or standing, were half clothed echoed judgments against the sartorial cultures of African civilizations, even as enslaved people themselves had little control over the state of their own clothing. More troubling was the sexualized implication of the naked body at this time. While anti-slavery activists sought to lay the blame on enslavers for the inadequate clothing, sexual abuse, and traumatic family separations that enslaved people experienced, the images were troublesome signals to those less amenable to the anti-slavery argument, reenforcing that people of African descent were unequal to whites. Whether that inequality was environmental or innate seemed to matter little to those who sought to keep Blacks enslaved and without citizenship rights.[5]

The anti-slavery movement would struggle with the utility and limitations of such images in their attempts to argue for the emancipation, humanity, and citizenship of people of African descent. For most white anti-slavery activists, the slave ship and Wedgewood images were powerful arguments against slavery. Some Black activists agreed. When presented with an image of the slave ship created by the Plymouth Anti-Slavery Society, Olaudah Equiano, an anti-slavery activist who had experienced the

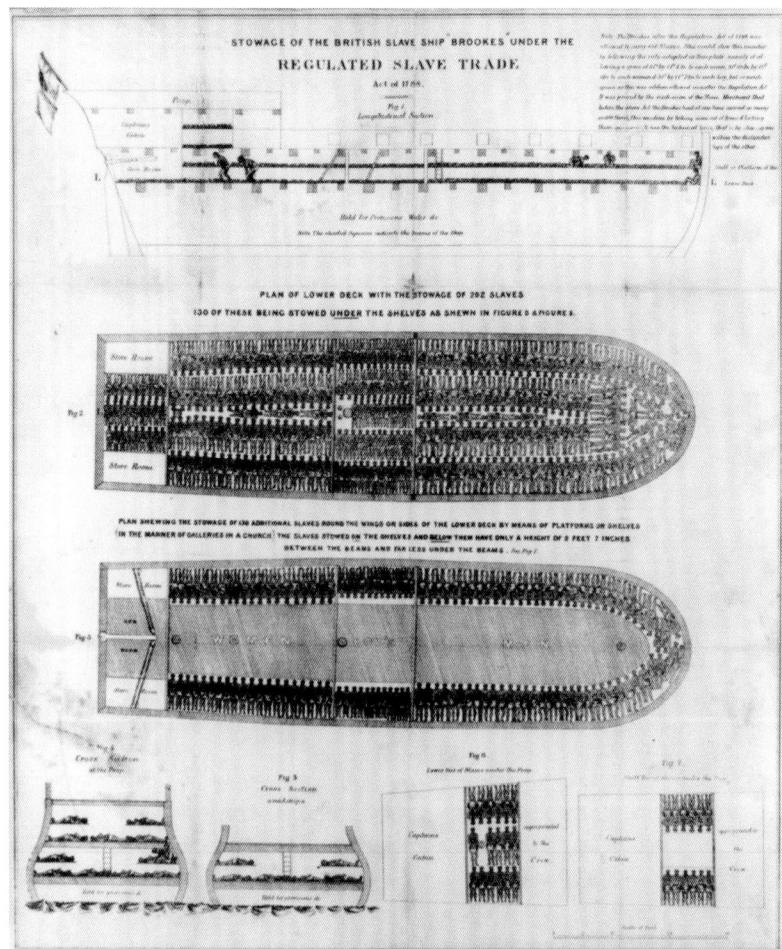

Fig. 2.1 *Stowage of the British Slave Ship "Brookes" under the Regulated Slave Trade Act of 1788*, 1789, etching, 18⁵⁷⁄₆₄ × 15¾ inches. Courtesy of the Library of Congress.

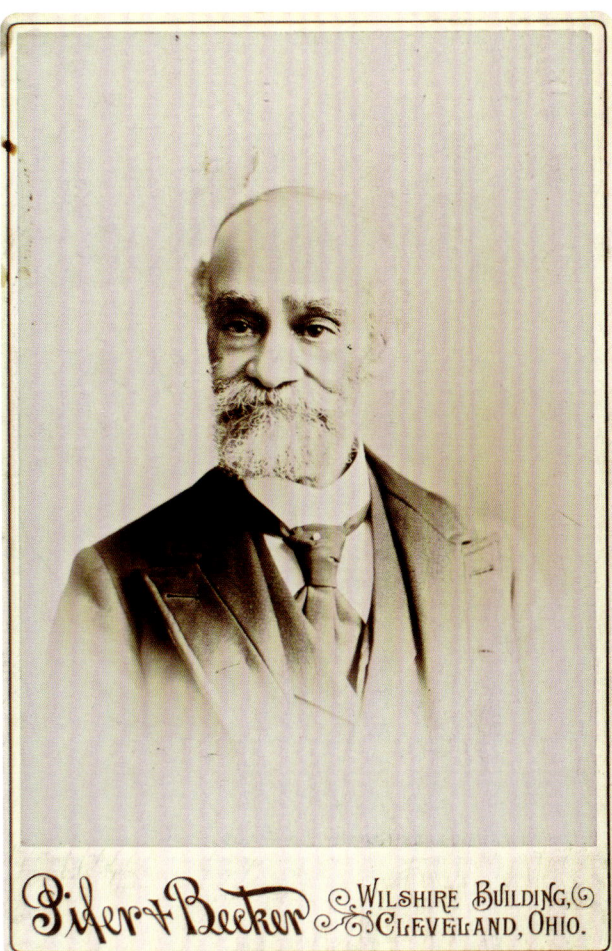

Fig. 2.2 Pifer and Becker, Cleveland, Ohio, *Studio Portrait of Patrick H. Reason*, ca. 1890–99, photograph. Cabinet card collection, courtesy of the Schomburg Center for Research in Black Culture, Photographs and Prints Division, the New York Public Library Digital Collections.

Middle Passage as a child, stated in a publicly published letter that he felt "love and gratitude" for the society for publicizing the brutality of the Middle Passage and for its work on behalf of enslaved people. As art historian Cheryl Finley writes, this public proclamation is probably only part of the range of emotions Equiano experienced upon seeing this image. No doubt his own memories of his time aboard a slave ship returned to him—experiences he described in detail in his autobiography.[6] And by the 1830s, Patrick Henry Reason (fig. 2.2), a Black engraver in New York City, had begun to publish his own versions of the Wedgewood engravings, albeit at the request of white abolitionists.[7]

Yet, some were troubled. Historian Paul Polgar states that the Wedgewood image caused concern among Pennsylvania's white anti-slavery activists as early as the 1780s. They believed the kneeling image reinforced negative ideas of people of African descent as passive and thus, within US ideals of freedom, less capable of being seen as equal citizens. They chose to depict a standing man, still half-clothed and partially in chains, but stepping toward freedom of his own volition.[8]

But the kneeling enslaved person and the cutaway slave ship were only part of what would become a flood of images depicting a range of physical punishments from the late eighteenth century through the antebellum period. The whipping of partially clothed or completely nude enslaved men and women was among the most common subjects of enslaver violence imagery, but implements of torture—whips, chains, iron masks, and other weapons—and other forms of cruelty were also detailed in anti-slavery print culture images and words. As more individuated images of enslaved people emerged in a range of anti-slavery publications, so did a more detailed accounting of the ways in which they were abused. Magazines for adults and children, newspapers, and books depicted an ever-wider range of accounts of slavery and, to a lesser degree, the racism that free Blacks experienced in the Northern states. The majority of white radical anti-slavery activists believed that these descriptions of bondage and oppression at the hands of white enslavers would be a powerful tool of moral suasion for the nation. The domestic slave trade, the labor that enslaved people performed, the punishments enslaved people endured, and the sexual and emotional abuses of enslaved people by enslavers—all were

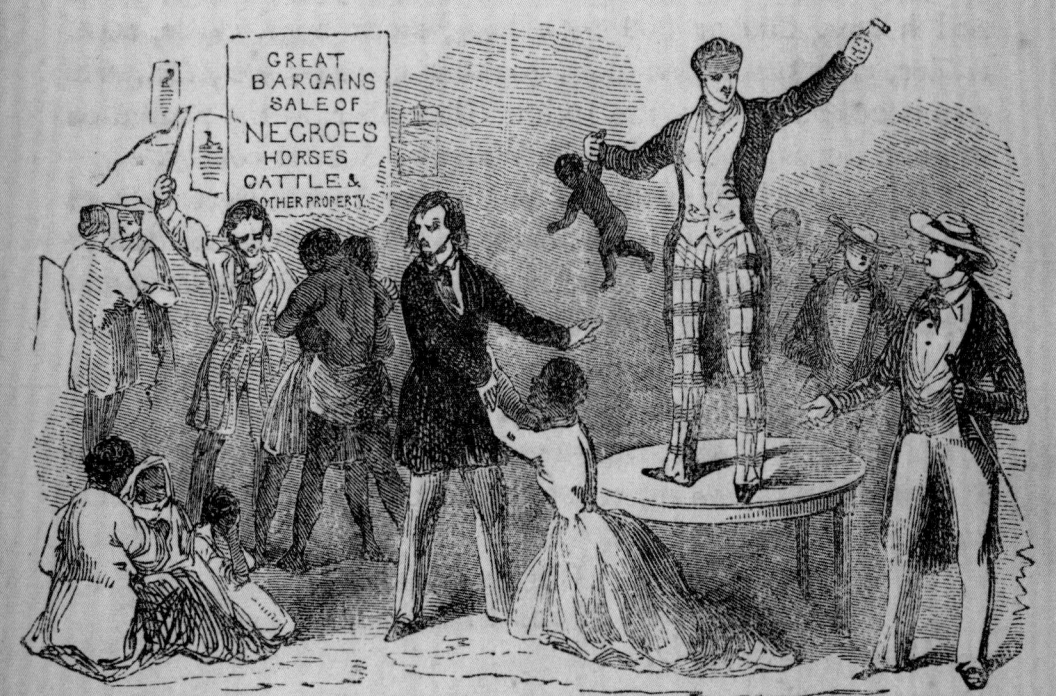

Leeds Anti-slavery Series. No. 9.

SALES BY AUCTION OF MEN, WOMEN, AND

CHILDREN,

WITH HOUSES, LANDS, AND CATTLE, &c.

Husbands, Wives, and Families sold indiscriminately to different purchasers, are violently separated—probably never to meet again.

"See the poor victim torn from social life,
The shrinking babe, the agonizing wife!"

The following is from the *Christian Index*, published at Penfield, Ga.:—

"EXECUTORS' SALE.—Will be sold at the late residence of Jesse Perkins, deceased, late of Greene county, on Wednesday, the 1st of March next, the following property, viz.:

Fig. 2.3 "Husbands, Wives, and Families sold indiscriminately to different purchasers, are violently separated—probably never to meet again," engraving published by W. and F. Cash, London, 1853. Courtesy of the Schomburg Center for Research in Black Culture, Manuscripts, Archives and Rare Books Division, the New York Public Library Digital Collections.

detailed by anti-slavery activists (fig. 2.3). The success of the slave ship and Wedgewood images and the rise of an increasingly accessible press led activists to produce reams of images of enslavement for consumption by the general public, in the hopes of achieving the abolition of slavery itself, as had previously been achieved with the trans-atlantic slave trade.

Some today see these images as reinforcing such brutality, rather than leading to liberation. But at the time of their production, white pro-slavery supporters North and South critiqued anti-slavery activists, and particularly white women, for speaking of such brutality because it aligned them politically with Black liberation and racial equality. Beginning in the 1830s and perhaps earlier, pro-slavery Southerners burned anti-slavery materials and passed laws against their circulation in the South. Pro-slavery and white supremacist supporters in the North also burned pamphlets and rioted against anti-slavery activists repeatedly in Philadelphia, New York, and other locales, destroying churches and other buildings where anti-slavery activists gathered, schools that offered to welcome Black children, and symbols of whites offering Blacks equality. White supremacists also produced caricatured images that reflected their beliefs that Blacks were unworthy of freedom. Edward Clay of Philadelphia and Anthony Imbert of New York were two of the most well-known cartoonists who lampooned the emerging Black middle class as outlandishly dressed and functionally illiterate, and thus unable to be equal citizens. They depicted white anti-slavery activists as seeking sexual favors and interracial marriages with Blacks. Indeed, one of the most violent demonstrations of the antebellum period was the New York City amalgamation riots, a three-day melee against Black and white businesses, churches, and homes perceived to be sites of activism on behalf of emancipation and racial equality.[9] Pro-slavery and white supremacist activists throughout the country understood the images produced by anti-slavery and anti-racist activists for what they were—a call to a new morality that truly saw all as equal before the eyes of God and nation. Arguments about equality before God were more easily refuted with concepts of earthly hierarchy, and even earthly suffering. But squaring racial hierarchies with the new ideologies of freedom and human equality called into being with the Revolutionary era was much more difficult.

Still, the abjectness of many anti-slavery images could not alone do battle against pro-slavery and racist ideologies. As Jasmine Cobb has argued, white anti-slavery activists used visual culture to depict the violence of slavery, but in focusing on the critique of white-inflicted violence, they often avoided depicting the possibilities of Black freedom. This left a gap that Northern free African Americans attempted to fill in a variety of ways.[10] Black anti-slavery activists emerged as a critical public voice by the 1840s and pushed back against this limited framing. The fugitive slave narratives that mostly male activists produced became one of the most popular literary genres of the nineteenth century. In addition to full-length books, anti-slavery periodicals published interviews, pamphlets, and short stories that largely "gave voice" to formerly enslaved people. These often-autobiographical works featured formal portraits of the authors or chief subjects of the narratives, as well as images from their experiences of slavery and escape. The publication and distribution of the vast majority of these works were controlled by white anti-slavery activists, and historians still struggle to determine the degree to which white activism shaped the focus of such texts and the imagery they used. But there is no doubt that the collaboration between white publishers and Black producers presented to the public a wider range of images and sentiments directly from people of African descent than had been available before.[11]

Among the earliest of these pairings of humanity and violence was in the work of Olaudah Equiano, whose 1789 *Interesting Narrative* stretched from his childhood in Africa, traversing the Middle Passage and his enslavement in the Atlantic World, to his self-purchase of his freedom and his life as an anti-slavery activist in Great Britain. His

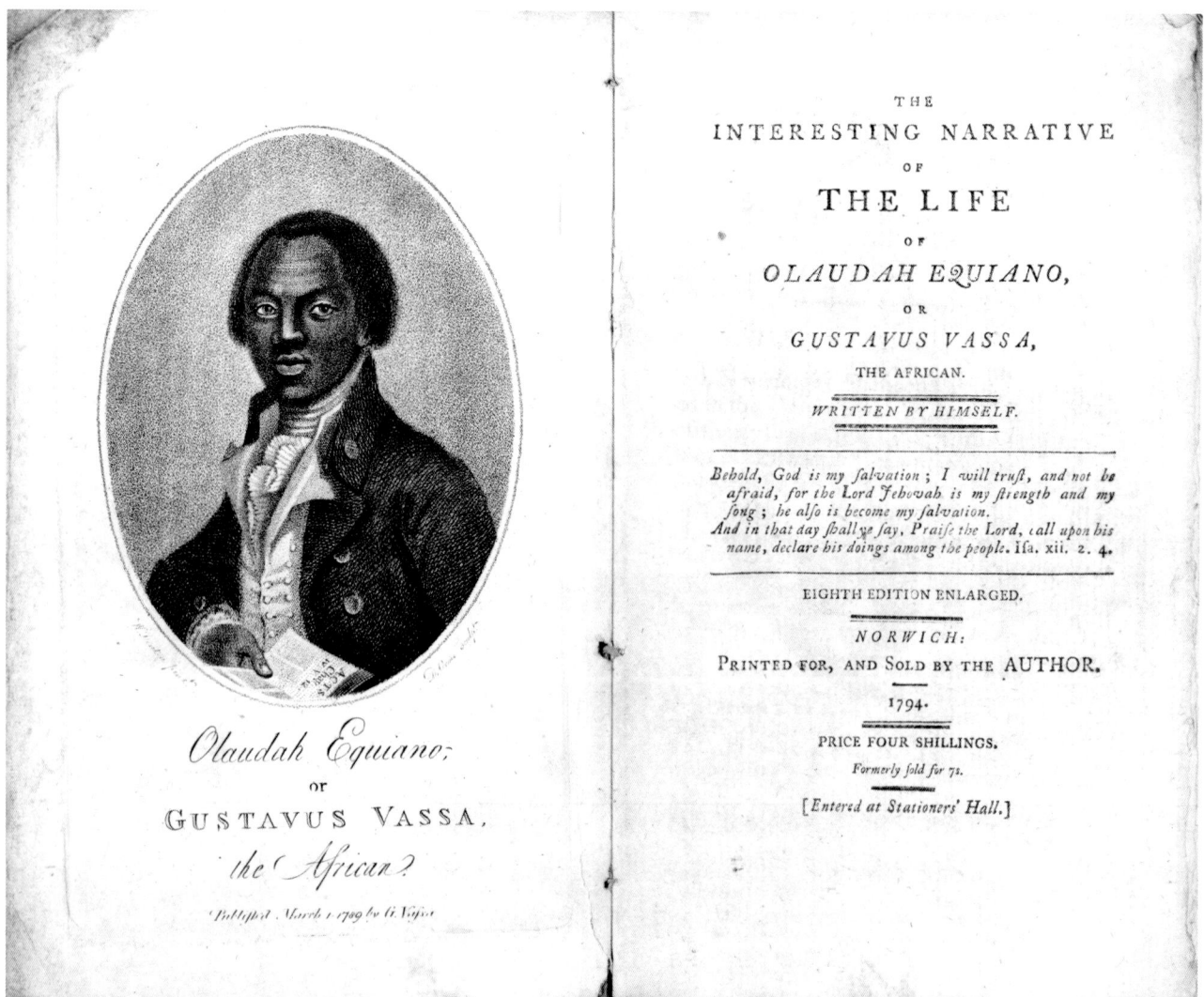

THE
INTERESTING NARRATIVE
OF
THE LIFE
OF
OLAUDAH EQUIANO,
OR
GUSTAVUS VASSA,
THE AFRICAN.
WRITTEN BY HIMSELF.

Behold, God is my salvation; I will trust, and not be
afraid, for the Lord Jehovah is my strength and my
song; he also is become my salvation.
And in that day shall ye say, Praise the Lord, call upon his
name, declare his doings among the people. Isa. xii. 2. 4.

EIGHTH EDITION ENLARGED.

NORWICH:
PRINTED FOR, AND SOLD BY THE AUTHOR.
1794.

PRICE FOUR SHILLINGS.
Formerly sold for 7s.

[Entered at Stationers' Hall.]

Olaudah Equiano;
or
GUSTAVUS VASSA,
the African?

Published March 1 1789 by G. Vassa

frontispiece portrait depicts him in full eighteenth-century European dress (fig. 2.4), and the narrative itself details his ability to be a full member of European society: his conversion to Christianity; acquisition of literacy; the business acumen he possessed as an enslaved person, which allowed him to earn the money to purchase his freedom; and his ability to use all these talents to address British society on the issue of slavery. For most Europeans, his assimilation to European life would have contrasted sharply with his childhood in Africa and the treatment he experienced at the hands of his enslavers in Africa and in European colonies. Although his portrait is the only image of Equiano in the book, he sought to draw attention to the tension between his image and his experiences in slavery—this was central to his political work.[12]

Fig. 2.4 Engraved frontispiece portrait of the author, *The Interesting Narrative of the Life of Olaudah Equiano, Or Gustavus Vassa, the African*, 1789. Courtesy of the British Library.

Fifty-odd years later, Frederick Douglass, Sojourner Truth, and a host of other formerly enslaved people in the United States worked with white anti-slavery activists to inaugurate a body of narratives—both book length and in periodicals—that sought to do the same political work against slavery. For the vast majority of these works, the author's self-presentation, textually and visually, proved that people of African descent were able to take advantage of the best that American culture had to offer in terms of dress, comportment, religiosity, education, and labor, and thus economic independence.[13] The illustrations in these books were drawings and engravings for the most part, and Patrick Reason was a popular choice to create such images. Douglass, Truth, and others also availed themselves of the emerging technology of photography, which they believed gave them even more control of their public presentation. Douglass, for example, was fascinated by the new technology and, according to historians John Stauffer, Zoe Trodd, and Celeste-Marie Bernier, he was the most photographed American of the nineteenth century. Douglass believed photography to be democratic in its accessibility; unlike portrait painting, a portrait photograph could be purchased by any working person. But he also believed photographs to be truthful representations of humanity and, thus, able to expose the lies of the pro-slavery and racist depictions of African Americans that proliferated in this era. The numerous photographs taken of Douglass over the course of his life were, in his view, nearly as important as his writings.[14]

While Sojourner Truth's photographic images of herself performed a similar function, anti-slavery activists were even less likely to depict free Black women than they were to depict free Black men as individuals. As noted above, anti-slavery images of free Black men largely accompanied fugitive slave narratives; women published far fewer of these works, and thus were less visible. Truth was no doubt one of the most photographed Black women of the nineteenth century, and her images among the most well circulated. Unlike the racist caricatures by whites like Edward Clay, who depicted Black women in garishly hued clothing and excessively beribboned hats, Truth's prim, dark-colored dresses, lace shawls, and simple, lace-trimmed caps implied feminine modesty, if not a Quaker-like religiosity (fig. 2.5).[15] Such portraits asserted the possibility of the transcendence of the violence enslavers and enslavement had inflicted on African Americans. But the power of the portrait for white America was rooted as much in the violence of slavery as in the gentility of the images.

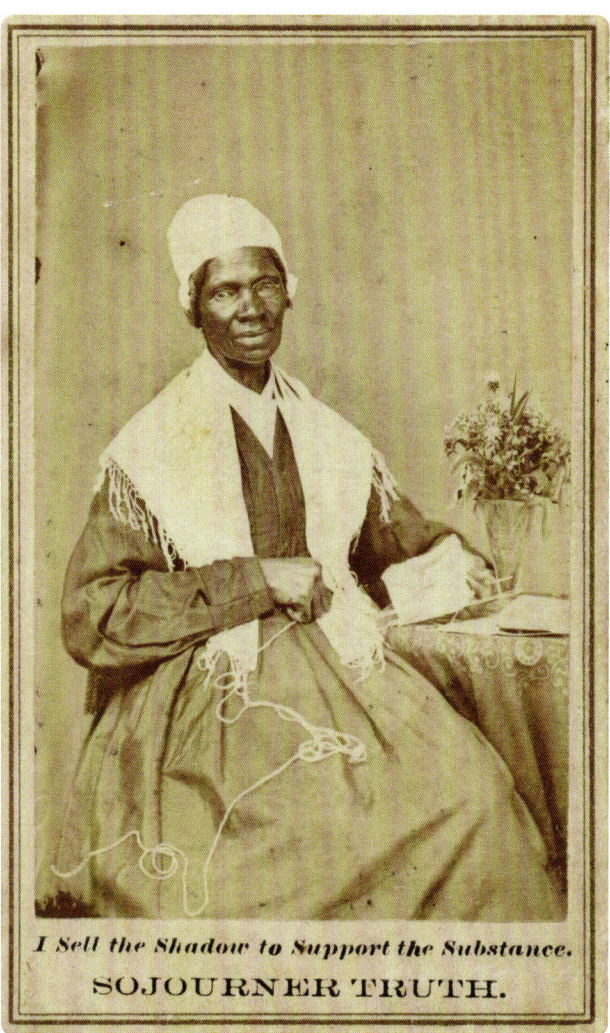

I Sell the Shadow to Support the Substance.
SOJOURNER TRUTH.

Fig. 2.5 *Sojourner Truth, I Sell the Shadow to Support the Substance,* ca. 1864, Eastern District, Michigan, carte de viste, 2⅜ × 3¹⁵⁄₁₆ inches. Courtesy of the Alfred Whital Stern Collection of Lincolniana, Library of Congress.

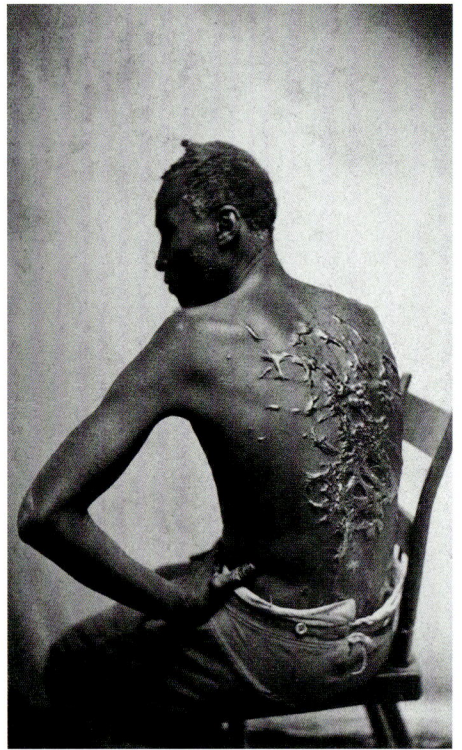

Fig. 2.6 McPherson and Oliver, *Escaped slave Gordon, also known as "Whipped Peter," showing his scarred back at a medical examination, Baton Rouge, Louisiana,* 1863, albumen print on card mount, mount, 4⅓ × 2¾ inches. Courtesy of Liljenquist Family Collection, Library of Congress.

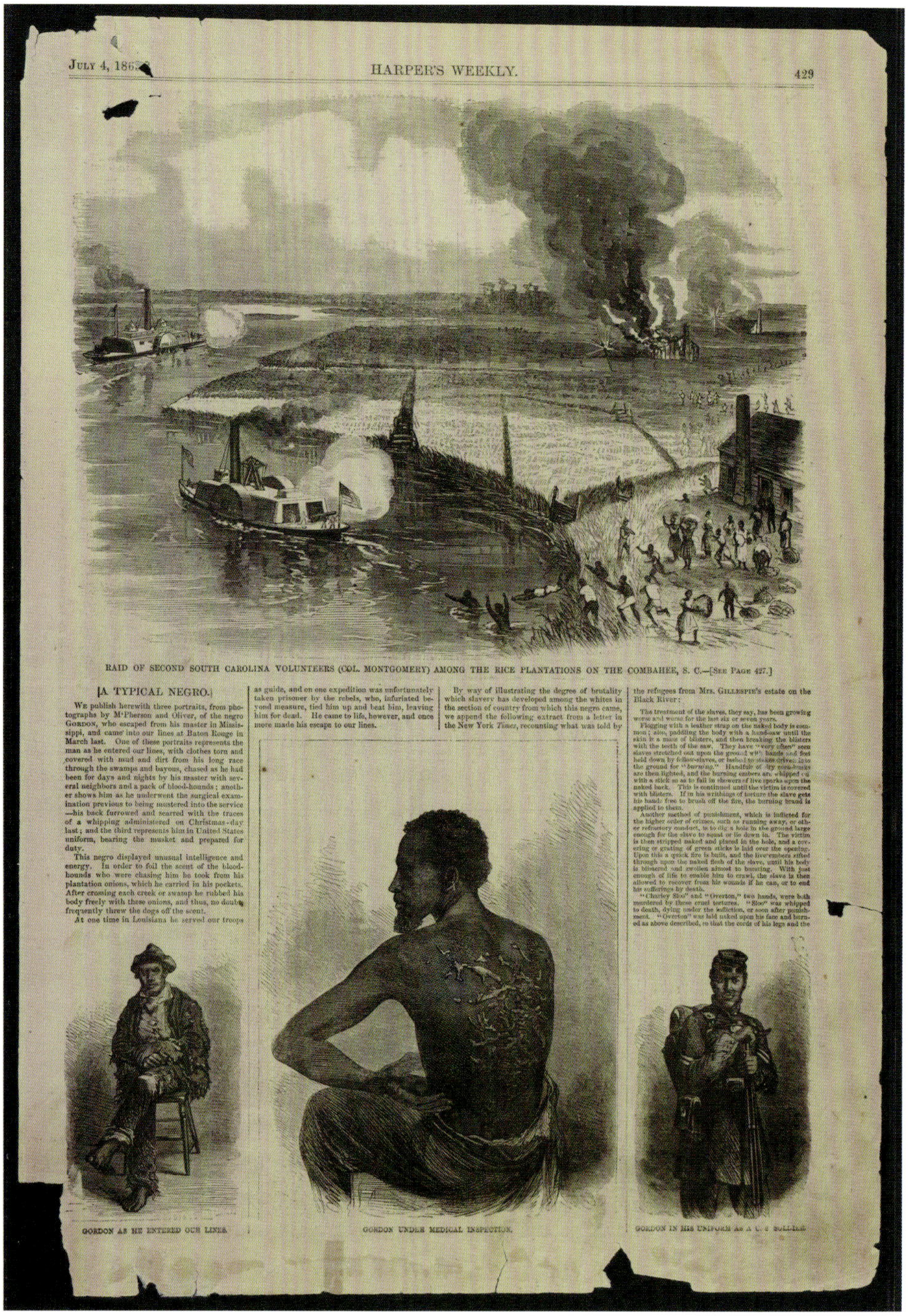

Fig. 2.7 McPherson and Oliver, ["2nd South Carolina Infantry Regiment Raid on Rice Plantation" and] "Escaped Slave Named Gordon," *Harper's Weekly*, July 4, 1863. Courtesy of the Library of Congress Prints and Photographs Division, Washington, DC.

Frederick Douglass and Sojourner Truth were only the most well-known African Americans to embrace photography and other forms of visual culture for political and personal reasons. African Americans in the North and South engaged in drawing, engraving, and painting, creating images for pleasure and amusement, or to build community. As photography historian Deborah Willis has documented, with others, African Americans also took their places in front of and behind the camera as the field of photography developed and expanded in the second half of the nineteenth century. Similarly, Douglass was but one of many African Americans who developed his own newspaper; others established publishing houses or worked as artists, creating images in text and in drawing that sought to engage the total humanity of people of African descent.[16] But the images of African Americans that dominated the public sphere were more likely to depict abjection than the wide range of Black life.

The events of the Civil War era challenged this constrained visual culture. The actions of enslaved people seeking their own freedom were startling and impossible to ignore as Union armies moved south and were met with thousands of enslaved people fleeing to Union lines and offering their labor for the Union cause and for freedom. On the one hand, propagandists against slavery still sought to use the old language of violence to denounce enslavers. Even today, perhaps the most well-known image of an African American Union soldier from the Civil War era is not of a man standing proudly in uniform fighting for freedom, but a dramatic physical representation of the punishments that were common under enslavement. Private Gordon, who escaped slavery to join the Union army, is known for the photograph taken of his back, riddled with raised scars—the result of a whipping he received (fig. 2.6). Through repeated depictions of such "scenes of subjection and terror," as scholar Saidiya Hartman has termed them, anti-slavery activists had emblazoned images of Black

people in abject situations on the minds of the general public.[17] They had also supported the self-presentation of people of African descent as more than abject, but the difficulty of dissociating slavery from African Americans was true in image and in fact. And amid the Civil War, some Northerners saw this photograph of Gordon's "scourged back"—not a photograph of Gordon as a Union soldier fighting for freedom—as the most effective way to prove that slavery should end. Ironically, the image forms one of a triptych published in *Harper's Weekly* (fig. 2.7), in which Gordon is first depicted upon his arrival at Union lines in Baton Rouge, Louisiana, dressed in the clothing he wore while enslaved; then half dressed, with his naked back exposed; and finally, in full Union uniform. Abolitionists had thousands of reprints created of only the central picture, as propaganda to inspire Northerners to support the Union cause. By focusing on the wrongs done by whites, communicated through the depiction of the suffering Black body, instead of on the labor completed by Black men, women, and children on behalf of emancipation and the Union cause, propagandists continued to reinforce the idea of African Americans as passive recipients of freedom and rights that could only be bestowed by whites. Such imagery was repeated in monuments celebrating emancipation and the Union victory after the war's end, as Kirk Savage has discussed in his aptly named *Standing Soldiers, Kneeling Slaves.*[18]

But the full experience of African Americans, in the North and South, seeking freedom and equality during the war was not entirely displaced by images of abjection. Over the course of the 1860s, journalists, reformers, engravers, illustrators, cartoonists, and photographers captured the reality of African Americans transcending the violence of slavery and white supremacy to claim their place in the new nation that would emerge in the aftermath of war. Visual artists—from professionals who published in periodicals such as *Harper's Weekly* and the *Illustrated London News* or created paintings for museum exhibitions after the war, to those who sketched in their own private journals—left a record of the successes and the failures of these efforts (figs. 2.8, 2.9).[19] Nonetheless, as the nation emerged into a new sense of itself after emancipation, the visual vocabulary of violence that had expanded during the war would continue to be deployed in the ongoing struggle against white supremacist violence for decades to come.

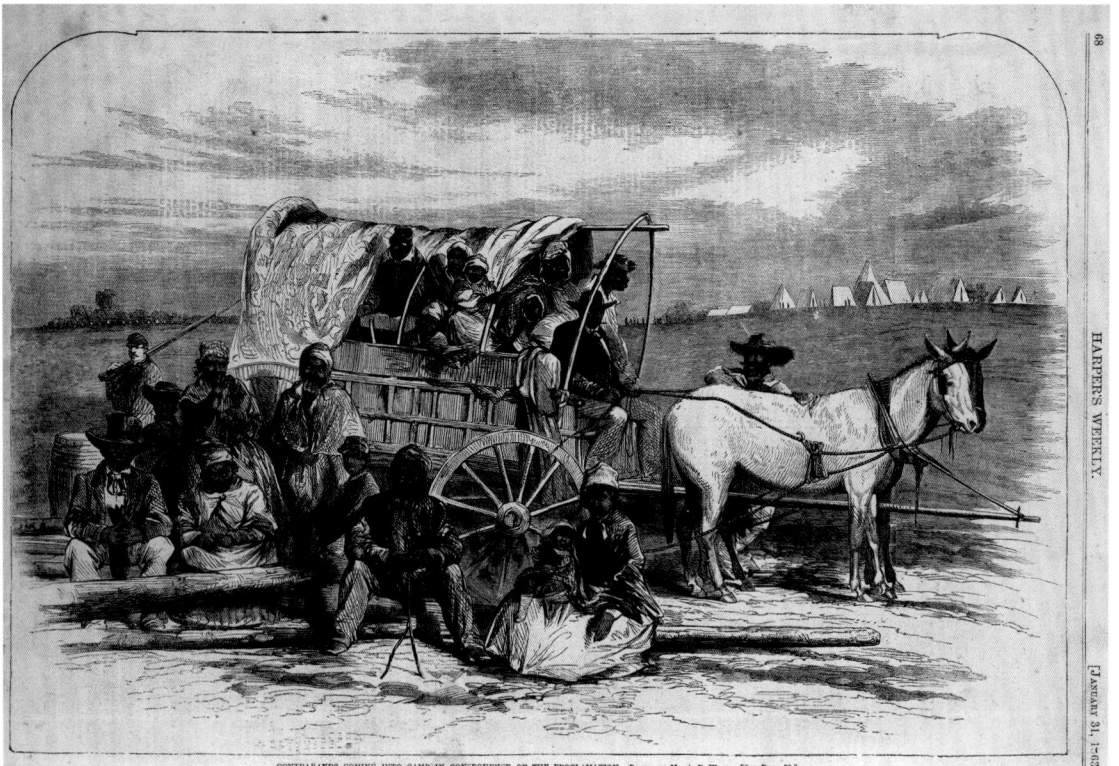

CONTRABANDS COMING INTO CAMP IN CONSEQUENCE OF THE PROCLAMATION.—DRAWN BY MR. A. R. WAUD.—[SEE PAGE 78.]

Fig. 2.8 Alfred Rudolph Waud, *Contrabands Coming into Camp in Consequence of the Proclamation*, 1863, wood engraving, in *Harper's Weekly*, January 31, 1863. Courtesy of Library of Congress.

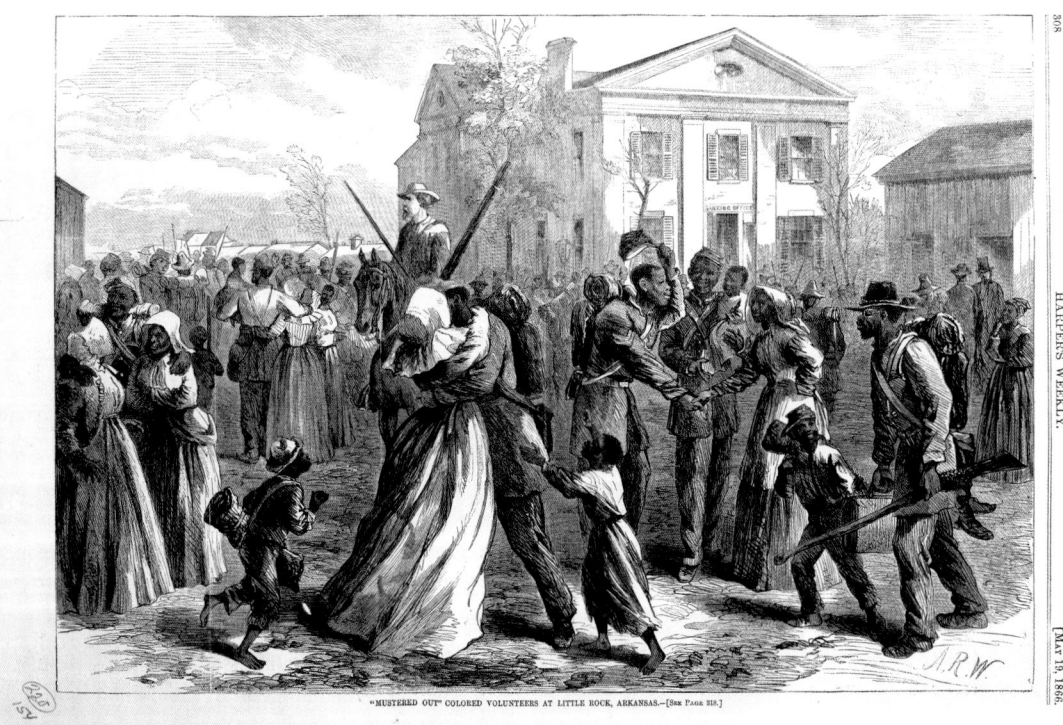

"MUSTERED OUT" COLORED VOLUNTEERS AT LITTLE ROCK, ARKANSAS.—[SEE PAGE 318.]

Fig. 2.9 Alfred Rudolph Waud, *"Mustered Out" Colored Volunteers at Little Rock, Arkansas*, 1866, wood engraving, in *Harper's Weekly*, May 19, 1866. Courtesy of Library of Congress.

Notes

I'd like to thank Kate Masur and Barbara Krauthamer for their comments on an earlier draft of this essay, as well as Janet Dees and the anonymous peer reviewers for their suggestions.

1   For an introduction to these kinds of images, see *Slavery Images: A Visual Record of the African Slave Trade and Slave Life in the Early African Diaspora* website, accessed December 20, 2020, http://slaveryimages.org/. Jennifer L. Morgan's "'Some Could Suckle over Their Shoulder': Male Travelers, Female Bodies, and the Gendering of Racial Ideology, 1500–1770," *The William and Mary Quarterly* 54, no. 1 (1997): 167–92, is a foundational work on the ways that Europeans "saw" people in Africa, particularly women. See also Stephanie M. H. Camp, "Early European Views of African Bodies: Beauty," in *Slavery and Sexuality: Reclaiming Intimate Histories in the Americas*, ed. Daina Ramey Berry and Leslie M. Harris (Athens: University of Georgia Press, 2019), 9–32; and the multivolume work by David Bindman, Henry Louis Gates, and Karen C. C. Dalton, *The Image of the Black in Western Art* (New ed., Cambridge, MA: Belknap Press of Harvard University Press, 2010–11). Africans also created depictions of themselves and of their interactions with Europeans, but in this essay, I focus on the cultural language created in Europe and the Americas.

2   There is a voluminous literature on the rise of mass culture in the late-eighteenth and nineteenth centuries. Probably the most complete synthesis in the United States is Daniel Walker Howe, *What God Hath Wrought: The Transformation of America, 1815–1848* (New York: Oxford University Press, 2007). On the rise of the anti-slavery movement generally, see Manisha Sinha's masterful *The Slave's Cause: A History of Abolition* (New Haven, CT: Yale University Press, 2016).

3   The best work on the development and rise of the slave ship image is Cheryl Finley, *Committed to Memory: The Art of the Slave Ship Icon* (Princeton, NJ: Princeton University Press, 2018), 1–108.

4   Finley, *Committed to Memory*. On the politics of anti-slavery imagery generally, and this image in particular, see Marcus Wood, *Blind Memory: Visual Representations of Slavery in England and America, 1780–1865* (Manchester, UK: Manchester University Press, 2000); on the production of the slave ship *Brookes*, see Wood's second chapter, "The Irrecoverable: Representing the 'Middle Passage.'" For detailed explorations of the Middle Passage, see Marcus Rediker, *The Slave Ship: A Human History* (New York: Viking, 2007); Sowande´ Mustakeem, *Slavery at Sea: Terror, Sex and Sickness in the Middle Passage* (Urbana: University of Illinois Press, 2016); and Stephanie Smallwood, *Saltwater Slavery: A Middle Passage from Africa to American Diaspora* (Cambridge MA: Harvard University Press, 2007).

5   Jasmine Nichole Cobb's *Picture Freedom: Remaking Black Visuality in the Early Nineteenth Century* (New York: New York University Press, 2015) is among the most thorough explications of the limits of anti-slavery imagery in the United States.

6   Finley, *Committed to Memory*, 19ff.

7   Aston Gonzalez, *Visualizing Equality: African American Rights and Visual Culture in the Nineteenth Century* (Chapel Hill: University of North Carolina, 2020), Kindle version: Location 874–90; 1,031–45.

8   Paul J. Polgar, *Standard-Bearers of Equality: America's First Abolition Movement* (Chapel Hill: University of North Carolina Press, 2019), 1, doi:10.5149/9781469653952_polgar. For a fuller discussion of this image and others of the period, see Wood, "The Irrecoverable," in *Blind Memory*; and Maurie McInnis, "Representing the Slave Trade," in *Slaves Waiting for Sale: Abolitionist Art and the American Slave Trade* (Chicago: University of Chicago Press, 2011). Regarding gender and sexuality in these images, see McInnis, *Slaves Waiting for Sale*, 33.

9   Glenn McNair, "The Elijiah Burritt Affair: David Walker's *Appeal* and Partisan Journalism in Antebellum Milledgeville," *Georgia Historical Quarterly* 83, no. 3 (Fall 1999): 448–78; Leslie M. Harris, "From Abolitionist Amalgamators to 'Rulers of the Five Points': The Discourse of Interracial Sex and Reform in Antebellum New York City," in *Sex, Love, Race: Crossing Boundaries in North American History*, ed. Martha Hodes (New York: New York University Press, 1999), 191–212; Emma Jones Lapsansky, "'Since They Got Those Separate Churches': Afro-Americans and Racism in Jacksonian Philadelphia," *American Quarterly* 32, no. 1 (1980): 54–78; Phillip Lapsansky, "Graphic Discord: Abolitionist and Antiabolitionist Images," in *The Abolitionist Sisterhood: Women's Political Culture in Antebellum America*, ed. Jean Fagan Yellin and John C. Van Horne (Ithaca, NY: Cornell University Press, 1994), 219–30; Gonzalez, *Visualizing Equality*, location 1,312–54; Cobb, *Picture Freedom*, 157–60.

10   On racist caricatures and the limits of anti-slavery visual culture in the antebellum North, see Cobb, "Racial Iconography: Freedom and Black Citizenship in the Antebellum North," in *Picture Freedom*, esp. 205–40. Both Wood, *Blind Memory*, and McInnis, *Slaves Waiting for Sale*, describe in critical detail the ways in which anti-slavery images developed over this time period. See also Huey Copeland and Krista Thompson, eds., "New World Slavery and the Matter of the Visual," special issue of *Representations* 113, no. 1 (Winter 2011).

11   On anti-slavery publishing, see Lapsansky, "Graphic Discord," 202ff.

12   *The Interesting Narrative of the Life of Olaudah Equiano, Or Gustavus Vassa, the African. Written By Himself* (London: The Author, 1789).

13   On slave narratives, see William L. Andrews, *To Tell a Free Story: The First Century of Afro-American Autobiography, 1760–1860* (Urbana: University of Illinois, 1986); Charles T. Davis and Henry Louis Gates Jr., eds., *The Slave's Narrative* (New York: Oxford University Press, 1991).

14   John Stauffer, Zoe Trodd, and Celeste-Marie Bernier, *Picturing Frederick Douglass: An Illustrated Biography of the Nineteenth Century's Most Photographed Man* (New York: Liveright, 2015), esp. x–xiii.

15   On the failure of anti-slavery activists to depict free Black women in antebellum visual culture, see Cobb, *Picture Freedom*. On Sojourner Truth, photography and self-making, see Nell Irvin Painter, *Sojourner Truth: A Life, A Symbol* (New York: Norton, 1991), esp. chapter 20; and Nell Irvin Painter, "Representing Truth: Sojourner Truth's Knowing and Becoming Known," *Journal of American History* 81, no. 2 (1994): 461–92, esp. 482–88.

16   For examples of visual culture among African Americans beyond the anti-slavery movement, see Erica Armstrong Dunbar, "A Mental and Moral Feast: Reading, Writing, and Sentimentality in Black Philadelphia," *Journal of Women's History* 16, no. 1 (Spring 2004): 78–102; Deborah Willis, *Reflections in Black: A History of Black Photographers, 1840 to the Present* (New York: Norton, 2000); Deborah Willis and Barbara Krauthamer, *Envisioning Emancipation: Black Americans and the End of Slavery* (Philadelphia: Temple University Press, 2013); Samella Lewis, *African American Art and Artists* (Berkeley: University of California Press, 1990); Cobb, *Picture Freedom*; Gonzalez, *Visualizing Equality*.

17   Saidiya V. Hartman, *Scenes of Subjection: Terror, Slavery, and Self-Making in Nineteenth-Century America* (New York: Oxford University Press, 1996). Aliyyah Abdur-Rahman argues for the ethical witnessing of the physical violence that the anti-slavery movement sought to encourage as a path to ending slavery in "'This Horrible Exhibition': Sexuality in Slave Narratives," *The Oxford Handbook of Slave Narratives*, ed. John Ernest (New York: Oxford University Press, 2014), doi: 10.1093/oxfordhb/9780199731480.013.009.

18   On Private Gordon in the context of a longer history of depictions of physical violence before and after US slavery, see Wood, *Blind Memory*, 260–71. See also McInnis, *Slaves Waiting for Sale*, 130; and Willis and Krauthamer, *Envisioning Emancipation*, 36–37 and 54–55. On the ways in which post–Civil War–era monuments enshrined ideas of Blacks as passive recipients of freedom and reinforced white supremacy, see Kirk Savage, *Standing Soldiers, Kneeling Slaves: Race, War, and Monument in Nineteenth-Century America* (1997, 2nd ed., Princeton, NJ: Princeton University Press, 2018).

19   Accounts of African Americans' centrality to seizing their own freedom during the war are numerous. An excellent introduction to this history and the ways in which Black freedom was interpreted politically and culturally is Kate Masur's "'A Rare Phenomenon of Philological Vegetation': The Word 'Contraband' and the Meanings of Emancipation in the United States," *Journal of American History* 93, no. 4 (March 2007), 1,050–84. See also Marcus Wood, *The Horrible Gift of Freedom: Atlantic Slavery and the Representation of Emancipation* (Athens: University of Georgia Press, 2010); Kirk Savage, *Standing Soldiers, Kneeling Slaves*; Willis and Krauthamer, *Envisioning Emancipation*; and Pennee Bender, Joshua Brown, Donna Thompson Ray et al., *Visual Culture of the Civil War* website, http://civilwar.picturinghistory.gc.cuny.edu.

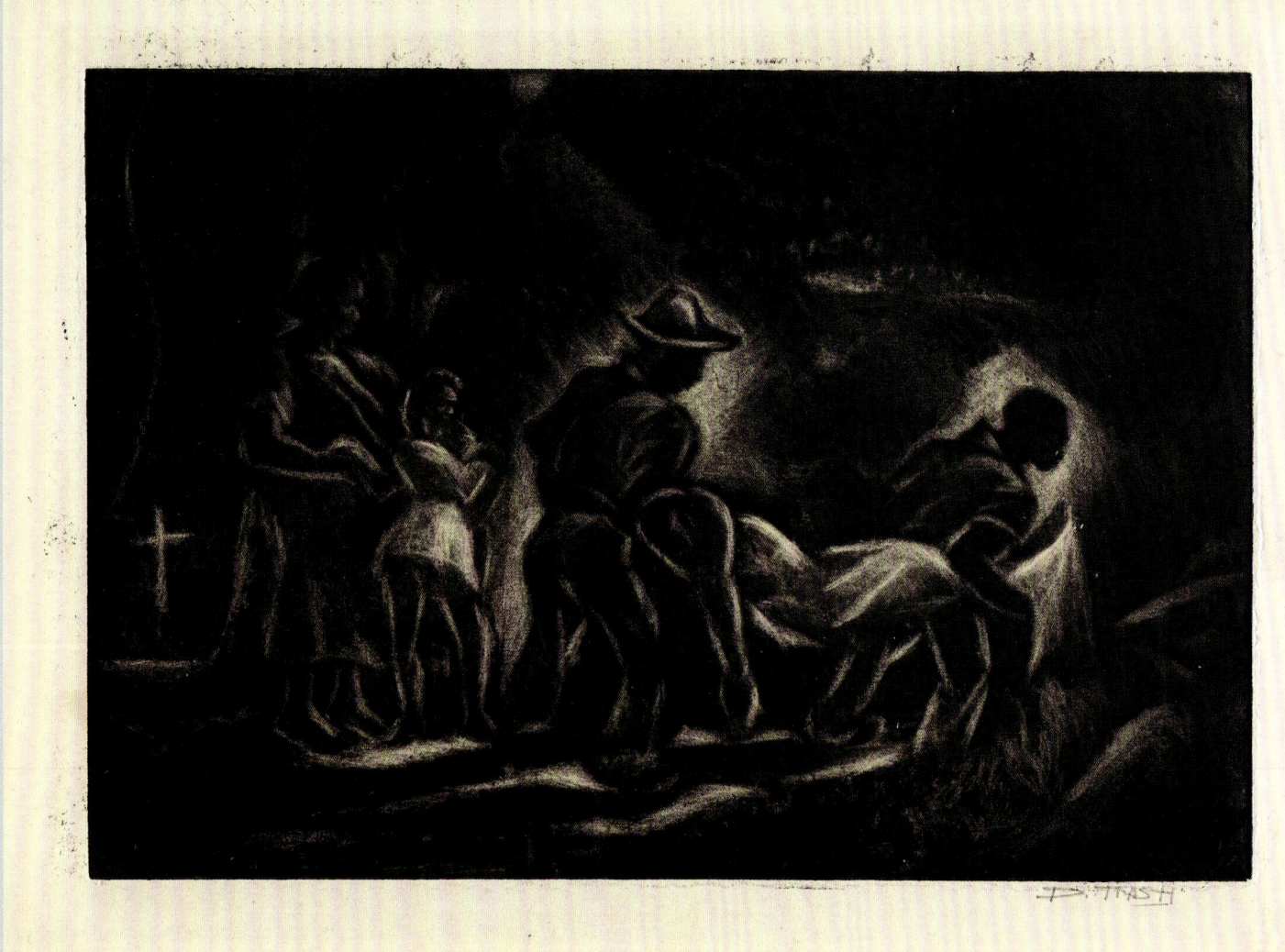

Dox Thrash

(American, 1893–1965)
After the Lynching,
late 1930s

Carborundum mezzotint printed in
black ink on wove paper
6¹⁄₁₆ × 8⅞ inches (plate); 8¹⁄₁₆ ×
11¹³⁄₁₆ inches (sheet)
Virginia Museum of Fine Arts,
Kathleen Boone Samuels
Memorial Fund, 2017.27. Photo by
David Stover. © Virginia Museum
of Fine Arts.

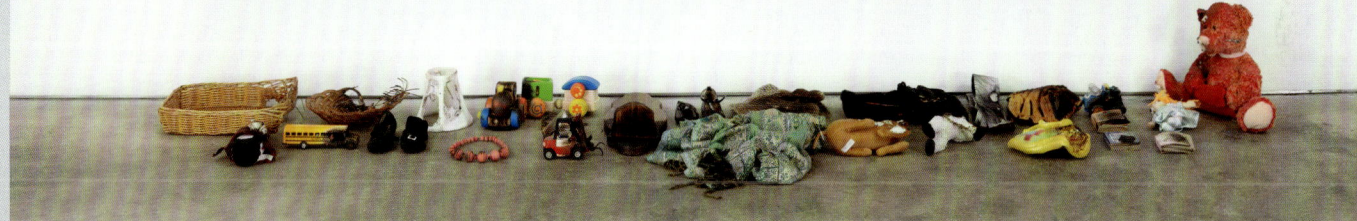

Howardina Pindell
(American, b. 1943)
Four Little Girls, 2020

Mixed media on canvas
96 × 108 × 25 inches
Courtesy of the artist and
Garth Greenan Gallery.

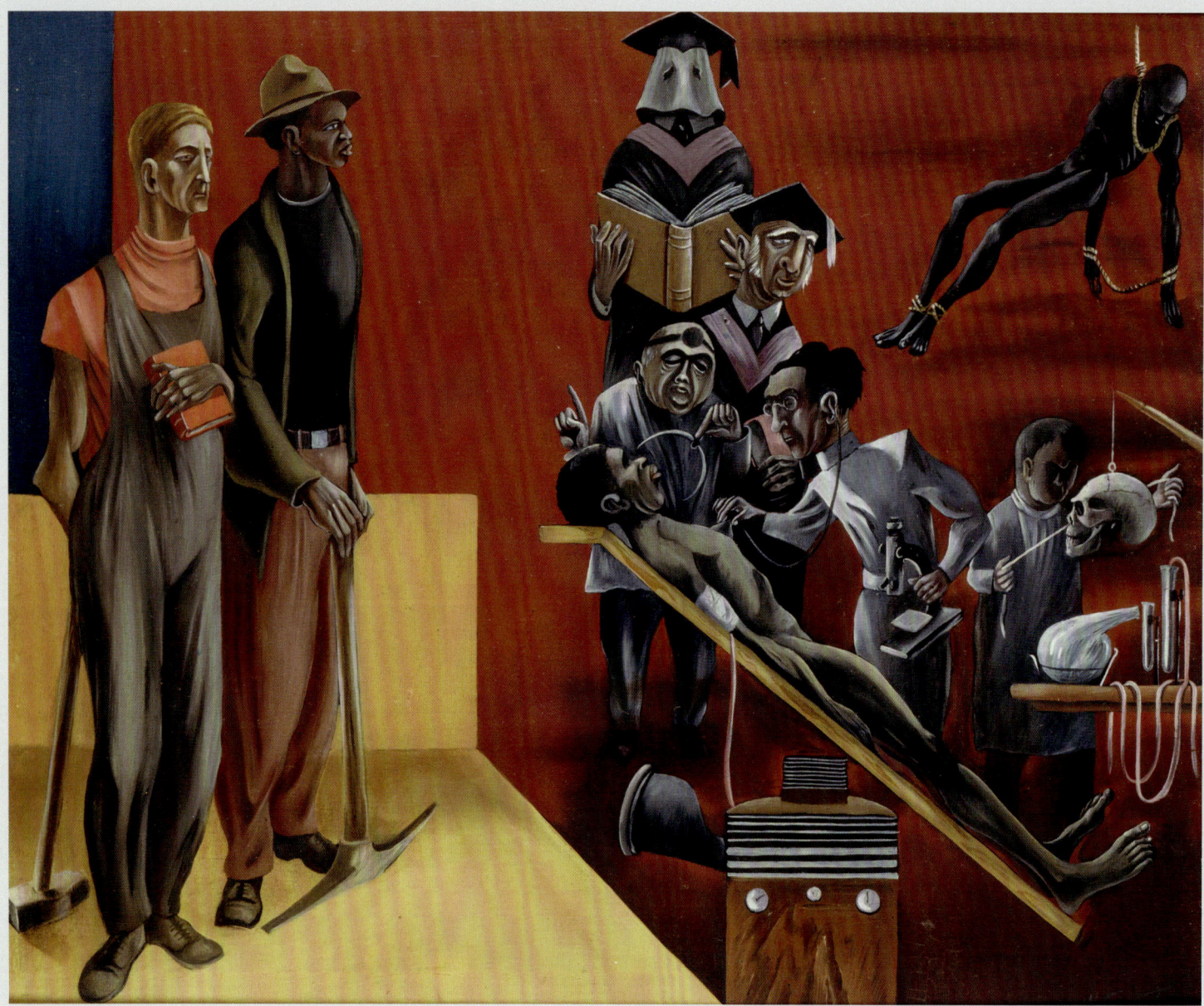

Walter Quirt

(American, 1902–1968)

The Clinic, 1935

Oil on composition panel
12⁵⁄₁₆ × 15 inches
The Wadsworth Atheneum
Museum of Art, The Ella Gallup
Sumner and Mary Catlin Sumner
Collection Fund, 1937.208
© Estate of Walter Quirt and
Wadsworth Atheneum Museum of
Art, Hartford, CT. Photo by Allen
Phillips / Wadsworth Atheneum.

Hale Woodruff

(American, 1900–1980)

Giddap!, 1935

Linocut
12 × 9 inches
Collection of Spelman College, Gift
of Kathryn C. and Kenneth I.
Chenault, 2001.1.006
© 2021 Estate of Hale Woodruff /
Licensed by VAGA at Artists Rights
Society (ARS), NY.

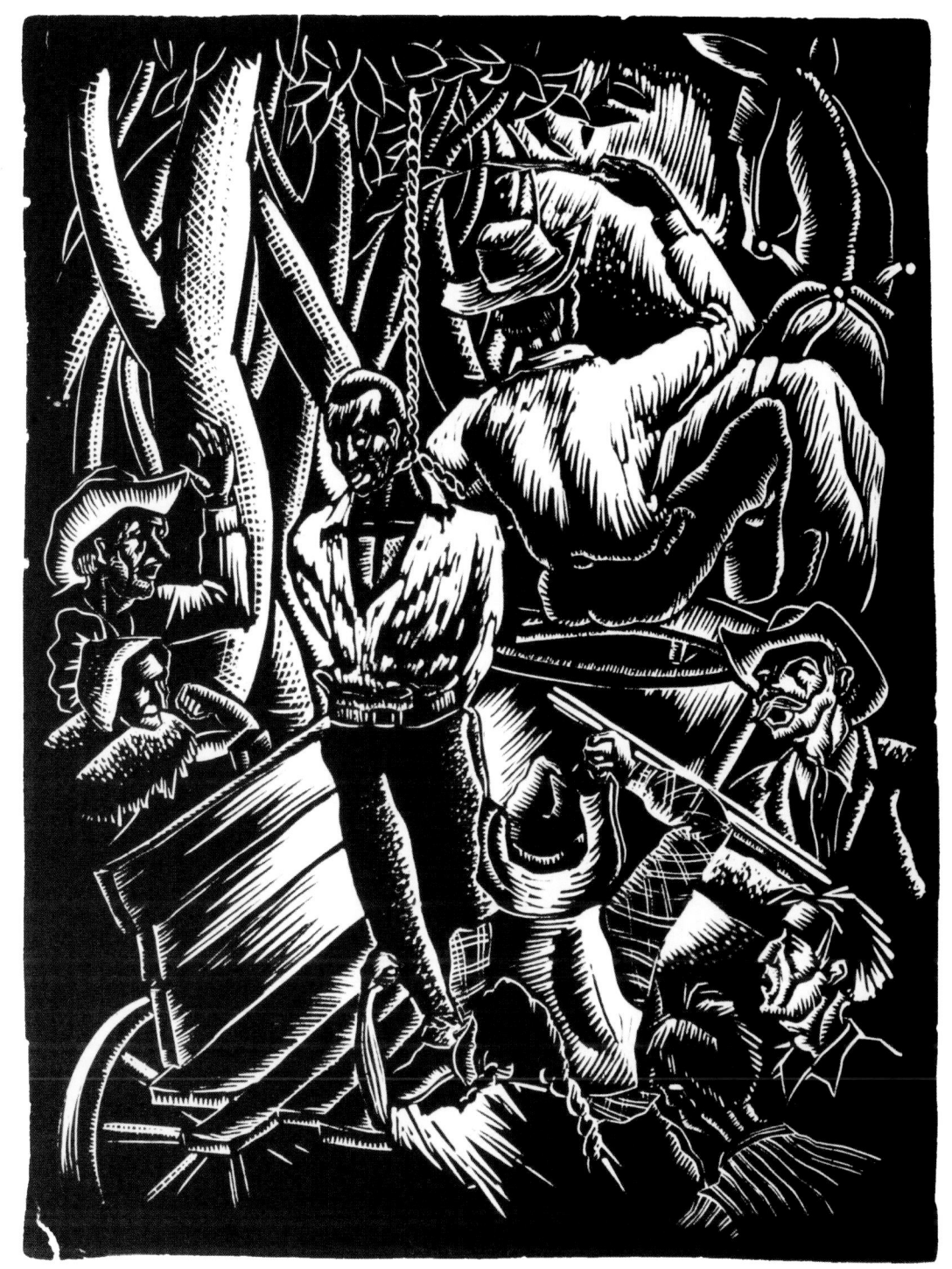

Functional Abstractions

Sensorial Afterlives
of the Black Body
Sampada Aranke

Earlier this year, before the swell of a world gone even more awry than before, as I was working on my forthcoming book, I was reminded by art historian Krista Thompson of a linocut by Elizabeth Catlett called *. . . And a special fear for my loved ones* (1946, fig. 3.1), the penultimate print in the artist's series of fifteen titled *The Black Woman* (formerly *The Negro Woman*). In this piece, we are thrown into the midst of an act of violence, a lynching. The only subject visible in his entirety is the lynching victim, angled and bent, right palm facing the viewer. Depicted from ground level, he lies with a noose encircling his neck as the perpetrators, represented by three pairs of men's shoes, stand on the rope, making escape—and thus survival— impossible. Diagonal and curved marks jolt across the print while, in contrast, its supine subject is restrained by his captors. Catlett brilliantly captures the frenzy and chaos of the violent scene through the shock of what it means both to endure and to witness such brutality. This print mobilizes a particularly Black aesthetic approach to the pitfalls and potentials of visualizing, and thus calling upon viewership of, such events. By Black aesthetic approach, I mean to highlight traditions of art making that work within and against an understanding of Blackness as solely in relation to the policies and practices of white supremacist violence. Instead, these practices offer a deep and nuanced encounter with the sensorial, material, political, and social elements of Black life, a reencounter with a shared past, creating a pathway in the present tense that might lead us toward a more liberated future.

When I most recently encountered Catlett's linocut, I was in the throes of revising my book's final chapter, which examines the 1971 killing of Black Panther George Jackson in California's San Quentin State Prison and the political posters made in the wake of his death to galvanize revolutionary action against his and so many Black radicals' murders.[1] Jackson, who had received an indeterminate sentence of one year to life for stealing $70 during an armed robbery at a gas station, was radicalized while serving time. He very quickly became one of the most prolific theorists of US imperialism, capitalism, and the prison-industrial complex through writings and interviews that circulated outside the prison walls. The posters made in response to his murder visually centralize Jackson's

dead body as a way to activate a fugitive imaginary, one grounded in a Black radical tradition with an eye toward freedom (1971, fig. 3.2). My book grapples with how these posters, made collectively and collaboratively, embodied formal qualities and visual strategies from across a Black art historical canon. Thompson thoughtfully asked me to consider Catlett's print in relation to these works. Upon reencounter, I realized how deeply sensorial her lynching image is. Each cut in the linoleum block seemed to mark an aspect of experience from the position of the subject enduring violence: the continuous, trembling folds of skin and cloth, the shaking terror of the ground. What makes this print so exceptionally constructed is an acute awareness of how Black bodies are seen and felt. Catlett's gesture spawns a radical Black aesthetic genealogy: generations of works that balance the sensorial *and* the visual, the embodied and the illustrated, the deeply abstracted and representational qualities of Black life.[2]

As a functional abstract, depictions of the Black body have long been caught between the pains and pleasures of seeing and being seen. While too long to engage here, these storied histories have been accounted for by first-person narratives, scholars, and makers in the long twentieth century. The ways, for example, that photography has been used to both surveil and provide historical agency reflects the vexed representational conditions Black people have had to navigate.[3] The functional abstract, in my formulation, operates despite and within this bind as the abstract form functions to serve as a modular stand-in for a sense, a body, a people. I call this burden of representation a functional abstract because Black visual histories have long accounted for the ways that Blackness itself throws into crisis a Western epistemological hardline between the representational and the abstract, the material and the conceptual, the embodied and the cerebral. By activating the lived sensorial experiences of Black life, a functional abstract activates a spectrum of sensations that cohere around Blackness as a political and aesthetic force that structures the very ground upon which we view the works in front of us. Earth-shattering yet subtle, the functional abstract often requires a quiet attention that troubles our presumptive logics about the world we have inherited; it centers Blackness not only as a condition that is colored by white supremacy but as a concrete and aesthetic modality that exceeds the violence that structures it. This isn't the place to replay the entirety of this story, but parts of it are necessary for understanding how (and possibly why) many of the artists presented in *A Site of Struggle* draw upon a Black radical aesthetic approach to considering the sensorial afterlives of anti-Black violence.[4]

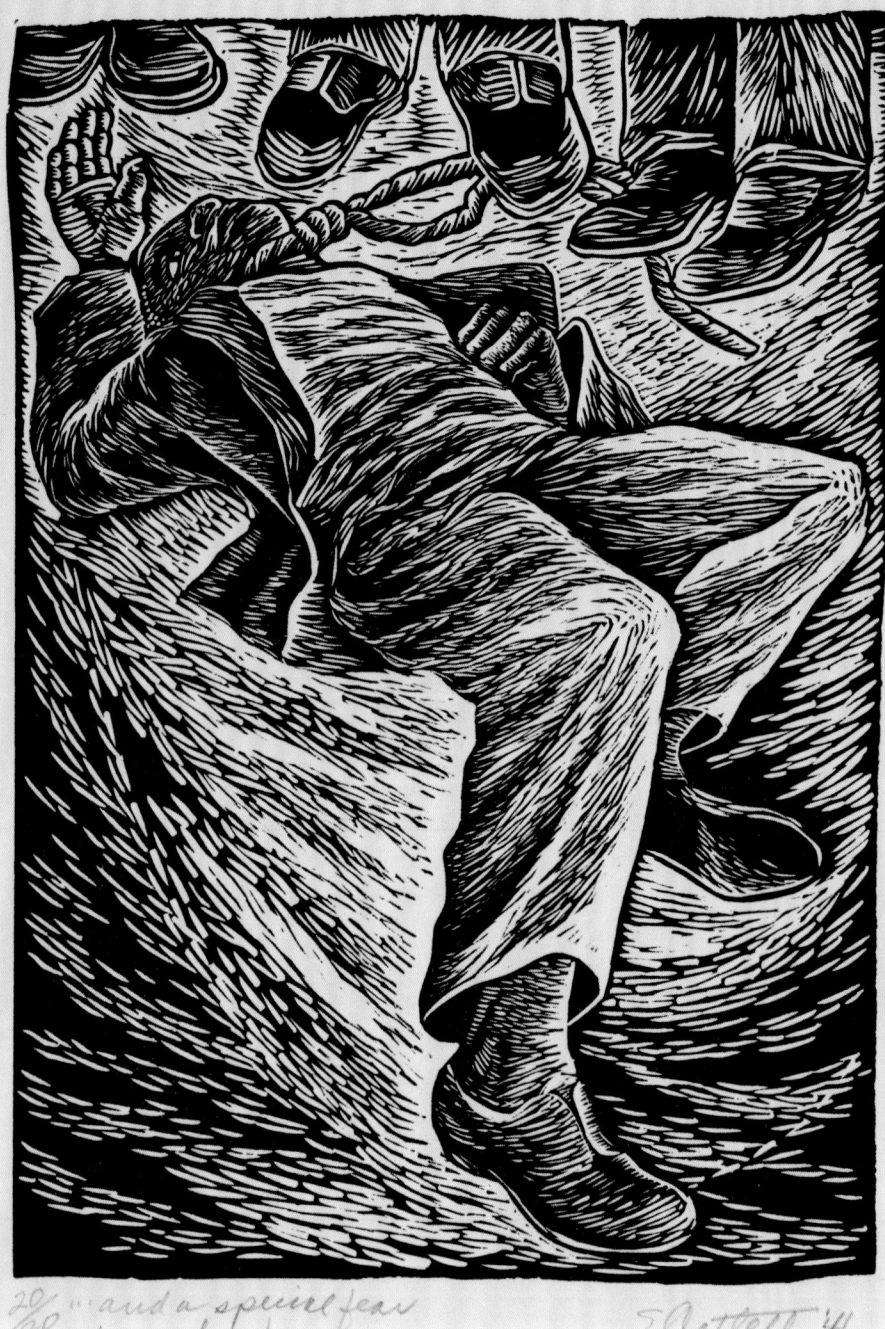

20/20 "...and a special fear for my loved ones.

ECatlett '46

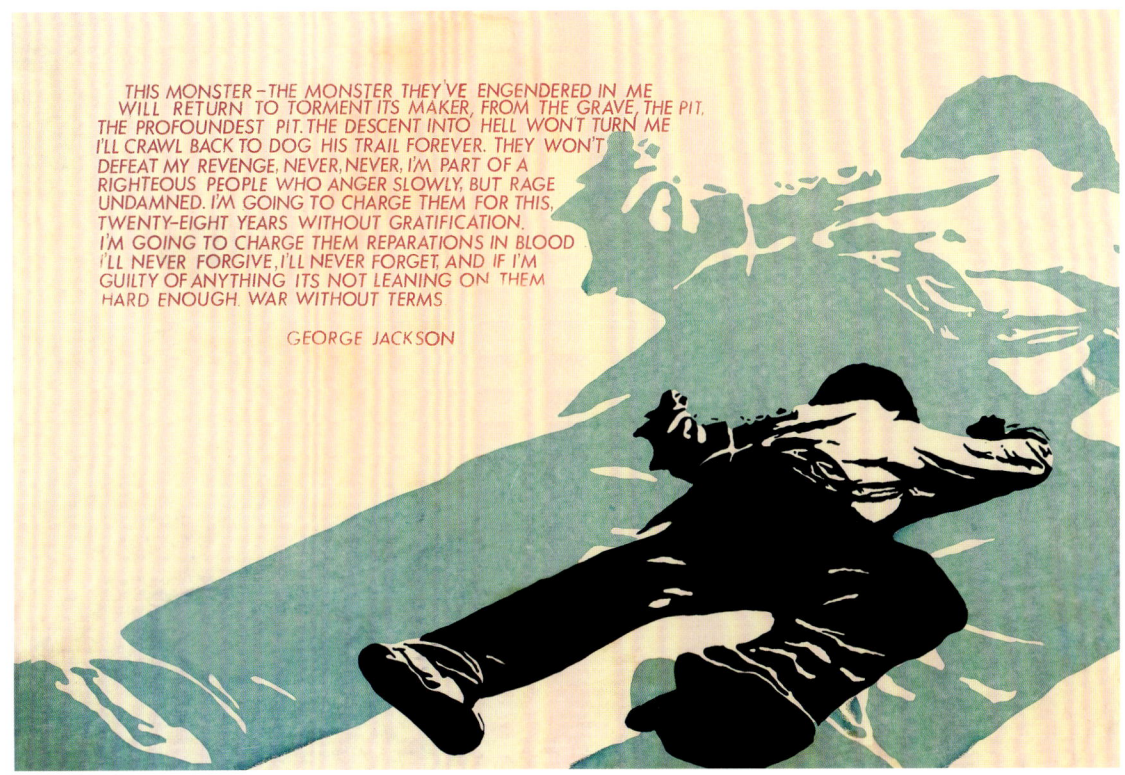

Fig. 3.2 Doug Lawler / East Bay Media Collective, *This Monster*, 1971, paper screen print, 20 × 30 inches. All of Us or None Archive, Gift of the Rossman Family. Image courtesy of the artist and Lincoln Cushing / Docs Populi.

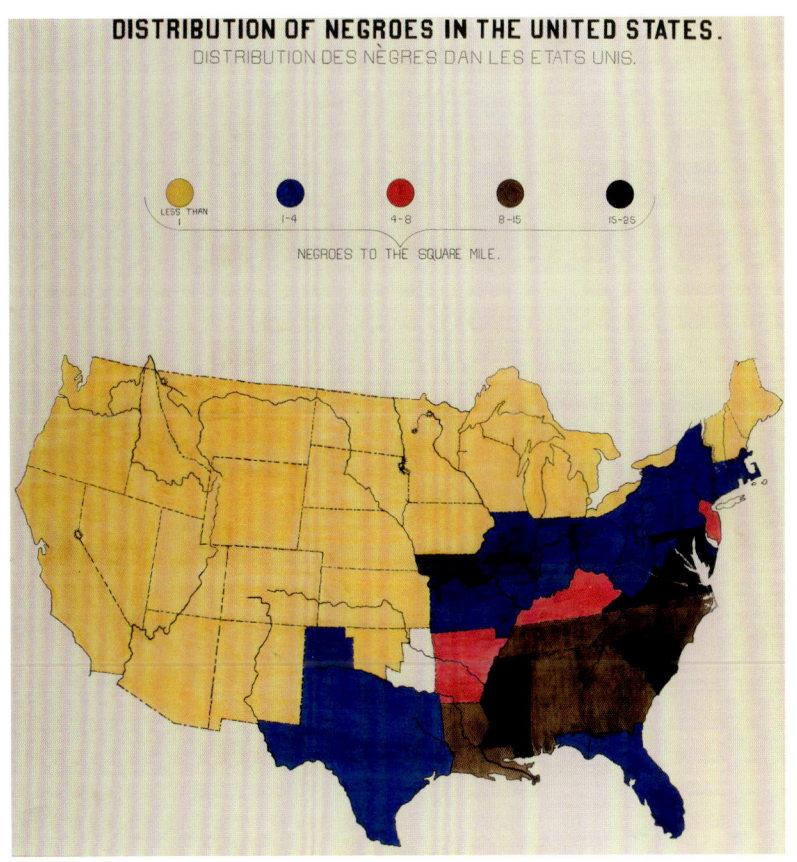

Fig. 3.3 W. E. B. Du Bois, "Distribution of Negroes in the United States," from *A series of statistical charts illustrating the condition of the descendants of former African slaves now in residence in the United States of America*, ca. 1900, ink and watercolor, 28 × 22 inches. Image courtesy of the Library of Congress.

W. E. B. Du Bois's 1897 statistical charts offer a prime case for the functional abstract.[5] Du Bois and his team made two sets of infographics: the first focused on Black Americans in Georgia, and the second charted the "Distribution of Negroes in the United States" (fig. 3.3).[6] These works take statistical information on the political, economic, and social conditions of Black Americans since the Civil War and translate seemingly objective calculations into abstracted data visualizations. These visualizations offer an approach to the statistics that speaks across multiple types of literacy. The graphs and charts seem to anticipate Du Bois's legendary 1900 proclamation that "the problem of the twentieth century is the problem of the color line."[7] Said to engage an "aesthetics of the color line," these works clearly embody a functional abstract.[8] Indeed, line and color are two of the most striking formal qualities in these works, making for an aesthetic manifestation of the famed scholar's poetic political prose; social and political meaning take shape through these formal traits as Du Bois and his collaborators translate the sociological data at hand into abstracted figures—what I see as bodies in their own right. As such, these forms amount to a kind of "racialized abstraction" in which the data is transformed into graphic embodiments of a people in order to communicate information otherwise reduced to depersonalized, often illegible statistics.[9]

These are *graphic* abstractions, and as such these works enact the full scope of that term: bringing ink to paper as a form of drawing, engaging the graph to translate verbal and numerical information into visual information, and vividly indicating the violences that structure the conditions for Black life. In his lucid account of these works, Alexander Weheliye carefully tracks how Du Bois's infographics "mark out the abstract forces of the color line, while simultaneously putting under erasure its primary function, which is to create and maintain hierarchical caesuras between different groups of humans, especially between black and white subjects."[10] He goes on, "The displacement of the angle of vision prompted by the partitioning of the graphics in *The Philadelphia Negro*, Du Bois's rhythmic criteria of color lined art, makes possible the theorization and visibilization of how abstract physiognomies of power produce the Negro as an abject yet central figure of modern civilization."[11] Here, Weheliye makes a brilliant assertion: that these graphics not only

draw upon abstraction as an aesthetic modality but also act as *physiognomies*, or facial characteristics often associated with racial demarcation and classification. For Weheliye, these "physiognomies of power" point directly to the ways that Blackness is central to the making of the modern even while cast as antimodern and abject. The abstract forces of the color line that Weheliye unpacks are indeed aesthetic in their formation, which is why they are crucial for understanding Black artistic practices in the twentieth century and beyond. Weheliye's reading here is key because he moves Du Bois's graphics into an embodied aesthetics of abstraction, one where the data enables an understanding of Black lived experience that makes visible the broader conditions in which that life takes place. By putting Weheliye's reading of Du Bois's infographics in conversation with Black artists whose aesthetic practices centralize the nonrepresentational and activate the sensorial, I suggest that these artists offer not physiognomies but functional abstractions. In their works, the Black body is figured as a series of substitutive, sensorial objects that give rise to a sense of how Black life is aesthetically imagined and lived despite the conditions that aim to kill that life.

Catlett's gripping print offers one strategy in which the sensorial is visualized as a kind of functional abstract. The grooves and swerves of ink on paper index an initial indentation, one that required the artist's careful hand to carve and scrape away to form a relief in her linoleum block. The quality of Catlett's staccato marks gestures toward skin, each groove and dip resembling the crevices of flesh, networks of pores and follicles that erupt in goosebumps when one is terrorized. Catlett's print visualizes fear as it simultaneously approximates the sensorial embodiment of such a fear. These indentations mark the central figure's body even as the edges of cloth that drape his body blur with the boundary of the ground, making for a discernible yet organic continuity between figure and ground, body and atmosphere. This approach suggests a forceful argument: that the anti-Black violence pictured is a result of foundational logics that structure the very ground upon which Black life is sought and lived. Thus, the specificity of *who* is violated is instead categorial. This is not a representation of a particular person; the figure instead comes to stand in for an abstracted body writ large, shorthanded as "the Black body." For this essay, the Black body constitutes an ultimate functional abstract: it can be substituted as a stand-in for a collective experience, and it serves as an activator of one's experiential and sensorial apparatus. Put another way, the bodies we see in these works serve as modular archetypes that activate a sense of a people.

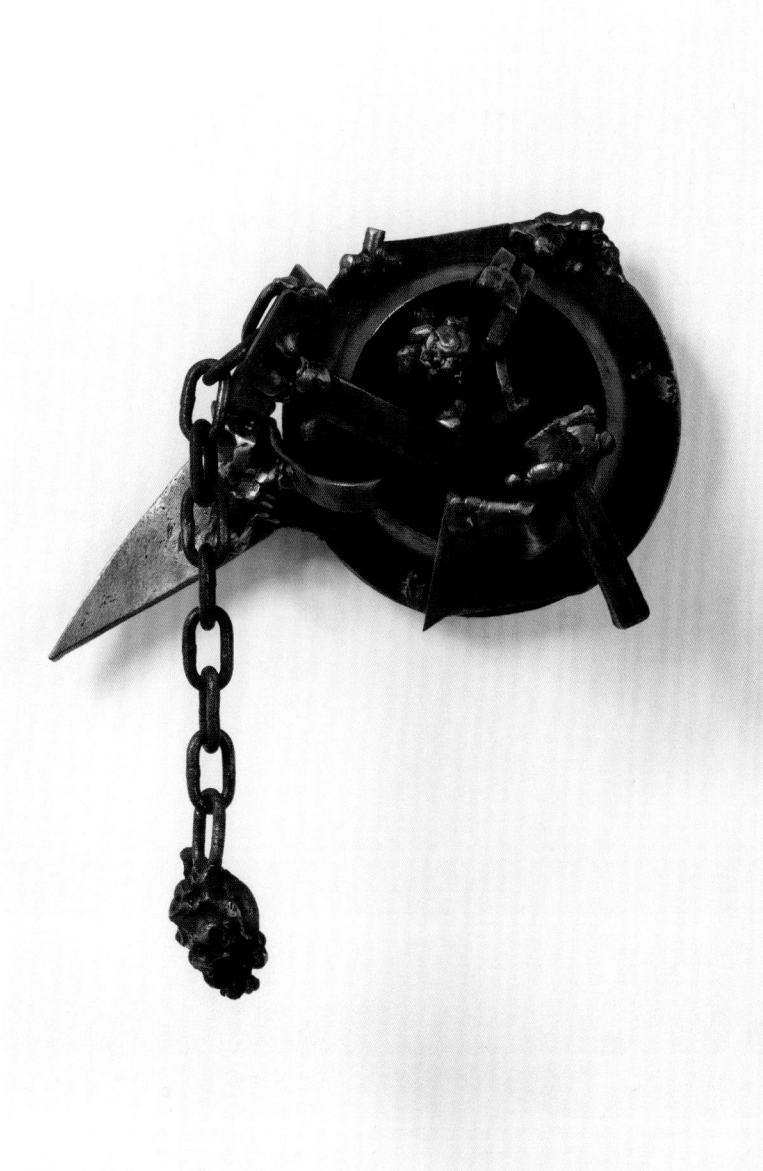

I mean sense doubly here, as both a sensual facet of everyday life (taste, smell, touch, etc.) and as a feeling about something's truth. Modular and material, abstract and representational, the Blackness of the bodies presented activates a shared, lived experience that undoubtedly touches viewers to various degrees. Each artist covered in this essay approaches vision as a sense that is often deployed toward acts of anti-Black violence. Yet rather than reproduce this logic, they seek instead to deform vision in order to account for the sensorial possibilities that exist within and despite the violent qualities of sight.

Melvin Edwards's *Lynch Fragments* series (figs. 3.4–6) is composed of multiple sculptures made of welded steel. These sculptures, in conceptual apparatus and form, compose bodies that speak to the poetic and material violences that accompany Black life. Edwards started this decades-long series in the 1960s and focused on ongoing white supremacist violence in the United States. Utilizing both the found and the made, the artist's method, somewhat akin to assemblage, accounts for how material itself can be manipulated to reflect the structure and meaning of violence.[12] Edwards cut, forged, and welded steel components with the aim of developing an entirely new form. As the artist notes in a 1994 statement: "This book contains fragments of my sculptural ideas as expressed by a group of works collectively titled *Lynch Fragments* (1963). They have been freely constructed of flame cut, welded and forged steel from bar, plate, and angle stock combined with prefabricated forms and objects (chain, barbwire, railroad spikes) to form a new abstract relief sculpture."[13]

Alex Potts has richly recounted how Edwards's material method was an attempt to develop a visual language that could somehow make space for the various processes, meanings, and outcomes of anti-Black violence.[14] In calling these works "freely constructed," the artist gestures toward the improvisational method of assemblage he employs, bringing together objects that have differing associations elsewhere and recontextualizing them in his dense forms. Edwards is very particular about how his *Lynch Fragments* are presented to an audience. The works are relatively small in scale and require the viewer's focused attention. Installed to resemble heads, as Potts notes, they "are to be fixed to the wall, facing a viewer at eye level."[15] Positioned face-to-face with the sculptures, viewers are encouraged to stare into the forms, to revel in their complexity, and to engage in a kind of eye contact that puts viewers in bodily relation to the fragments in front of them.[16] What I find most compelling is Edwards's notion of a "new abstract relief sculpture," which connects directly to the notion of functional abstract.

Fig. 3.4 Melvin Edwards, *Some Bright Morning*, 1963, from the *Lynch Fragments* series, welded steel, 14¼ × 9¼ × 5 inches. Courtesy of Melvin Edwards and Alexander Gray Gallery. © 2021 Melvin Edwards / Artists Rights Society (ARS), New York.

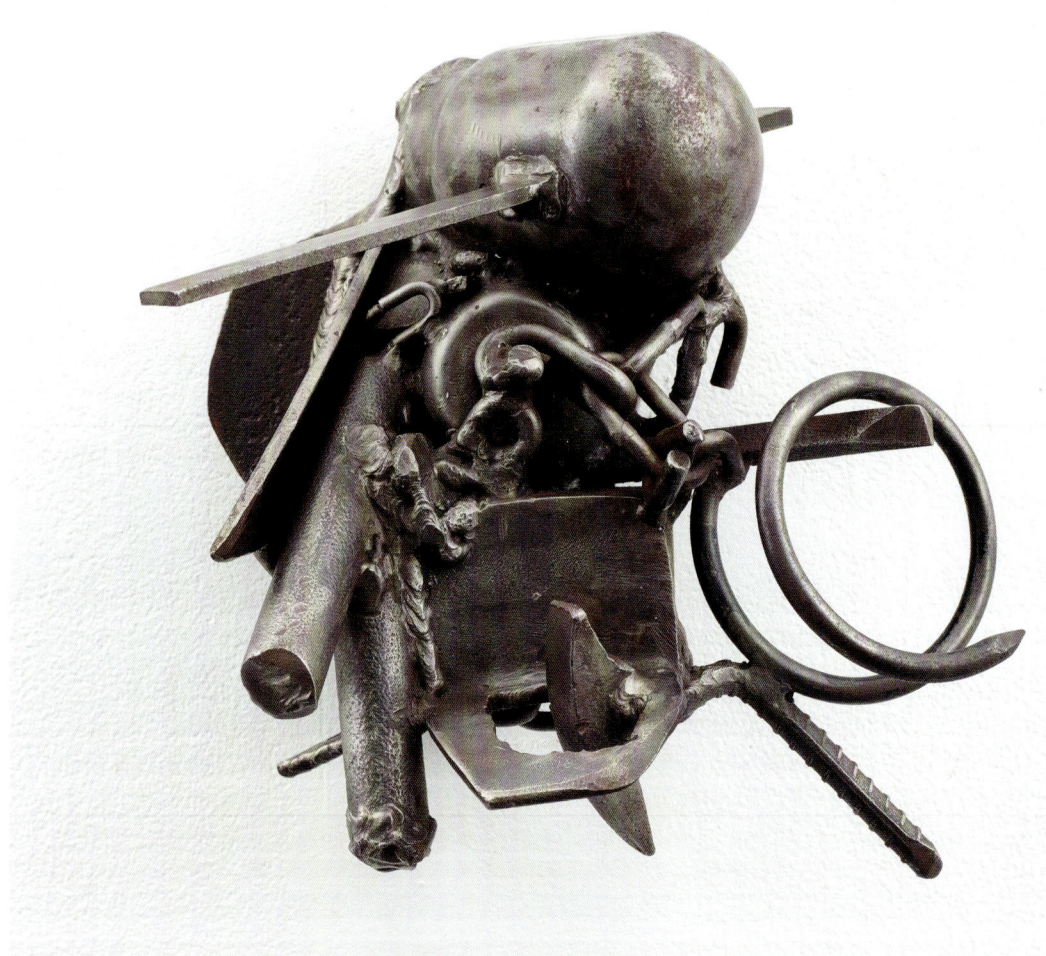

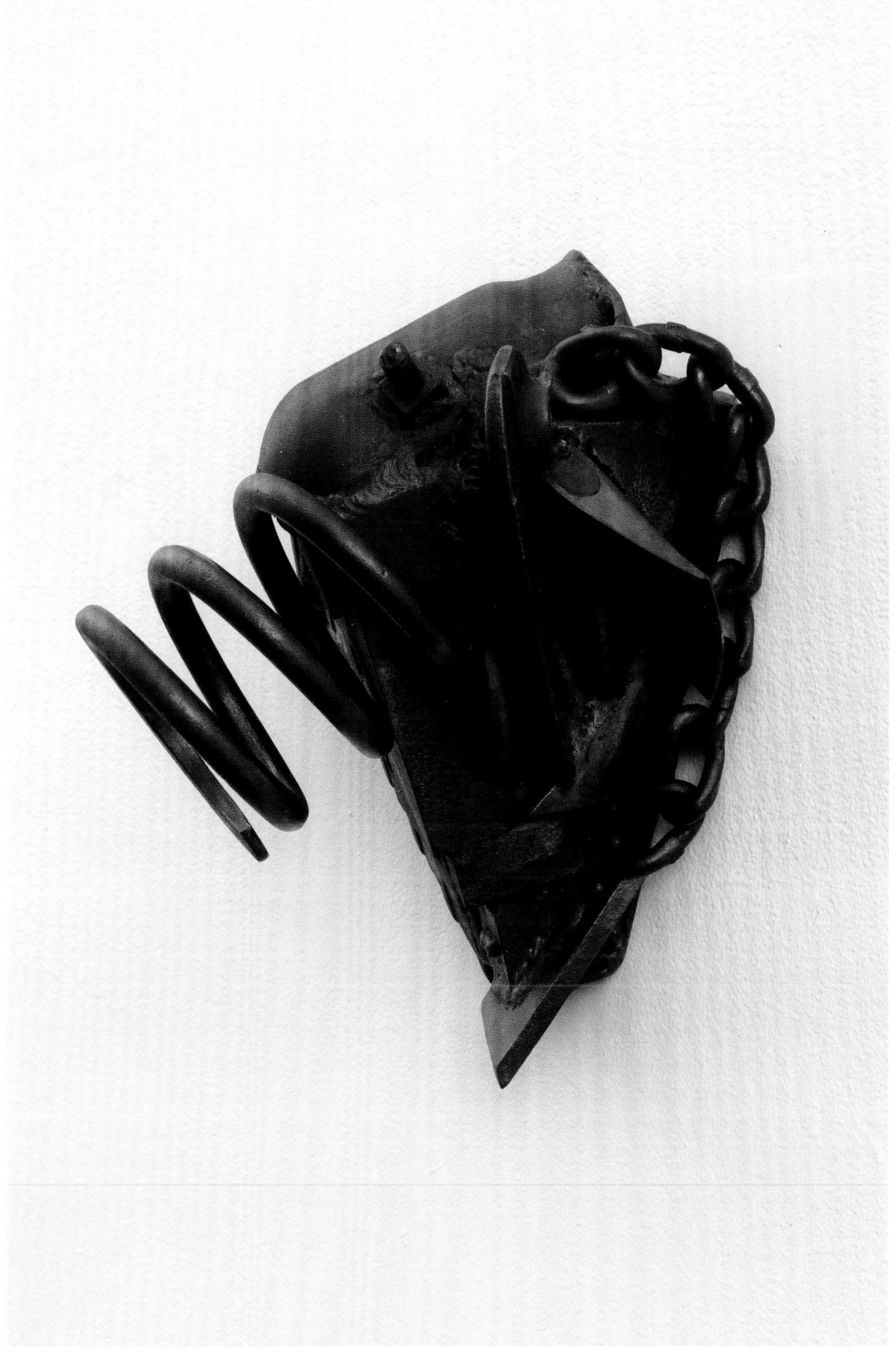

The *Lynch Fragments* series works within the language of a Black abstraction, built through deconstructed elements associated with racial terror. As indicated by the title, we are given a series of compositions, relatively small in scale, that signal acts of lynching, a particular form of terrorization that is undoubtedly associated with anti-Black violence. Like Catlett's print, these sculptures point us to the intimate and ghastly methods of attacks upon Black people. Yet unlike Catlett, who depicts a scene in progress, Edwards chooses the vocabulary of the fragment—that partial, broken-off element connected to an act. The fragment, too, is an abstraction, a floating signifier that derives the fullness of its meaning from the grammar and syntax that surround it. Put differently, the meaning of the fragment is tethered to context, and the viewer's imaginative capacity to place the fragment in that context amplifies its force. In Edwards's series, individual work titles clue the viewer into how each fragment serves as a functional abstract pointing us back to the act that it signifies—lynching.

Various components of each sculpture have been weaponized against Black people—chains and ax heads to name but two. What makes these works "new abstract relief sculptures" is not only their newness as a visual language, but also that they are built from a series of materials that form a new kind of racialized body out of refuse materials considered of no use. In Edwards's works, discarded materials are transformed, abstracted from both their original purpose and their status as trash into composite, layered, and dense bodily wholes. Destruction and construction serve as both material processes and functional meanings in these works, which communicate the sensorial weight of anti-Black violence. It is almost as if the "eye contact" Edwards stages between the viewer and these works emphasizes the *contact* over the ocular. Goosebumps—again, that fleshly manifestation of fear or the uncanny—surface across the viewer's body when confronted with these objects that allude to the lynching act: coldness of the material as it might hit warm skin, the imagined metallic clanking of steel crashing into steel, the tension of chain links and metal rope as it tightly circles parts of the body. Yet apart from any kind of literal reference, the constitutive elements also form another bodily possibility entirely. The compacted steel components sit delicately together, layering and touching each fragmented element with care, the metallic pieces offering an imagined progression of percussive sounds, like jazz, rubbing together as a kind of warmness exudes from these uncanny shapes. Touch is signaled in these work as a sense attributed both to the violences of lynching and to the kinds of intimate modalities that affirm modes of living. The steel serves as

a kind of surrogate material, an abstracted skin, that functions to alert the viewer to how the material makes meaning out of the violence to which it is central. Much like Weheliye's invocation of the infographic as a kind of physiognomy, the *Lynch Fragments* are abstracted bodies that signpost the sensorial modes of Black life, within and despite the violences that often construct their meaning.

If Edwards's abstract sculptures offer up an emergent quality of contact and touch, then Theaster Gates's works suggest a haptic contemplation of *force*. I want to close with a meditation on Gates's *In Case of Race Riot II* (2011, fig. 3.7), which can be understood in tandem with the artist's *Minority Majority* (2012, fig. 3.8). Both works use decommissioned fire hoses to create quiet, poetic compositions that cite white midcentury modernism. *In Case of Race Riot II* features a rolled-up fire hose housed behind a glass covering, within a wood frame. The hose wraps around itself, looping to form a tightly layered spiral. One end of the hose is cocooned into a center navel, while the other drapes from right to left along the bottom of the case. The drooping hose looks exhausted; its textured and dirtied exterior skin suggests a weathered and storied past. This object likely derives from an era when fire hoses were made of cotton, a raw material whose history undoubtedly dovetails with Black experience in the United States. Cotton, associated with enslaved Black labor, remains a ubiquitous fiber, breathable, light, and durable, which touches everyday life. In order to achieve maximum durability for an object like a fire hose, cotton would need to be bound into a tight weave, though most cotton hoses were nonetheless easily torn, vulnerable to abrasion due to water pressure or external ruptures.[17] The hose we see in *In Case of Race Riot II* was likely decommissioned because of such wear and tear. Gates's display case implies that it is now merely a museum piece, null and void: here we have a historical object trapped in its bodily incapacity.

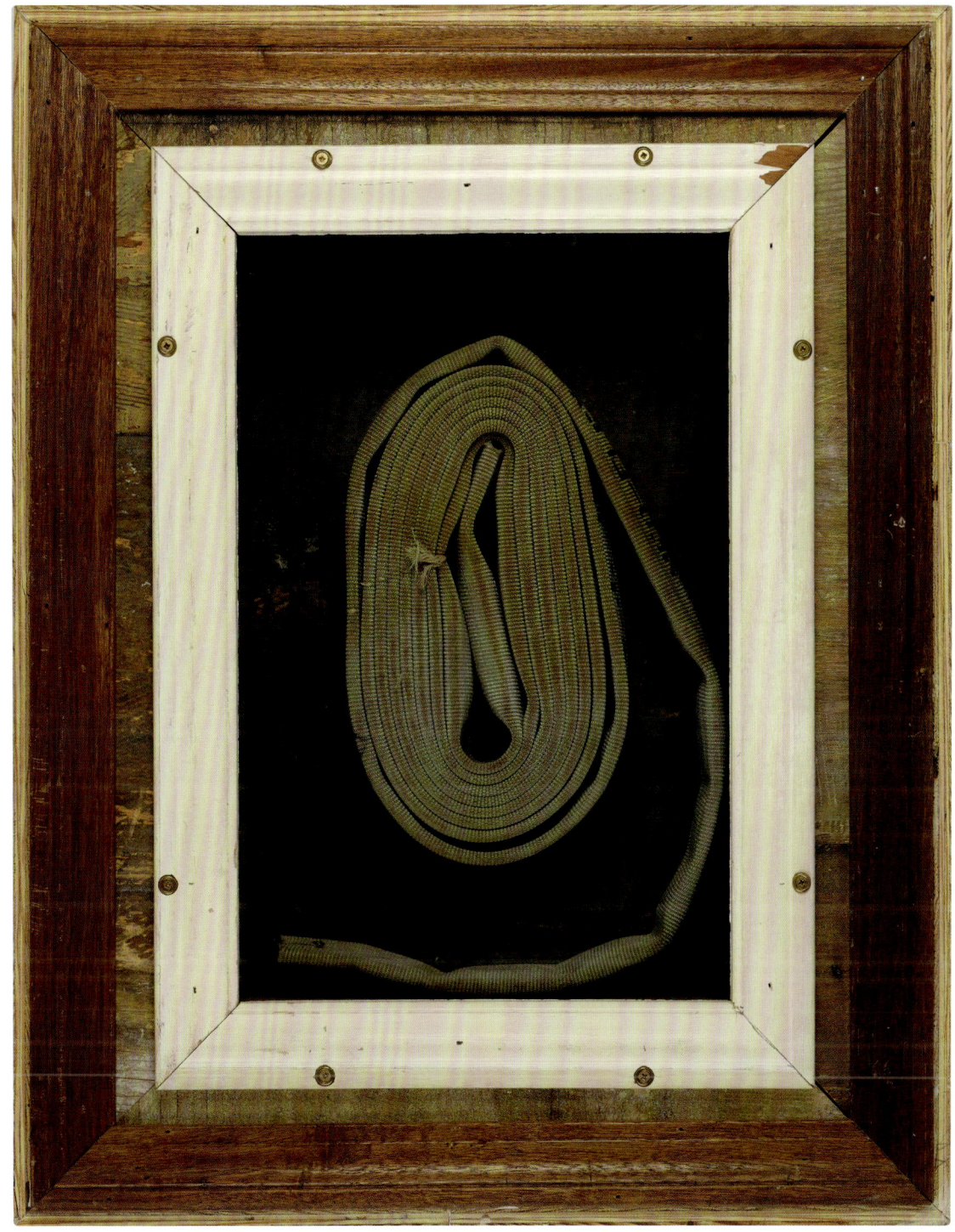

Fig. 3.7 Theater Gates, *In Case of Race Riot II*, 2011, wood, pigment, plastic, metal, adhesive, 33½ × 26⅝ × 6 inches. Brooklyn Museum of Art, Purchase gift of Jill and Jay Bernstein, 2011.9. © Theater Gates. Image courtesy of the Brooklyn Museum.

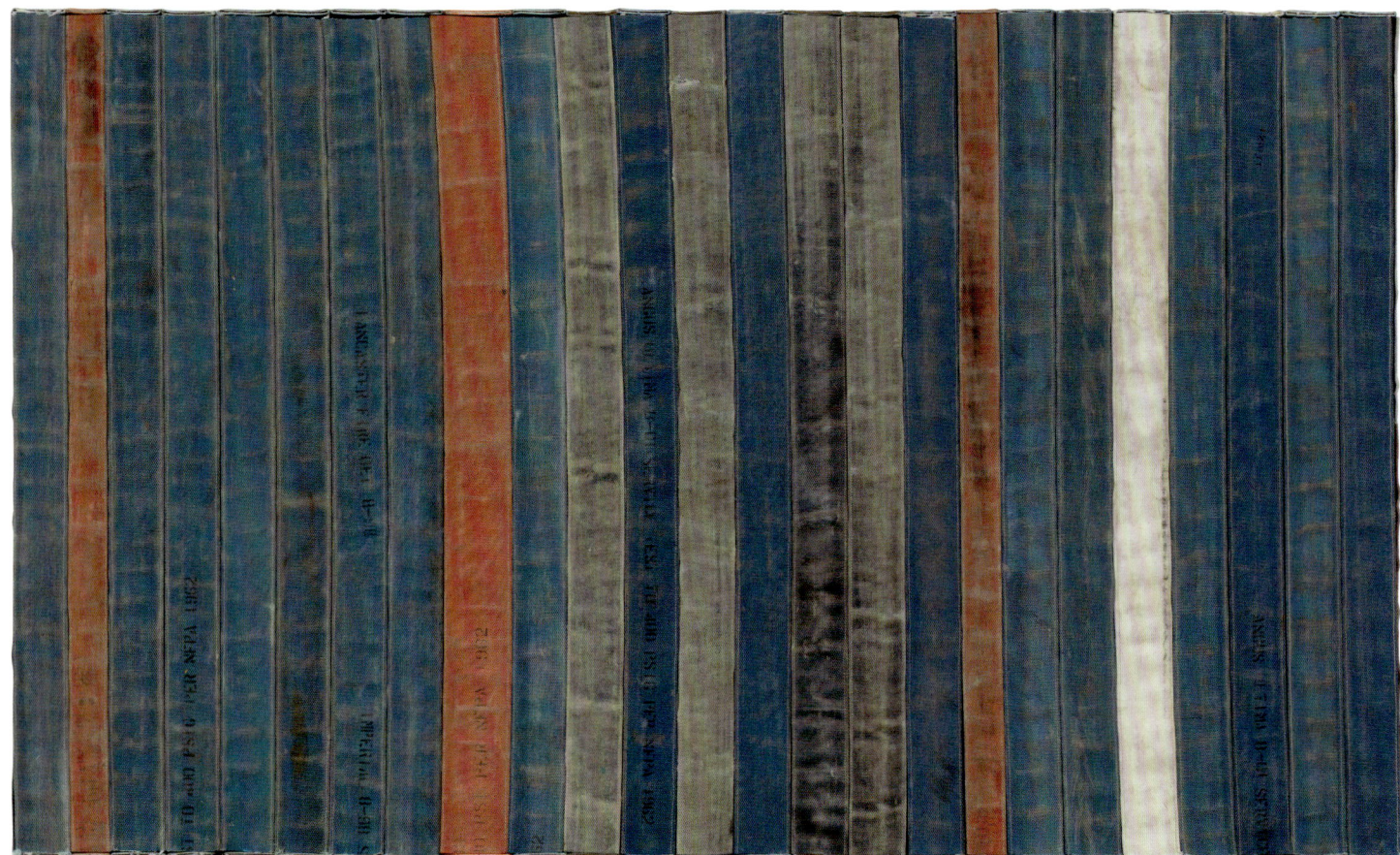

Fig. 3.8 Theaster Gates, *Minority Majority*, 2012, decommissioned fire hoses and vinyl on plywood, 66 × 111½ × 3¾ inches. Whitney Museum of American Art, New York, Gift of Barbara and Michael Gamson, 2016.262. © Theaster Gates. Digital image courtesy of the Whitney Museum of American Art, New York / Licensed by SCALA / Art Resource, NY.

Gates's use of decommissioned fire hoses is prompted by the artist's deep inquiry into the history of civil rights in the United States. The work's instructive title prompts the viewer to associate it with the widely disseminated 1960s documentary photographs that capture nonviolent protestors being aggressively attacked by vigilantes, police, and firefighters. Some of the most shocking of these depict protestors being blasted with water speeding out of fire hoses with irresistible force. These images are seared into a collective national memory of anti-Black violence aimed at Black Americans and their allies who were merely fighting for the fullness of the civil rights guaranteed by the law. The fire hose, meant to be an instrument of public safety, was weaponized against a people as a way to violently neutralize demonstrators. Gates's associative presentation of the fire hose allows for a kind of abstraction that activates a haptic sensibility in order to tap into the contemporary resonance of historical events. The ominous title raises the specter of its future use in a possible race riot, an object rendered still in a frame, caught up in a sinister history that might reappear in our present. Thus, abstraction here engages the viewer's sense of touch—how it must have felt to have water blasted onto your body, how it must have felt to hold the hose still, how it might feel now to break open that glass. . . . These haptic encounters move us toward another kind of understanding of the historical anti-Black violences that structure our present.

Here, the hose acts as a body whose materiality alerts us to a past in order to prompt us to make another kind of future. "Certain materials make you grapple with those histories and you can use those materials to make modest gestures that are really monumental," notes Gates, "I'm interested in reconstructing histories and intervening in futures."[18] Such change requires taking seriously how the Black body might be untethered from the weight of violences that structure the world from which that body is formed. This approach to materiality is decidedly a Black aesthetic endeavor: artists from Catlett to Edwards to Gates have prioritized the exceptional scope of anti-Black violence, particularly focusing on how histories of presenting the Black body have been and often are a function of white supremacist desires. They point us to the very places where those desires could be and are being escaped, resisted, or outright denied. In these modalities, the material and the sensorial converge to open up a set of aspirations toward Black freedom. Functional abstractions might look to a horizon line where the future is not only an accumulation of recalled violences but also an abundance of sensed possibilities.

Notes

1   My book, *Death's Futurity: The Visual Life of Black Power* (Durham, NC: Duke University Press, forthcoming), examines images of death in the Black Power era. The project focuses on three murders of Black radicals—Bobby Hutton (1968), Fred Hampton (1969), and George Jackson (1971)—and the visual objects made in the wake of their deaths.

2   Melanie Herzog, *Elizabeth Catlett: An American Artist* (Seattle: University of Washington Press, 2005); Samella Lewis et al., *Elizabeth Catlett: Works on Paper, 1944–1992* (Hampton, VA: Hampton University Museum, 1993); Samella Lewis, *Elizabeth Catlett* (Claremont, CA: Hancraft Studios, 1984).

3   Matthew Fox-Amato, *Exposing Slavery: Photography, Human Bondage, and the Birth of Modern Visual Politics in America* (Oxford: Oxford University Press, 2019); Tina Campt, *Listening to Images* (Durham, NC: Duke University Press, 2018); Avery Gordon, *Ghostly Matters: Haunting and the Sociological Imagination* (Minneapolis: University of Minnesota Press, 1997); David Marriott, *On Black Men* (New York: Columbia University Press, 2000); Leigh Raiford, *Imprisoned in a Luminous Glare: Photography and the African American Freedom Struggle* (Chapel Hill, NC: University of North Carolina Press, 2011); Maurice O. Wallace and Shawn Michelle Smith, eds., *Pictures and Progress: Early Photography and the Making of African American Identity* (Durham, NC: Duke University Press, 2012); Krista Thompson, *An Eye for the Tropics: Tourism, Photography, and Framing the Caribbean Picturesque* (Durham, NC: Duke University Press, 2006); Michele Wallace, *Dark Designs and Visual Culture* (Durham, NC: Duke University Press, 2004); Deborah Willis, *Picturing Us: African American Identity in Photography* (New York: New Press, 1996); and Harvey Young, "Still Standing: Daguerreotypes, Photography, and the Black Body," in *Embodying Black Experience: Stillness, Critical Memory and the Black Body* (Ann Arbor: University of Michigan Press, 2010).

4   "Black radical aesthetic," in the context of this essay, signposts a critical position and approach to Black artistic practices that reconceptualize, puncture, or trouble the reductively panoptic qualities of sight as these qualities play out in relation to Black experience and creative life. I consider writings that turn toward the deconstructing of the relationship between the representational and the nonrepresentational with an eye toward the "abstract" in Black studies: Huey Copeland, *Bound to Appear: Art, Slavery, and the Site of Blackness in Multicultural America* (Chicago: University of Chicago Press, 2013); Adrienne Edwards, *Blackness in Abstraction* (New York: Pace Gallery, 2016); Philip Brian Harper, *Abstractionist Aesthetics: Artistic Form and Social Critique in African American Culture* (New York: New York University Press, 2015); Kellie Jones, *South of Pico: African American Artists in Los Angeles in the 1960s and 1970s* (Durham, NC: Duke University Press, 2017); Kobena Mercer, *Discrepant Abstraction* (London: Institute of International Visual Arts, 2006); Fred Moten, *In the Break: The Aesthetics of the Black Radical Tradition* (Minneapolis: University of Minnesota Press, 2003); Hortense Spillers, "Mama's Baby, Papa's Maybe: An American Grammar Book," *Diacritics* 17, no. 2 (Summer 1987): 64–81.

5   Whitney Battle-Baptiste and Britt Rusert, eds., *W. E. B. Du Bois's Data Portraits Visualizing Black America: The Color Line at the Turn of the Twentieth Century* (Hudson, NY: Princeton Architectural Press, 2018).

6   Battle-Baptiste and Rusert, *W. E. B. Du Bois's Data Portraits*, 11.

7   W. E. B. Du Bois, "To the Nations of the World" (1900), in *W. E. B. Du Bois: A Reader*, ed. David Levering Lewis (New York: Henry Holt, 1995), 639.

8   Battle-Baptiste and Rusert, *W. E. B. Du Bois's Data Portraits*, 13.

9   Battle-Baptiste and Rusert, *W. E. B. Du Bois's Data Portraits*, 13.

10   Alexander Weheliye, "Diagrammatics as Physiognomy: W. E. B. Du Bois's Graphic Modernities," *CR: The New Centennial Review* 15, no. 2 (2015): 39.

11   Weheliye, "Diagrammatics as Physiognomy," 49.

12   "Melvin Edwards, *Lynch Fragments*, 1960s–Present," Alexander Gray Associates website, accessed April 7, 2021, http://www.alexandergray.com/series-projects/melvin-edwards3.

13   Melvin Edwards, as quoted in Alex Potts, "Melvin Edwards's Sculptural Intensity," in *Melvin Edwards: Five Decades*, ed. Catherine Craft (Dallas: Nasher Sculpture Center, 2015), 48.

14   Potts, "Melvin Edwards's Sculptural Intensity," 48.

15   Potts, "Melvin Edwards's Sculptural Intensity," 47.

16   For more on the ways that Edwards encourages the viewer take up a bodily position in relation to his work, see Sampada Aranke, "Blackouts and Other Visual Escapes," *Art Journal* (Winter 2020): 62–75.

17   Sam Goldwater and Robert F. Nelson, "Large-Diameter Super Aquaduct Flexible Pipeline Applications in the Fire Service," *Fire Engineering* (April 1997): 147–49.

18   Theaster Gates and Lilly Wei, "Theaster Gates," *Art in America* (December 2011), http://www.artnews.com/art-in-america/features/theaster-gates-62915/.

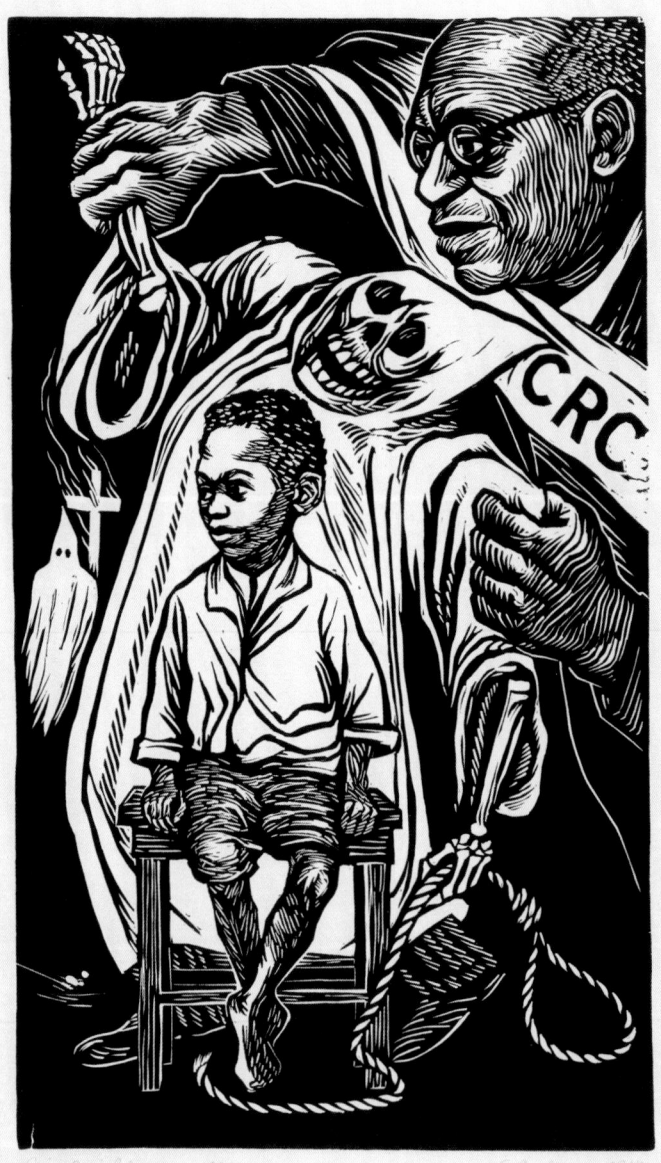

Elizabeth Catlett

(American, 1915–2012)

Target Practice, 1970

Bronze, wood, and metal
19½ × 12 × 15¾ inches
Amistad Research Center, Tulane
University. © Catlett Mora Family
Trust / Licensed by VAGA at Artists
Rights Society (ARS), NY.

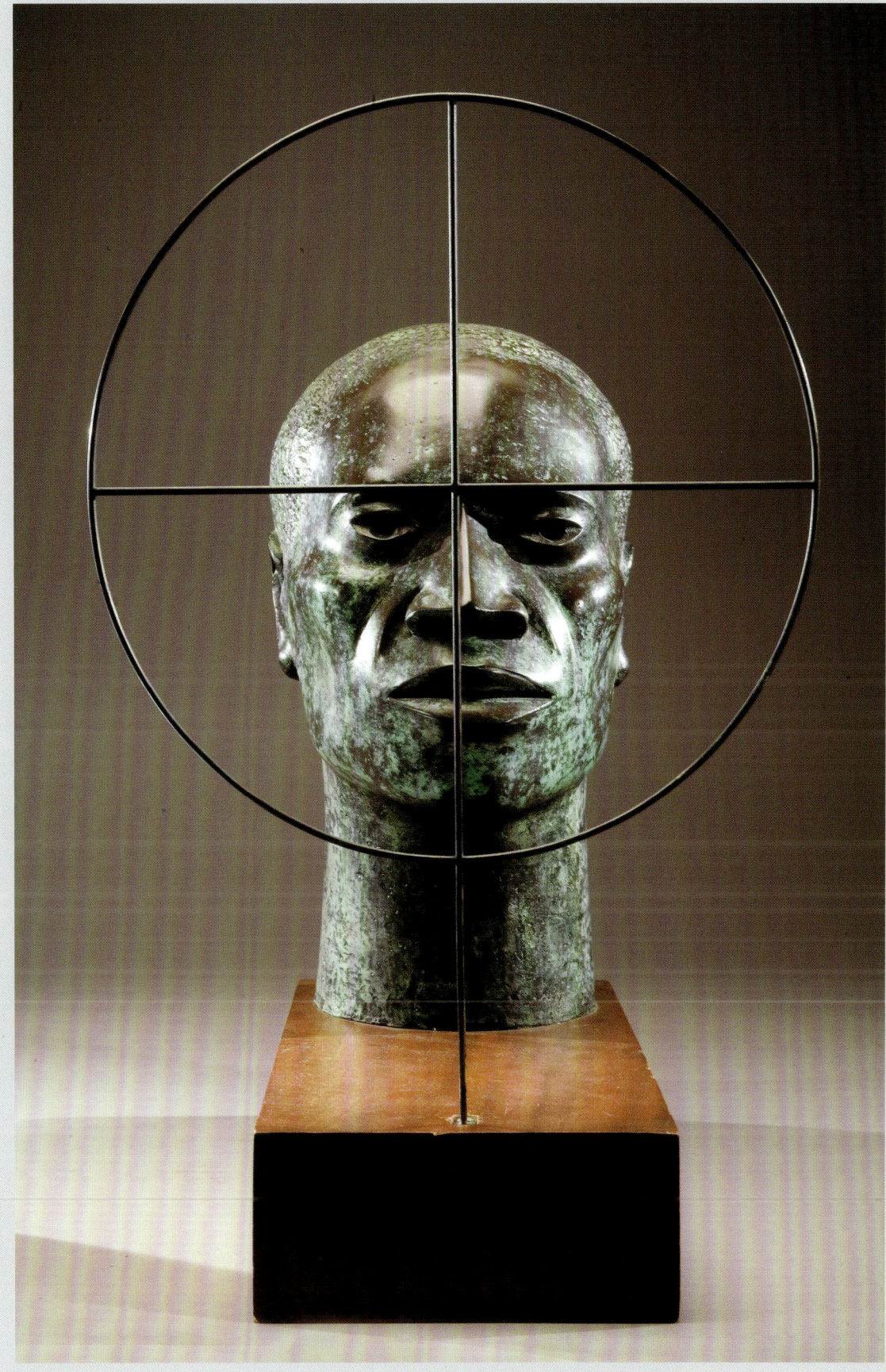

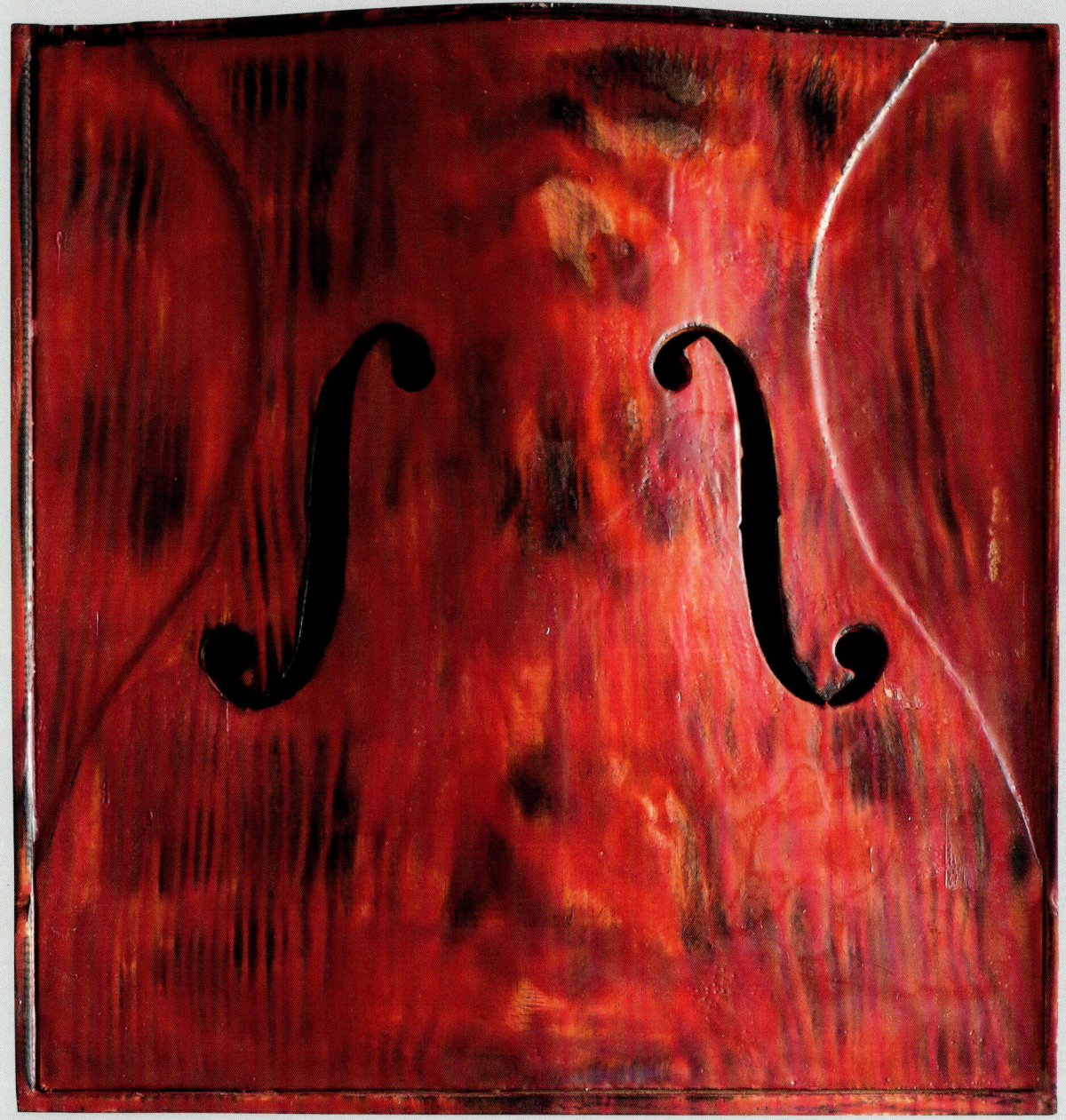

Paul Rucker
(American, b. 1968)
January 1–September 14, 1919,
Red Summer, from the series
Soundless, 2015

Pine, blowtorch, encaustic, acrylic
16 × 16 × 2 inches
Courtesy of the artist.

Paul Rucker
(American, b. 1968)
May 15, 1916, Waco, Texas, from
the series *Soundless*, 2015

Plywood, blowtorch, encaustic, acrylic
16 × 16 × 2 inches
Courtesy of the artist.

Black Redaction, Black Evidence

Another Testimony
of Black Life
LaCharles Ward

How do objects, especially human remains and ruins, become significant—start to signify—when they are identified, introduced, enlisted, and fought over, as evidence in political and juridical forms?

—Thomas Keenan

What happens when Blackness enters the frame? The ontological status of those who are racialized as Black is of paramount importance to the possibility of a legible, functional and operative Black Testimony. The fact or phenomenon of Blackness should be considered as a form of evidence that, due to its blurring of subject and object positionality, requires distinct modes of attention, just as bones do within forensic discourse.

—Imani Robinson

I.

In an article published in the *Columbia Journalism Review*, multidisciplinary artist Alexandra Bell asks: "Is there a way to train people how to question?"[1] Indeed, questions about the ways images and terminology are used not only are asked of the viewers who engage her work but also lie at the heart of Bell's artistic practice. They guide her critical and aesthetic investigation of how racism, anti-Black violence, and the wages of whiteness are covered in mainstream journalism. In her popular series *Counternarratives*, produced in 2017, Bell troubles how certain narratives are consumed and offers an alternative narrative through aesthetic practices of redaction and annotation. The series was influenced by Chilean artist Alfredo Jaar, whose 1995 series *Untitled (Newsweek)* challenged the absence of the Rwandan genocide from magazine covers in the United States, and by George Lipsitz, a scholar of whiteness and social movements, namely for his notion of counter-memory.[2] Each of Bell's five *Counternarratives* works, which range in size, considers a different story that was published in the *New York Times*, all centering on themes of racism, white supremacy, and violence. At its core, in the artist's words, the series "deconstructs language and imagery to explore the tension between marginal experiences and dominant histories."[3]

The diptych *A Teenager With Promise* (2017, fig. 4.1), the first work to be produced in the series and Bell's most popular, centers on the life of Michael Brown. The artist's goal was to challenge how the *Times*'s attempt to present an objective narrative of two lives: that of Officer Darren Wilson of the Ferguson Police Department, who is still alive, and Michael Brown, the Black teenager he killed. The original article, titled "Two Lives at the Crossroads in Ferguson," published on August 25, 2014, appeared under bolded headlines and featured two different stories by two different staff writers.[4] The title of the first story read "A Low-Profile Officer with Unsettled Early Days," and the second read "A Teenager Grappling with Problems and Promise." Bell has argued that the subtitles constructed a false equivalency and presented Wilson more favorably while reverting to normative racist tropes and terminology to describe Brown. In the first story, Wilson is a "low-profile officer" whose whiteness and anti-Blackness the title veils in its attempt to render him unremarkable. In the second, however, Brown's teenage problems come before his promise, the headline writer clinging to a trite but dangerous controlling narrative about familial dysfunction and Black male social pathology à la Daniel Patrick Moynihan.[5] Black studies scholar Hortense Spillers has importantly challenged assumptions that underpin both of these

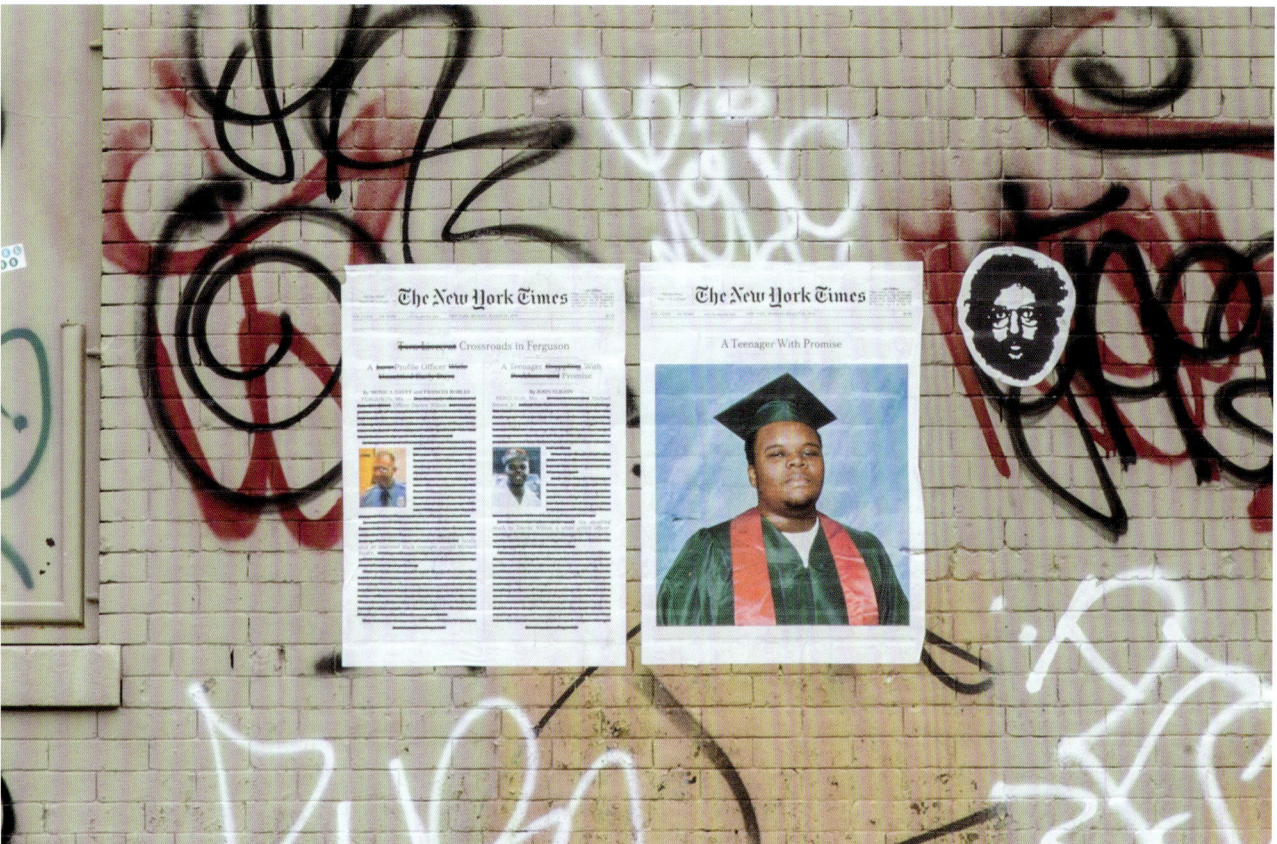

narratives, namely that Black women are to blame for the supposed dysfuntion of Black men and, more broadly, the Black family.[6]

Responding directly to Black critical theorist Christina Sharpe, who asks, "What might practices of Black annotation and Black redaction offer?"[7] this essay considers practices of redaction and annotation by Black people, artists, and cultural producers as contributing to a framework of evidence where Blackness and the expansiveness of Black people's lives are centered. In doing so, we refuse the anti-Black terms imposed upon Black people that "reduce black life to always already suspect."[8] Likewise, this essay proposes that Black art constitutes one form of evidence necessary for imagining Black life within and against the grain of a brutal anti-Black world.

The legal conception of what counts as evidence has long been a site of struggle for Black people (consider, for example, the exoneration of police officers for acts of violence against Black individuals, despite the Rodney King video or eyewitness testimony of Michael Brown's death).[9] To reimagine evidence from the position of Blackness, I turn to artists such as those here to illuminate how Black people continue to produce archives that redefine evidence with what I call Black evidence, which draws on a distinct mode of attention in order to hang on to Black testimonies. This echoes the important work of London-based artistic duo Languid Hands, which includes writer and artist Imani Robinson and filmmaker and curator Rabz Lansiquot. In their video installation *Towards a Black Testimony: Prayer/Protest/Peace* (2019), the artists examine how Black testimonies of anti-Black violence are obscured, ignored, and erased by the State.[10] The work insists on new forms of evidence that instead of appealing to the State appeal to a Black forum of global Black communities. One of the major suppositions of Black evidence is that Black people have long produced evidence grounded in the experiences of their daily lives, but that has loitered in the typographical and visual margins of the legal archive and moved outside of legal conceptions of evidence.

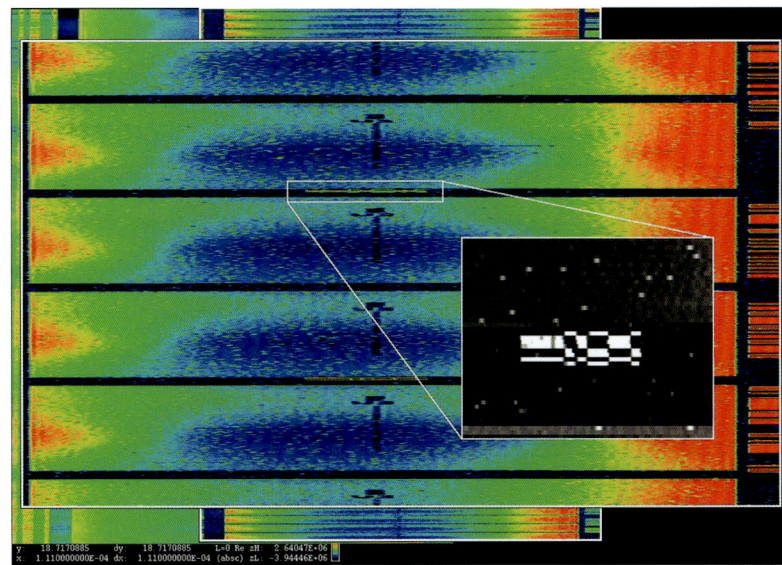

Fig. 4.1 Alexandra Bell, *A Teenager With Promise*, 2017, installation view, Brooklyn, New York, 2017. Photo courtesy of the artist.

Fig. 4.2 Laura Poitras, *ANARCHIST Israeli Drone Video Signal (Intercepted February 24, 2009)*, 2016, film still, from the installation *Disposition Matrix (2016)*. Courtesy of Laura Poitras in collaboration with Henrik Moltke.

In the subsequent pages, I discuss practices of redaction and gesture to artists who draw on redaction aesthetics more broadly. I then move to consider several works by artists of color who engage in practices of Black annotation and redaction, paying particular attention to Alexandra Bell but also discussing artists M. NourbeSe Philip, Steve McQueen, Titus Kaphar, and Reginald Dwayne Betts. Sharpe's conceptual work forms the backdrop for my discussion of each of these artists and their works. I bring the essay to a close with a set of thoughts about what the work of Black redaction as a form of Black evidence might offer as a means of holding onto testimonies of Black life.[11]

II.

Redaction has been understood as the act of "bringing or putting into a definite form," such as the drafting of source material in a distinctive, written form; the act of revising or editing a text; or the presentation of a new version of a text.[12] Most people, however, think of redaction as "the act of censoring a document . . . or blacking out certain words," images, or series of texts, "especially for legal, high security," or other secrecy purposes.[13] The characteristic appearance of declassified government documents released to the public with redacted information has inspired redaction art and poetry, or what others have called "erasure aesthetics."[14] Cultural producers mobilize redaction as a way to get us to look again, see differently, and read that which is not there but is present in its absence.[15] The use of redaction as an aesthetic practice not only asks questions of a text, broadly construed, through erasure or omission, it also asks the viewer to ask critical questions. Indeed, redaction asks us to see and read in new ways and, importantly, to attend to the complex dynamics between what is absented and presented. In short, redaction might be understood as a practice to reveal power relations, draw our attention to the hegemony of language, and allow for a speculative reimagining of sites of inquiry. Bell's *Counternarratives* series can be understood within a growing body of artistic and cultural work that draws on the aesthetic practices of redaction. For example, we might recall Jenny Holzer's *Redaction Paintings* from the early 2000s, which probe the boundaries of censorship and transparency and invite viewers to scrutinize the notion of documentary evidence, or Laura Poitras's installation *Disposition Matrix (2016)* (2016, fig. 4.2), where visitors navigate through an effectively redacted space—a blackened corridor—with several illuminated spots displaying a range of government documents. We can think here, too, of poetry by Solmaz Sharif,

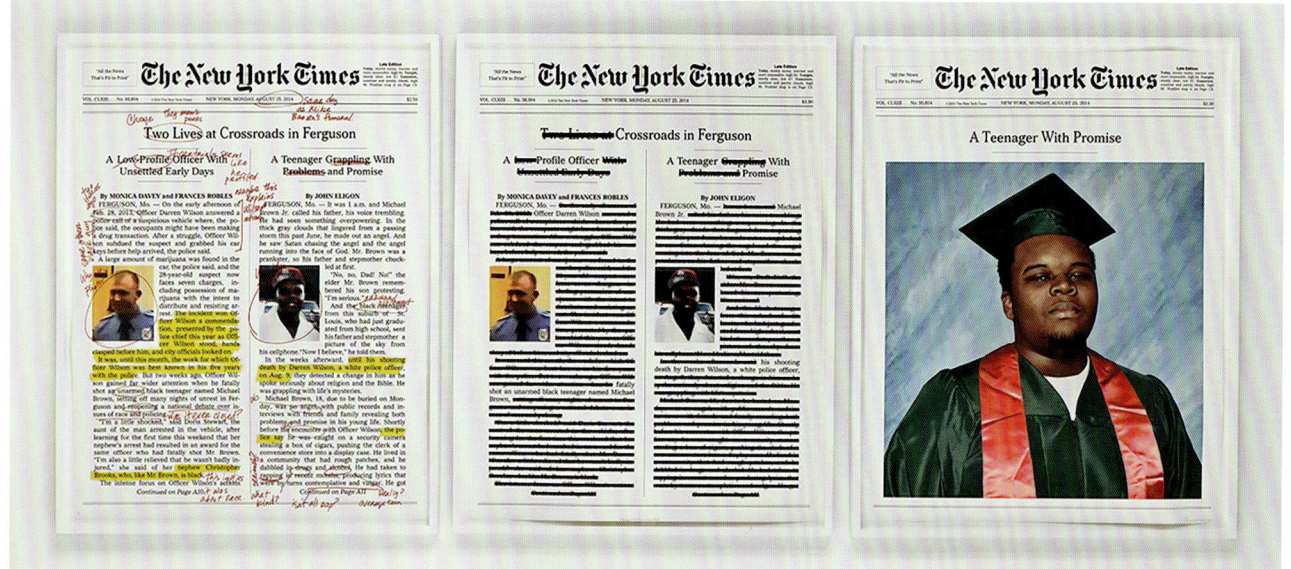

Fig. 4.3 Alexandra Bell, *A Teenager With Promise (Annotated)*, 2017, inkjet print and wheat paste, 96 × 216 inches. Courtesy of the artist.

whose 2016 collection *Look* draws on practices of redaction and erasure to explore the terror wrought by war. Her poems also examine how the *Department of Defense Dictionary of Military and Associated Terms* conducts violence against language by simultaneously deploying and eschewing particular phrases and terminology.

Bell's followed the diptych *A Teenager With Promise* with a triptych titled *A Teenager With Promise (Annotated)* (2017, fig. 4.3), which visualizes the process of annotation. By annotation, I refer to the written explanation, edits, critical comments, and thought-in-motion that appears in the margins of a work or text. In this three-panel work, the original *New York Times* article appears on the left panel with Bell's annotations and edits in red ink and yellow highlighting; the center panel reveals lines of text completely obfuscated by thick black bars, its uniformity in black overwhelming the viewer; and in the final panel, Bell replaces the article in its entirety with an enlarged portrait of Michael Brown, notably a photo that was not in the original *Times* article. Even before the redaction, Bell's annotations call into question so much about whiteness, the unequal value of life, and the inhumaneness of journalistic writing when it comes to Black people. In the left column of the center panel, Bell uses black bars to redact text that paints Officer Wilson as a person who was simply known for doing police work, calling attention to the language of whiteness and its propensity to enact anti-Black violence. Indeed, the only text she leaves unredacted reads, "Officer Darren Wilson fatally shot an unarmed black teenager named Michael Brown." In the adjacent column, she redacts text in the story of Brown that references "dabbling in drugs and alcohol" and "[producing] lyrics that were by turns

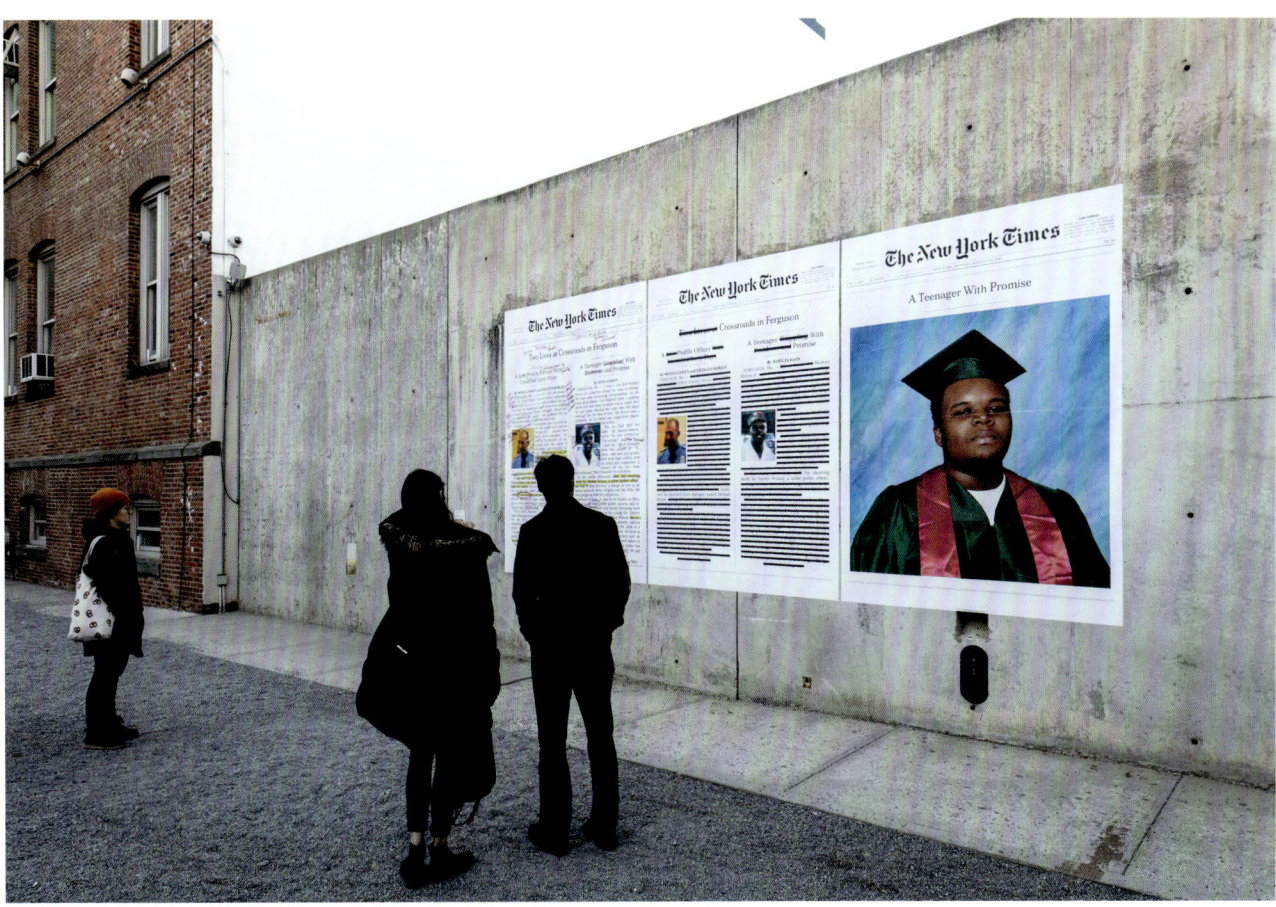

Fig. 4.4   Alexandra Bell, *A Teenager With Promise (Annotated)*, 2017, installation view, MoMA PS1, Queens, New York, 2017. Photo by Charles Roussel.

contemplative and vulgar." In the wake of her redaction, what remains is: "Michael Brown Jr. his shooting death by Darren Wilson, a white police officer," alongside a photograph of Brown wearing a red baseball cap and a white shirt. In the striking final panel, Bell substitutes a portrait of Brown in a graduation robe, enlarged and centered under the newspaper's nameplate—an act that signifies it as the cover story, not relegated to a side column—pointedly replacing "Two Lives at the Crossroads in Ferguson" with a new headline: "A Teenager With Promise." At the 2017 presentation of the work at MoMA PS1, Bell amplified her critique and brought it out of the museum space and into the public sphere, mounting the triptych's three 6 × 8–foot panels to the building's exterior (fig. 4.4).

Christina Sharpe lays the groundwork for understanding the work of redaction and annotation from the perspective of Black studies in her book *In the Wake: On Blackness and Being*. She argues that Black annotation and redaction calls on us—Black people and those committed to and caring for Black life—to do the work necessary for thinking, feeling, and acting "in the wake of slavery."[16] To be in the wake of slavery, writes Sharpe, is to live in the long history of anti-Black terror, from the enslavement of Africans to the present. It is to recognize how we are constituted "through and by continued vulnerability," as exemplified by the ongoing state-sanctioned legal and extralegal murders of Black people.[17] Yet, in the wake, we must still attend to the largeness of Black life and mobilize practices to hold on to Black life.[18] Sharpe refers to this as wake work: imagining new ways to live in the wake of slavery; new ways of seeing and attending to Black life despite Black death.

The work of Black annotation and redaction, then, is a practice of imagining what is deemed impossible in the wake of slavery, which is to say, following prison abolitionist and scholar Ruth Wilson Gilmore, how Black people strive to live "unbounded lives."[19] Accordingly, Black annotation and redaction "is another effort to try to look, to try to really see," to open that which has been abandoned—Black life— "out into a life"; indeed, it is to "make Black life visible, if only momentarily."[20] What marks practices of Black redaction as distinct from the commonplace understanding of redaction is an ethic of insistence: a practice of imagination that is grounded in refusal, it is one of the ways Black people stand their ground. This Black insistence indexes a labor of always striving for an idea of something else, entertaining the thought of that which is not but might be, or insisting on the traces of life where we are told life cannot exist. In short, it marks how Black people engage in what Zimbabwean poet and literary scholar Tsitsi Jaji enthrallingly phrased "archives of imagination."[21] It is what propels Geneva Veal-Reed, mother of Sandra Bland, to say, "She is still speaking, still."[22] Black British filmmaker and video artist Steve McQueen's video installation *End Credits* (2012–ongoing, fig. 4.5), for example, insists on a fundamental understanding of how far the US government went to surveil and harass twentieth-century African American performer and social activist Paul Robeson, drawing on the voluminous redacted FBI files regarding his everyday life. Yet it also reveals how Robeson refused to be hindered or intimidated by the state (knowing full well the

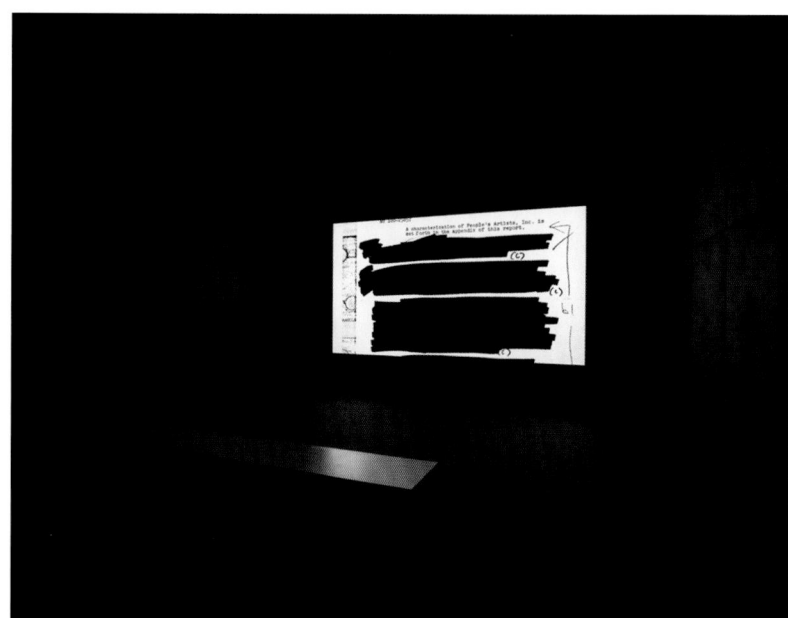

Fig. 4.5 Steve McQueen, *End Credits, Part 1*, 2012–ongoing, high-definition video sequence of scanned files (projection) with independent audio track, 5:38:00 loop. Courtesy of the artist and Marian Goodman Gallery, New York. Installation view, *Steve McQueen*, Art Institute of Chicago, 2017.

violent consequences). Indeed, his voice circulated (even as he physically could not, due the revocation of his passport) through the radio waves, and he sang and engaged in political work via hologram. This knowledge, or other way of being, cannot be erased by the FBI.[23]

In her own practices of Black annotation, Bell reorients the viewer's looking. To borrow a phrase from curator and Black visual theorist Nicole Fleetwood, Bell calls upon the spectator to "perform a function as arbiter, or decoder" of the presumed official record and to produce another record that centers Black life.[24] Bell not only disrupts and refuses the media's exculpation of the white officer, she also rejects the criminalization of Blackness by the state. Instead, she positions whiteness as the death-producing agent that it is and that the state allows. In one interview, she concedes that, sure, Michael Brown might have done drugs, cursed, and drunk, but none of these traits justify his death or should be used as reasoning to vindicate Wilson. Bell calls upon viewers to observe how anti-Black racism is codified and normalized in language and, importantly, how it is mobilized strategically in this context to decriminalize whiteness. Here, then, we might think of how Bell not only undermines the dominant narrative structures of journalism

and the ideological structure of feeling(s) and knowing that delimits it, which is to say whiteness, but also marks the failures of journalistic language to attend to the expansiveness of Black life. By redacting the problematic text, Bell paradoxically exposes those failures and opens up breathing room within the ellipses and annotations to locate a counter to the force of the State and, importantly, the anti-Black violence veiled under the gaze of objectivity that drives so-called good journalism.

Certainly, it is this counter to the force of state and what French sociologist Pierre Bourdieu called the force of law that informs not only Bell's work, but also that of other Black artists, writers, and poets who have turned to redaction as a way to offer another testimony of Black life—an art historical genealogy within which we can further locate Bell's important work.[25] Poet and trained lawyer M. NourbeSe Philip engages in a poetic form of redaction by stripping away words from the 1783 legal decision *Gregson v. Gilbert*, which justified the murder of more than 130 enslaved Africans by the crew of the slave ship *Zong*, in order to tell a different story of the crew's victims. Philip's poem *Zong!* excavates a truth in contradistinction to what the two-page eighteenth-century legal document sought to convey. Redaction here does not manifest in thick black bars; rather, it is embodied in the poem's distinctive, written form and in the unsettling organization of letters.[26]

Historical, journalistic, and legal documents serve as the source material for Bell, Holzer, Poitras, and Philip. This is also the case for McQueen, as well as for Titus Kaphar, a Black American painter, sculptor, filmmaker, and video installation artist. As noted above, McQueen's *End Credits* draws on thousands of declassified FBI documents to pay homage to the social, cultural, artistic, political, and intellectual life of Paul Robeson. Nothing short of an exercise in duration, the video layers thirteen hours of footage, including redacted FBI documents, and nearly nineteen hours of spoken word. If, as Shana Redmond brilliantly writes, "Robeson was the raw material that, in turn, made possible other types of building, both literal and figurative," then McQueen builds an audio and visual narrative of Paul Robeson's life that stands in contraposition to the "Black intramural life" the state sought to redact, erase.[27] When I first saw *End Credits* at the Art Institute of Chicago in 2017, I remember not only being overwhelmed by the scale of the redacted material, but even more important, being caught up in the timbre, enraptured by a "wall of sound," to use Redmond again, that McQueen built in order to offer another testimony—not outside of but in excess of the federal government's—of Robeson's life.[28] And while I agree with Redmond that there is no "otherwise evidence" to bring Robeson's life into these FBI documents, I wonder what would it mean to think of *End Credits* as a type of Black evidence that is itself a fundamental undoing of prevailing evidentiary theory.[29] If we accept Eyal Weizman's argument on negative evidence—that the very act of redaction is itself evidence, or that the absence of evidence (in this case of Black life) operates as evidence in its own right—then I am suggesting *End Credits* be read as a Black evidentiary object that mobilizes the FBI documents through practices of Black annotation to testify *otherwise*; against the state's imposition and its erasure of Black life.

In *Untitled (Redaction)* (2019, fig. 4.6), an installation project organized by Kaphar and attorney Reginald Dwayne Betts, viewers encounter not only multilayered black panels of text and image but also a meticulous and overwhelming history of how state and federal courts exploit and erase Black and incarcerated people from the public record. Specifically, *Redaction* examines those who have been incarcerated because of their inability to pay court fines and fees or, in other words, make cash bail—even though they have neither been tried nor convicted. Kaphar's etched portraits of incarcerated people on handmade paper are hauntingly layered with poems that Betts crafted by using the legal strategy of redaction. Kaphar and Betts note that their aim is to reclaim the "lost narratives" from legal documents and draw attention "to some of the many individuals whose lives have been impacted by mass incarceration."[30] For example, in *Redaction (In Missouri)*, one of the four redacted poems from Betts's *Felon* series[31] is collapsed on an anonymous portrait etched by Kaphar. Viewers are beckoned to dwell in the redacted space, to sit with absences and, at the same time, apprehend the meaning being conveyed by the artists. Words strain against their missing counterparts as each redaction erases an eye, part of a lip, or blocks out another part of the face—such as the mouth, thereby disabling speech—and erases human identity. Viewers, then, must strain, even if exhausted, too. They are compelled to perform the labor of deciphering. In this deciphering, if we are patient, we witness Betts's attempt—through his lithe economy of language—to reveal the particularity of the state's cruelty, the violence and exhaustion of incarceration.[32]

In *Marking Time: Art in the Age of Mass Incarceration*, Nicole Fleetwood contends that portraits produced by incarcerated and nonincarcerated artists "counterpose against the large state archive of mug shots and criminal indexes."[33] Kaphar's portraits and Betts's practices of

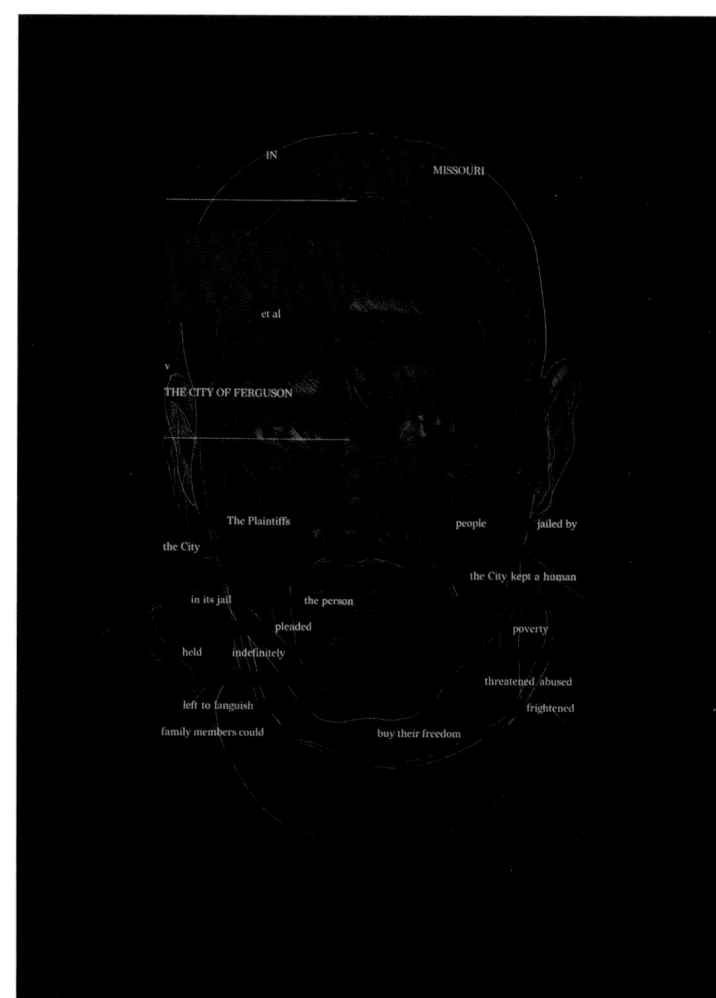

Fig. 4.6 Titus Kaphar and Reginald Dwayne Betts, *Untitled (Redaction)*, 2019, etching and silkscreen on paper, 30 × 22 inches, edition of 8. © Titus Kaphar. Courtesy of Gagosian. Photo by Rob McKeever.

redaction reveal the complex humanity of those incarcerated and, at the same time, expose the inhumanity and anti-Black violence of the prosecutors and the state archive. Intriguingly, the *Redaction* project's poems are screen printed using a "redaction" typeface that Kaphar and Betts created with designers Forest Young and Jeremy Mickel. Times New Roman and New Century Schoolbook were sedimented as foundational fonts in legal typography that, according to Young and Mickel, felt "default, functional, and familiar" and commanded a sense of authority. The "redaction" typeface, then, unsettles the typographical history of legal documents and subsequently disrupts, even if only typographically, the force of law and its signature of power.[34] If, as Betts has stated, "redaction is a rhetoric of law, of government," and he wanted to mobilize "redaction as a revelatory tool," to turn "this legalese into a song"[35]— by which he means *for Black people*—then I want to read his practice as one grounded in the specificity of Blackness and a refusal of law's violent anthem.

III.

I have been concerned with how Black people use strategies such as the legal tactic of redaction, Black annotation, and other similar aesthetic practices to reconceptualize evidence. Each of the works of art described here has not only mobilized a strategy unique to law—redaction—but also used those very evidentiary documents to thwart their supposed evidentiary weight. In doing so, they constructed a new evidentiary narrative of Black life that can only ever be one in an antagonistic entanglement with law and the signature of power it sought to invest in its redactions. The deconstructive strategies of Black redaction and the reconstructive practices of annotation are committed to Black life. Indeed, Alexandra Bell states that what she is doing is not simply a "grammar exercise" but an attempt to think critically and read aggressively the work of dominant histories.[36] I understand the practices of Black redaction and annotation as reading evidence aggressively

and, in turn, contributing to new ways of reading and seeing evidence from the position of Blackness. Objects that have hitherto been employed as specific types of evidence against the humanity of Black people are reread and reimagined as evidence of something else, such as Black people's longstanding ability to produce a counter-archive to normative evidentiary theory.[37]

Counternarratives, Bell states, is a striving to "disrupt subliminal messaging about who should be valued."[38] She strategically challenges the construction of narratives, especially those that become dominant and are simply assumed to be true, by saying, in effect, "Actually, nope, you're not getting it right, even if you are the *New York Times*."[39] She shifts and manipulates images and texts in order to unveil another truth, one that, for the most part, is grounded in the lived experiences of Blackness. But it is also not about the *Times*. Bell is not so much interested in trying to indict the media, per se, as she is in revealing the violence of language, distortion, and omission in journalism because it has "real consequences for people at the margins who are still suffering under the weight of unfair and biased representation."[40] Alongside the other artists discussed in this essay, Bell is engaged in a practice to produce Black visual evidence that not only humanizes Black people, but challenges how we see (fig. 4.7). Bell views her series as deeply committed to contending with something that is not there. That which is absent, invisible. In fact, across all her talks, Bell reminds listeners that what is not discussed in news articles does not mean that a narrative is not forming, it just means we have to read more critically.[41]

Individually and collectively, the works of Philip, McQueen, Kaphar and Betts, and Bell push us to consider, fundamentally, what remains to be seen. They direct our attention, to think with art historian Krista Thompson, to the evidence of things not seen.[42] Ultimately, to return to Sharpe's query, practices such as Black redaction and annotation enable us, like the tools of a forensic archaeologist, to search for the evidence of acts of Black living: *Black evidence*. These practices of redaction and annotation allow us to hold on to testimonies of Black life, to stay their continued erasure. Black artists, theorists, and cultural producers, such as those attended to here, reveal how Black people subsist under the weight of the law's brutality, never fully escaping its hold, but always performing a series of acrobatics to remain productively fugitive from and in open rebellion with it.

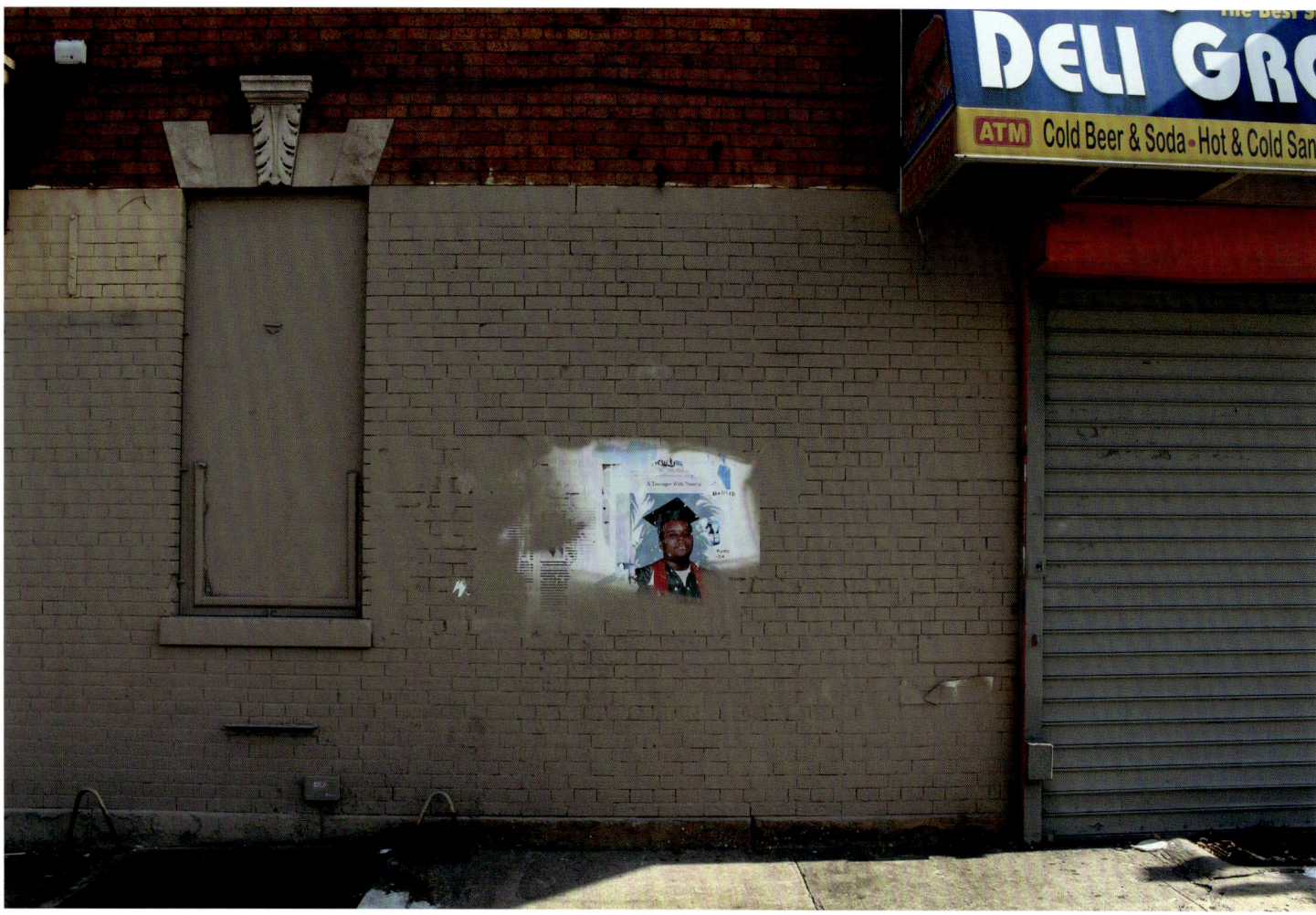

Notes

Epigraphs: Thomas Keenan, "Getting the Dead to
Tell Me What Happened: Justice, Prosopopoeia, and
Forensic Afterlives," in *Forensis: The Architecture
of Public Truth*, ed. Forensic Architecture (Berlin:
Sternberg Press, 2014), 38. Imani Robinson, *Objects
Who Testify* (London: PSS, 2019), 4.

1   Alexandra Bell, "Alexandra Bell's Revelations,"
Columbia Journalism Review (Fall 2018), http://www
.cjr.org/special_report/alexandra-bell-new-york
-central-park-five.php.

2   See, for example, George Lipsitz, *The Possessive
Investment in Whiteness: How White People Profit from
Identity Politics* (Philadelphia: Temple University Press,
2006/2018).

3   Alexandra Bell, artist website bio, accessed April
2021, http://www.alexandrabell.com/new-page/.

4   See the original *New York Times* article here:
http://www.nytimes.com/images/2014/08/25
/nytfrontpage/scan.pdf.

5   Authored by trained sociologist and United States
Senator Daniel Patrick Moynihan, *The Negro Family:
The Case for National Action*, known colloquially as
the 1965 Moynihan Report, suggested that the reason
for the dysfunction in Black communities was rooted
in the absence of a strong Black patriarchal figure. It
suggested that Black matriarchy, which Moynihan
argued was at the center of Black families, prevented
Black men from "realizing their manhood" and, in
effect, advancing in society. Stated simply, Moynihan
blamed Black women for the problems not only of Black
men but of the Black community more broadly. While
this report was quickly criticized by Black people for its
racism, it nonetheless had a massive impact on policies
and ideological perspectives that would shape the
experiences of Black people then and, arguably, now.

6   Hortense J. Spillers, "Mama's Baby, Papa's Maybe:
An American Grammar Book," *Diacritics* 17, no. 2
(Summer 1987): 64–81.

7   Christina Sharpe, *In the Wake: On Blackness and
Being* (Durham, NC: Duke University Press, 2016), 117.

8   Tina M. Campt, *Listening to Images* (Durham, NC:
Duke University Press, 2017), 113.

Fig. 4.7   Alexandra Bell, *A
Teenager With Promise*, 2017,
installation view showing work
partially covered, Brooklyn, New
York. Photo courtesy of the artist.

9 For a fuller discussion of the Rodney King beating and the subsequent verdict, see Kimberlé Crenshaw and Gary Peller, "Reel Time / Real Justice," in *Reading Rodney King / Reading Urban Uprising*, ed. Robert Gooding-Williams (New York: Routledge, 1993), 56–70.

10 In my larger book project, I spend considerable time arguing that we consider Languid Hands as crucial theorists of evidence and visual culture but, more important, as theorists of Black evidence. In mobilizing the entire corpus of Black critical theory and Black lived experiences, their work challenges the very philosophical and theoretical underpinnings of existing frameworks of evidence. To read about the work, which has only been exhibited in the United Kingdom so far, visit their website, http://languidhands.co.uk/Towards-A-Black-Testimony.

11 In April 2021, news broke that the University of Pennsylvania and Princeton University had been harboring and teaching with bones from one of the victims killed in the 1985 MOVE bombing in Philadelphia. This is not shocking within the larger history of physical anthropology, eugenics, and the use of science to locate so-called evidence of inferior and superior races. The disclosure was, however, a surprise to the public, especially to Black communities. In this context, the Thomas Keenan epigraph that opens this essay takes on a greater meaning. The idea of holding on to testimonies of Black life might, in this example, take the form of Black and other concerned people insisting that each of these institutions be held to account and, more importantly, that we humanize the life of Tree Africa, the presumed victim. Africa's remains have, until now, been mere teaching objects for a class on the "adventures of forensic anthropology." For more on this story, see Abdul-Aliy Muhammad, "Penn Museum Owes Reparation for Previously Holding Remains of A MOVE Bombing Victim," *Philadelphia Inquirer*, April 21, 2021, http://www.inquirer.com/opinion/commentary/penn-museum-reparations-repatriation-move-bombing-20210421.html.

12 *Oxford English Dictionary*, s.v. "redaction," accessed April 15, 2021, http://www-oed-com.proxy.library.upenn.edu/view/Entry/160141?redirectedFrom=Redaction#eid.

13 *Oxford English Dictionary*, s.v. "redaction."

14 For more on the phrase "erasure aesthetics," see Paul Benzon and Sarah Sweeney, eds., "The Aesthetics of Erasure," special issue, *Media-N: Journal of the New Media Caucus* 11, no. 1 (Spring 2015), http://median.newmediacaucus.org/the_aesthetics_of_erasure/. For a more theoretical account of erasure and its relationship to archives, see, for example, Jacques Derrida, *Archive Fever: A Freudian Impression* (Chicago: University of Chicago Press, 1998).

15 It is possible for us to understand this presence in absence as what Eyal Weizman calls negative evidence, or that which is marked as evidentiary because of its absence, because of its redaction. Negative evidence for Weizman can also be understood as the "withdrawal of evidence." For more discussion of redaction, absence, and evidence, see the work of Eyal Weizman and others associated with the Forensic Architecture Movement in *Forensis: The Architecture of Public Truth*, ed. Forensic Architecture (Berlin: Sternberg Press, 2014). See also Jordan H. Carver, *Spaces of Disappearance: The Architecture of Extraordinary Rendition* (New York: Terreform, 2018).

16 Sharpe, *In the Wake*, 116.

17 Sharpe continues, "Living in the wake means living in and with terror in that in much of what passes for public discourse *about* terror we, Black people, become the *carriers* of terror, terror's embodiment, and not the primary objects of terror's multiple enactments; the ground of terror's possibility globally." Indeed, "to be in the wake is to live in those no's, to live in no citizenship, to live in the long time of Dred and Harriet Scott; and it is more than that." Sharpe, *In the Wake,* 15–16.

18 These, following Tina Campt, might be understood as "the nimble and strategic practices that undermine the categories of the dominant." Tina Campt, *Listening to Images* (Durham, NC: Duke University Press, 2017), 32.

19 Ruth Wilson Gilmore, comments made at The Black Atlantic @ 50. "In the Wake of the Black Atlantic: Pedagogy and Practice," The Black Atlantic @ 50 Conference, Center for the Humanities, CUNY-Graduate Center, October 24, 2013, http://gcdi.commons.gc.cuny.edu/2013/12/12/in-the-wake-of-the-black-atlantic-pedagogy-and-practice.

20 Sharpe, *In the Wake*, 117–23.

21 Jaji briefly used this phrase in her discussion with Achille Mbembe and Laurent Dubois at Duke University Forum for Scholars and Publics, "'Critique of Black Reason': A Discussion with Achille Mbembe and Laurent Dubois," Duke University, March 29, 2017. http://www.youtube.com/watch?v=IQ8Vf70qVAg.

22 Veal-Reed made these remarks in a news article when discussing the death of her daughter, Sandra Bland. Sandra Bland was a twenty-eight-year-old Black woman who was found dead in her jail cell in Waller County, Texas, on July 13, 2015. Her death came three days after she was arrested following a minor traffic stop.

23 Shana L. Redmond, *Everything Man: The Form and Function of Paul Robeson* (Durham, NC: Duke University Press, 2020).

24 Nicole Fleetwood, *Troubling Vision: Performance, Visuality, and Blackness* (Chicago: University of Chicago Press, 2011), 7.

25 See Pierre Bourdieu, "The Force of Law: Toward a Sociology of the Juridical Field," *Hastings Law Journal* 38, no. 5 (1987): 805–53.

26 M. NourbeSe Philip, *Zong!* (Middletown, CT: Wesleyan Univeristy Press, 2008).

27 Redmond, *Everything Man*, 5. Sharpe, *In the Wake*, 114.

28 Redmond, *Everything Man*, 3.

29 I like this turn of phrase, used by Shana Redmond, because of its ambiguity. "Otherwise evidence" could connote an evidence that does not exist or, more compellingly, could indicate that there is no mechanism to truly bring the life of Paul Robeson into the legal narrative due to the very fact that the legal narrative is intent on erasing Black life. It could also suggest how Black life might remain fugitive from the constraints of legal and normative frameworks of evidence. Redmond, *Everything Man*, 93.

30 Quoted from MoMA PS1's exhibition text in *Pleading Freedom: An Exhibition by Titus Kaphar and Reginald Dwayne Betts* (August 12–September 26, 2020)," NXTHVN exhibition calendar, http://www.nxthvn.com/calendar/1906/.

31 For the full text of Betts's poem "In Missouri," see Amanda Newell, "Reginald Dwayne Betts: On Art, Poetry, the Particular Fucked Up Parts of Incarceration, and the Multitudes of I," *Plume*, no. 106 (June 2020), http://plumepoetry.com/reginald-dwayne-betts-on-art-poetry-the-particular-fucked-up-parts-of-incarceration-and-the-multitudes-of-i/.

32 In an interview with Amanda Newell, Betts was asked to speak about his poem "In Missouri" and the particular aim of his use of redaction. He responded: "And so a poem like 'Missouri,' in using redaction there, I am using it as a tool of revelation, and as a way to take a class action lawsuit that contains the multitudes of those harms, that as a form says this suit is representing these named folks and all the folks similarly situated, and say something in their voice about a particular fucked up part of incarceration." Newell, "Reginald Dwayne Betts."

33 Nicole Fleetwood, *Marking Time: Art in the Age of Mass Incarceration* (Cambridge, MA: Harvard University Press, 2020), 124.

34 For a more detailed account of this legal typography and how the "redaction" typeface developed by Kaphar, Betts, Young, and Mickel sought to challenge this history, see their essay, "Redaction—A Multiplicity of Typographic, Legal, and Human Histories," on the websiste dedicated to the project, http://www.redaction.us.

35 Rohan Preston, "In His Journey from Jail to Yale Law, Felon-Turned Poet 'Writes to Remember Who I Am,'" *Star Tribune (Minneapolis)*, March 6, 2021, http://www.startribune.com/in-his-journey-from-jail-to-yale-law-felon-turned-poet-writes-to-remember-who-i-am/600030677/?refresh=true.

36 Alexandra Bell, "2018 Infinity Award: Applied—Alexandra Bell," *International Center of Photography*, Youtube video, April 10, 2018, http://www.youtube.com/watch?v=-MHXY6vIoe4. This is not unlike the call for "an aggressive reading of evidence" (one that I return to and extend in my larger project) that Judith Butler makes in their essay about the Rodney King verdict. Judith Butler, "Endangered/Endangering: Schematic Racism and White Paranoia," in *Reading Rodney King / Reading Urban Uprising*, ed. Robert Gooding-Williams (New York: Routledge, 1993), 17.

37 Robinson, *Objects Who Testify* (London: PSS, 2019).

38 Doreen St. Felix, "How Alexandra Bell Is Disrupting Racism in Journalism," *New Yorker*, May 29, 2018, http://www.newyorker.com/culture/culture-desk/how-alexandra-bell-is-disrupting-racism-in-journalism.

39 Alexandra Bell, "Art that Forms New Narratives," Storytellers Summit 2019, *National Geographic Society*, YouTube video, May 7, 2019, http://www.youtube.com/watch?v=wXjkxdRtGe8.

40 Sandra Stevenson, "Analyzing Race and Gender Bias Amid All the News That's Fit to Print," *New York Times*, December 7, 2017, http://www.nytimes.com/2017/12/07/arts/design/artist-alexandra-bell-dissects-the-new-york-times.html.

41 See, for example, Alexandra Bell, "An Evening with Alexandra Bell," exhibition lecture, Spencer Museum of Art, YouTube video, March 6, 2018, http://www.youtube.com/watch?v=1sG54qALVrA; and Bell, "Art that Forms New Narratives."

42 Krista Thompson, "The Evidence of Things Not Photographed: Slavery and the Historical Memory in the British West Indies," *Representations* 113 (Winter 2011): 39–71. See also Shawn Michelle Smith, *At the Edge of Sight: Photography and the Unseen* (Durham, NC: Duke University Press, 2013).

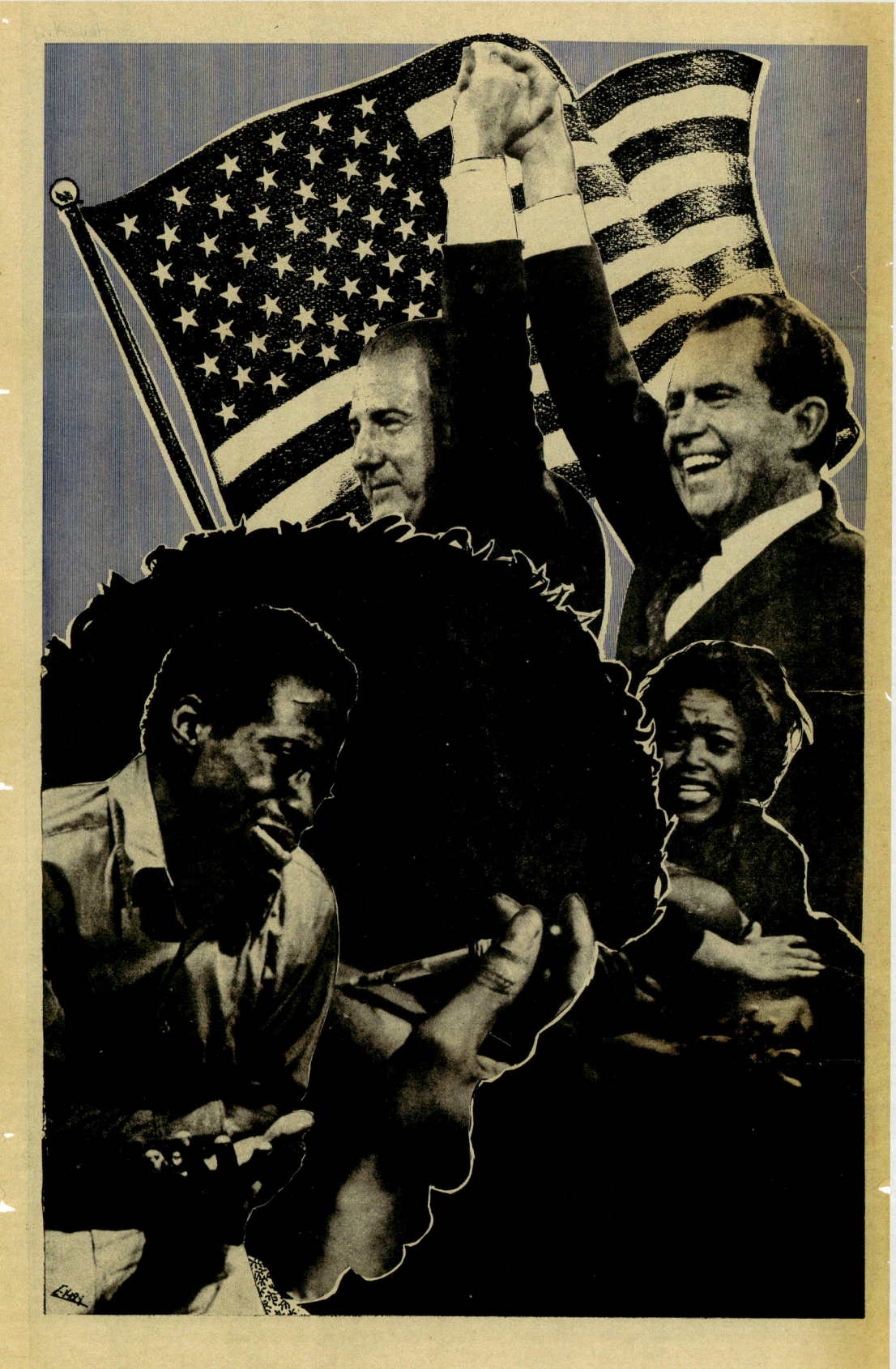

Emory Douglas
(American, b. 1943)
November 16, 1972, 1972

Photo collage
20 × 14 inches
Richard J. Daley Library, Special
Collections and Archives,
University of Illinois at Chicago.
Image Courtesy of the Center for
the Study of Political Graphics.
© 2021 Emory Douglas / Artists
Rights Society (ARS), New York.

Emory Douglas
(American, b. 1943)
May 26, 1973, 1973

Ink wash and graphite pencil
20 × 14 inches
Richard J. Daley Library, Special
Collections and Archives,
University of Illinois at Chicago.
Image Courtesy of the Center for
the Study of Political Graphics.
© 2021 Emory Douglas / Artists
Rights Society (ARS), New York.

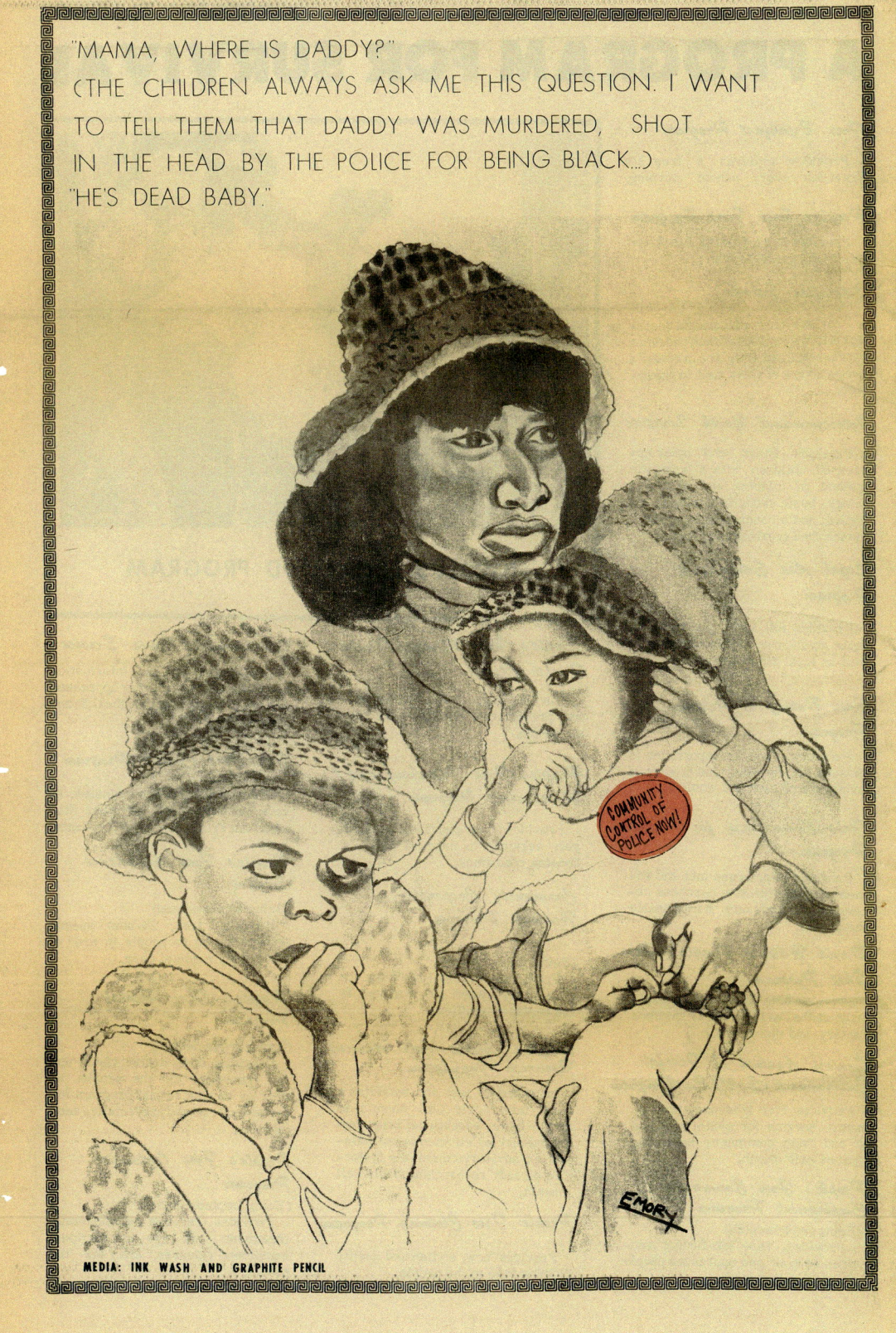

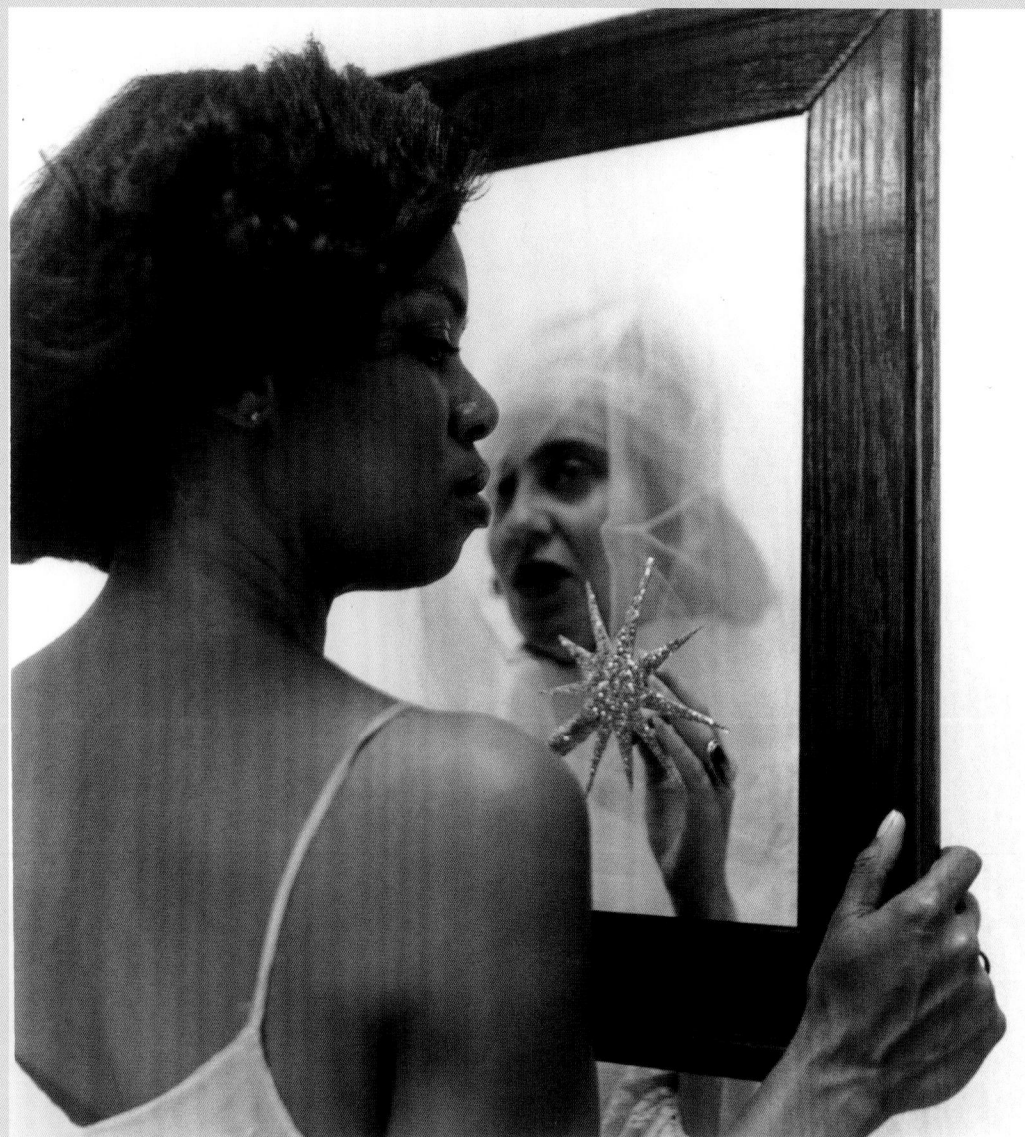

LOOKING INTO THE MIRROR, THE BLACK WOMAN ASKED,
"MIRROR, MIRROR ON THE WALL, WHO'S THE FINEST OF THEM ALL?"
THE MIRROR SAYS, "SNOW WHITE, YOU BLACK BITCH,
AND DON'T YOU FORGET IT!!!"

Carrie Mae Weems
(American, b. 1953)
Mirror, Mirror, 1987
Gelatin silver print with text panels
26 × 20¾ × 1½ inches (framed)
Courtesy of the artist and Jack
Shainman Gallery, New York.
© Carrie Mae Weems.

David Antonio Cruz
(American, b. 1974)
anotherroadblockinourway,
butifwegowegotogether,
the detroit kids, 2020
Oil and latex on wood panel
72 × 48 inches
Courtesy of the artist and Monique
Meloche Gallery, Chicago;
Collection of Hill Harper, Detroit.

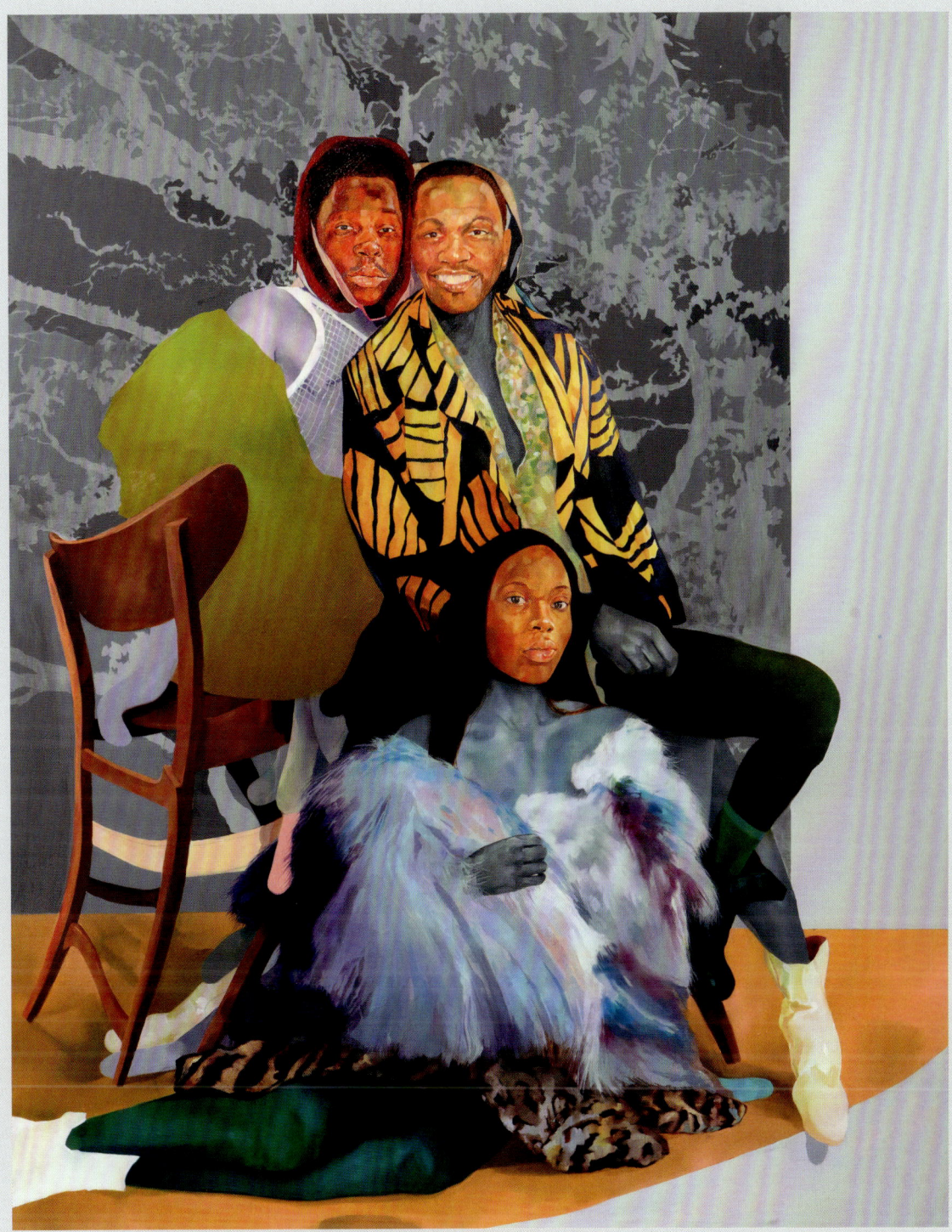

Courtney R. Baker

Pausing at the Threshold

It was the blood-stained gate, the entrance to the hell of slavery, through which I was about to pass. It was a most terrible spectacle.

—Frederick Douglass, *Narrative of the Life of Frederick Douglass* (1845)

Paul D tied his shoes together, hung them over his shoulder and followed her through the door straight into a pool of red and undulating light that locked him where he stood. . . .

"What kind of evil you got in there?"

"It's not evil, just sad. Come on. Just step through."

—Toni Morrison, *Beloved* (1987)

Are you sure, sweetheart, that you want to be well? . . . Just so's you're sure, sweetheart, and ready to be healed, cause wholeness is no trifling matter. A lot of weight when you're well.

—Toni Cade Bambara, *The Salt Eaters* (1980)

A Site of Struggle foregrounds the fact that artists—many, but not all, of African heritage—have long rejected the submission and silencing sought by the violence of white supremacy and anti-Blackness. Such an exhibition that highlights and solicits an unflinchingly deep look into the history and terrible present of anti-Black violence may inspire the question, What more is there to see?

From this, other questions arise: Is it even possible to repeat the motifs—to bring their visual semblance into the present of the (semi)protective gallery space—without repeating the injury and injustice of their origins? Is such an insulated view of these works and the brutality they invoke even to be desired? In its conscious foregrounding of enduring violence against Black people, a confrontation staged between the objects and the viewer, *A Site of Struggle* productively troubles the safety of the looking relations supposedly secured by the art institution. The act of curation—not only the selection of works, but also and primarily the task of caring for the works, the subject, the artists, as well as the viewers—is itself an act that hopefully intervenes into and reverses the originary violence of racism. The individual works and this exhibition as a whole are perhaps best viewed, then, not as confirming our ideas about racial violence but as providing us with new or alternative ways to perceive and respond to violent racial ideologies.

In my previous research, I considered the myriad and often conflicting responses that these spectacles of Black mortality have elicited in the gallery space.[1] Other African American visual culture scholars, including Nicole Fleetwood, Leigh Raiford, Cheryl Finley, Bridget Cooks, Sasha Torres, Shawn Michelle Smith, and Sarah Elizabeth Lewis have discussed the reception and circulation of iconographies of Black subjugation—from lynching's stagecraft to the slave ship icon to the photojournalism of the civil rights movement and much more.[2] Their work attends to the undervalued and frequently absented history of African American and Black visual engagement with scenes of our own destruction, in so doing underscoring the hush-harbor traditions called out by Elizabeth Alexander when she notes, in the wake of the video of Rodney King's beating by Los Angeles police officers, that "black people also have been looking, forging a traumatized collective historical memory which is reinvoked at contemporary sites of conflict."[3] Each of these studies defers an absolute moralist assessment of the image and instead excavates multiple truths, desires, and denials in order to expand the archive of Black collective ways of creating, seeing, and knowing.

Acknowledging that this struggle over aesthetics is not simply won by advancing some reproducible notion of authentic Blackness, this exhibition puts several strategies on display. Though works from some of the rare prior exhibitions on this subject are on view here, the conditions of spectatorship are importantly different. Works that appeared in *Art Commentary on Lynching* (1935)—a juried exhibition organized by the National Association for the Advancement of Colored People (NAACP)—are here as both art and artifacts of the antilynching movement of the Jim Crow era. The inclusion of artworks distinguishes *A Site of Struggle*'s retrospective gaze from James Allen and John Littlefield's more recent traveling exhibition, *Without Sanctuary: Lynching Photography in America* (2000–2018), which almost exclusively featured vernacular photographs and souvenirs from lynchings—thereby privileging a more sociological gaze. *A Site of Struggle* also resists the uplift strategy of W. E. B. Du Bois and photographer Thomas Askew's important *Georgia Negro Album*, presented at the 1900 Paris Exposition Universelle, in which portraits of African Americans advertised Black progress and humanity through signifiers of bourgeois finery that contrasted with illustrated statistics of contemporaneous lynchings.[4]

The artworks discussed below draw upon various aesthetic principles and practices yet are unified in both their source, the destruction of Black lives, and their aim, the condemnation of the lethal campaign against Black livelihood that has, for far too long, served as a primary pillar of global anti-Blackness. Ranging from the representational to the abstract, from social documentary to the metaphorical and synecdochic, each piece in *A Site of Struggle* identifies an aesthetics of atrocity specific to the conditions of anti-Blackness—with a particular emphasis on the American contours of that project—in order to magnify the horror. Even now, the state's routine commission and approval of anti-Black violence attempts to diffuse public outrage by making recourse to a logic of business as usual. These coercive conditions necessitate the work of the emotionally invested, compassionate onlooker. The literal or emotional reclamation of the brutalized Black body continues to be a crucial project of Black folks' psychic survival. In the face of a hostile or dispassionate non-Black population, African American activists, and especially African American women, wreathe our murdered beloveds in shrouds of compassion and care. As the sage James Baldwin instructs us, "If one can reach back, reach down—into oneself, into one's life—and find there some witness, however unexpected or ambivalent, to one's reality, one will be enabled, though perhaps not very spiritedly, to face another day."[5]

Aesthetics of Atrocity and Endurance

A Site of Struggle understands deeply that art is inseparable from politics—as though a uniquely human practice could ever be separated from the conditions of the humans who make, see, and labor with and through art. It illustrates how artists have identified and then shrewdly manipulated the recurring aesthetics and conventions of racial terrorism. While the mission is oriented singularly toward justice, the strategies for achieving this effect are many. Calling our attention to form, function, and the contours of our social relations, the various works in the exhibition incorporate social documentary photography, caricature, gender, martyrdom, and the motif of the lynch rope, supplying a variety of points of entry into the artistic rendering of anti-Black violence.

For example, the seemingly straightforward social documentary photographs of Bob Crawford (*Untitled*, 1966, fig. 5.1) and Darryl Cowherd (*Stop White Police from Killing Us—St. Louis, MO*, ca. 1966–67, fig. 5.2) are as powerful in their condemnation as the seemingly less-objective drawings, collages, and caricatures of Emory Douglas, illustrator for *The Black Panther* newspaper from 1967 to 1980. Though each of the works reveals something about the conditions of Black life in the United States in the 1960s, Douglas's hand-drawn illustration for the November 8, 1969, issue of the paper, in which a bound Bobby Seal raises an accusing finger toward a Confederate-flag-waving judge depicted as a rat and flanked by two sheriffs depicted as pigs, gives a clear indication of the individual artist's and the Black Panther organization's appreciation of anti-Blackness as a structural issue affecting the nation (fig. 5.3). As Rebecca Wanzo explains, "If we recognize that representational struggles often occur not in attempts at the realistic but in fantastic representations of 'real Americanness' in history, film, and news media, then caricature becomes a language used to demonstrate a citizen's value."[6] Here, Douglas transcodes what was meant to be an image of judicial dominance over a Black unruly subject into a scene in which the literal "little guy," who has been confined to the lower right quadrant of the page, is poised as ideologically and perhaps spiritually above the lawless menagerie and the racist fray.

Though unified in their implicit condemnation of unchecked racism brazenly displayed, the photographs by

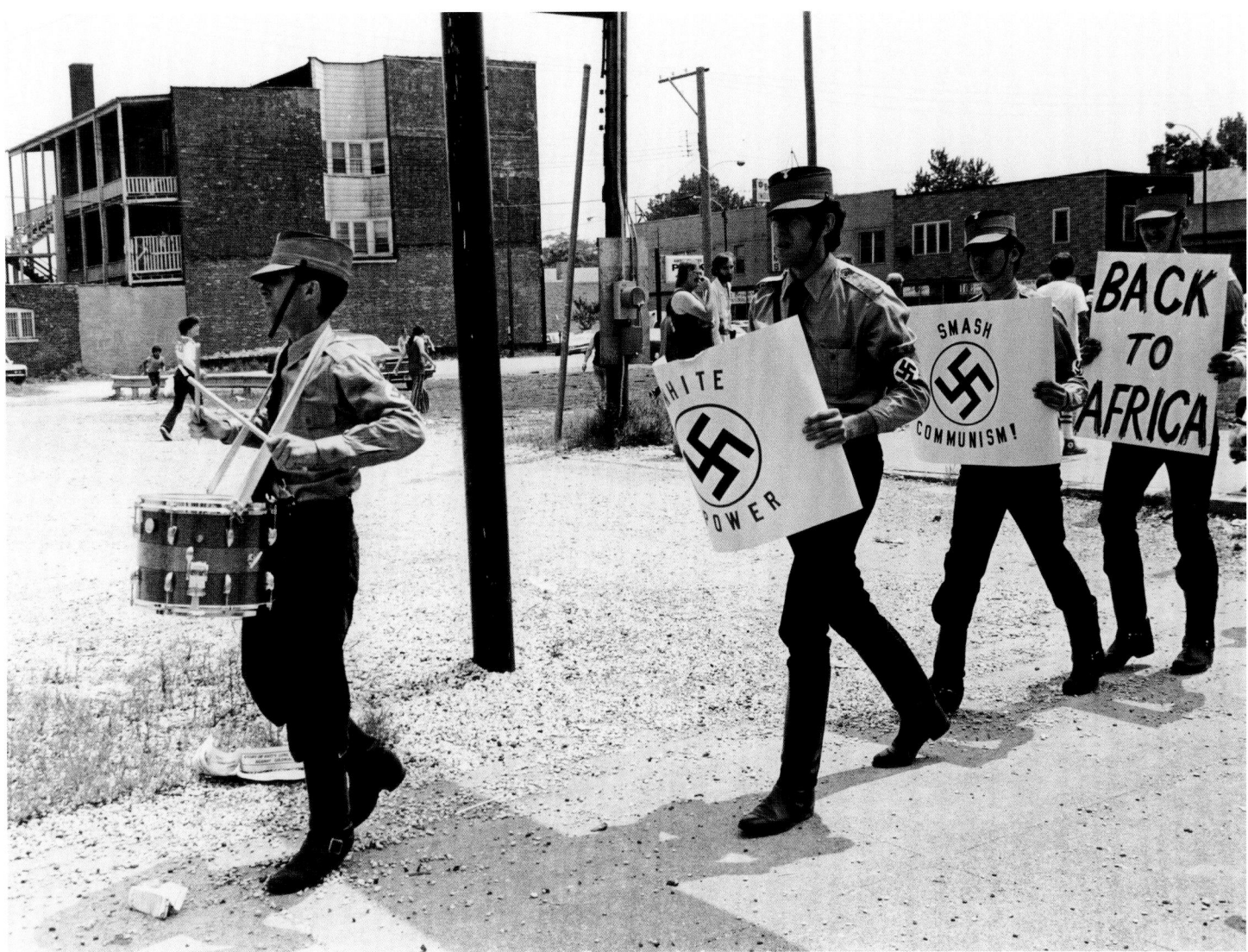

Fig. 5.1 Bob Crawford, *Untitled*,
1966, gelatin silver print, 5⅞ ×
7¹⁵⁄₁₆ inches (image); 7⅞ ×
9⅞ inches (sheet). Art Institute
of Chicago, through prior gifts of
Emanuel and Edithann M. Gerard
and Hugh Edwards, 2017.173.
Courtesy of the Estate of Bob
Crawford. Image courtesy of the
Art Institute of Chicago / Art
Resource, Inc.

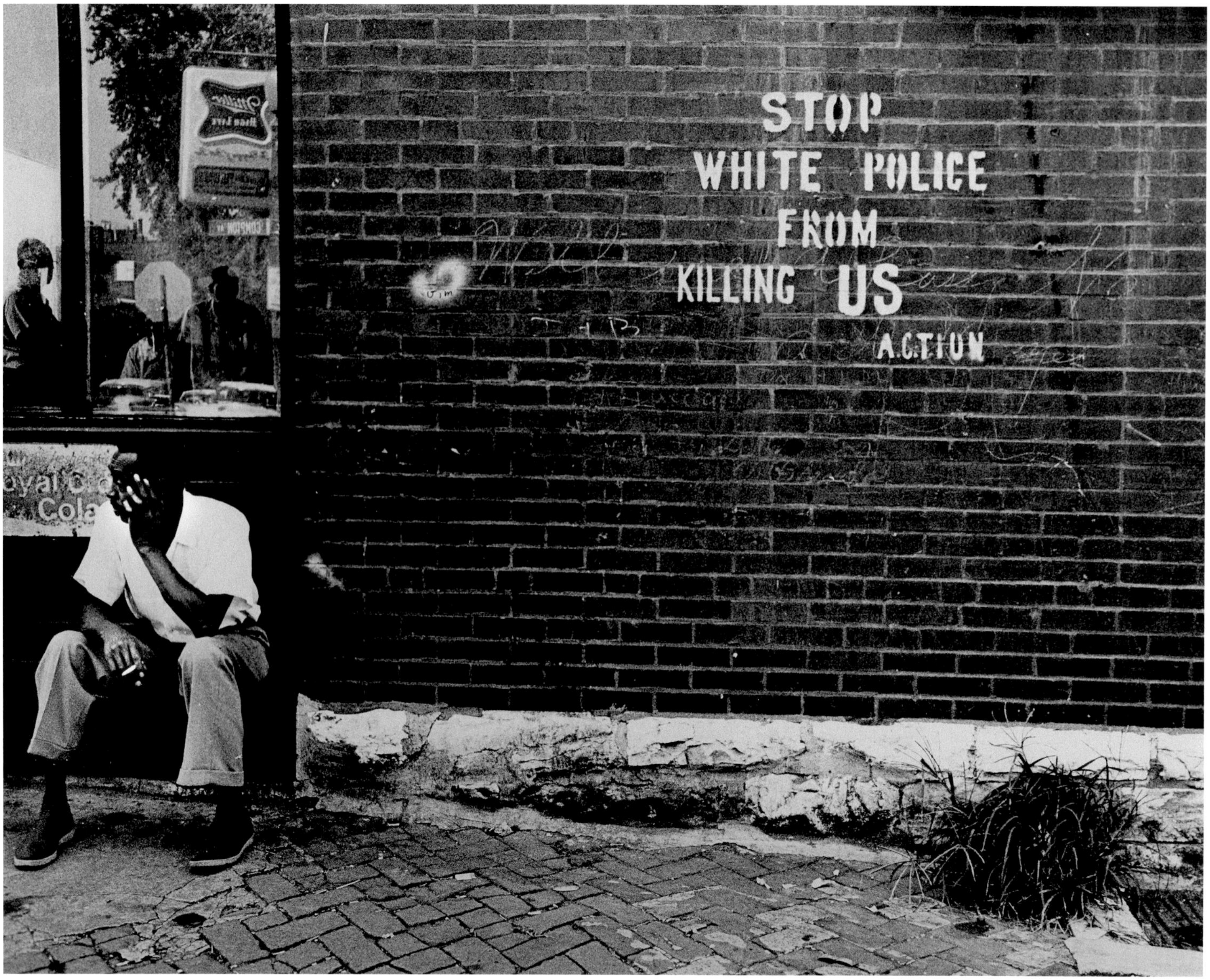

Fig. 5.2   Darryl Cowherd, *Stop White Police from Killing Us— St. Louis, MO*, ca. 1966–67, gelatin silver print, 15 × 19 inches (image); 16 × 20 inches (sheet). Museum of Contemporary Photography, Columbia College, Chicago, 2018.138. Courtesy of Darryl Cowherd.

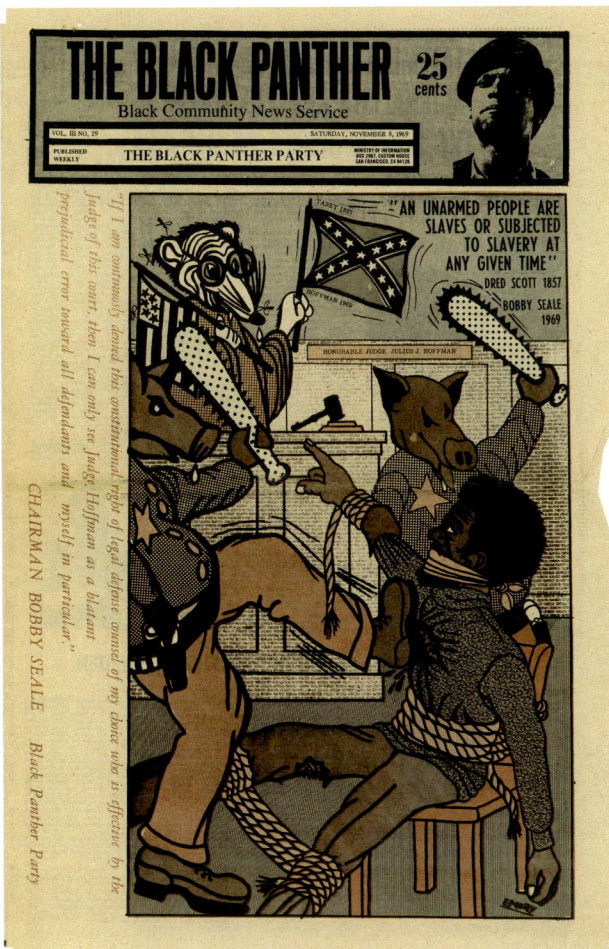

Fig. 5.3   Emory Douglas, *November 8, 1969*, 1969, ink drawing, 20 × 14 inches. Courtesy of the Center for the Study of Political Graphics. © 2021 Emory Douglas / Artists Rights Society (ARS), New York.

Crawford and Cowherd rely upon the rhetoric of the documentary photograph, in which the image is understood to be a consequence of happenstance—a photographer and a camera at the right time and the right place. Complementing Douglas's staged depiction (albeit one inspired by real life), these photographs capture goings-on that might otherwise go unexamined, stopping the moments so that we may scrutinize them for the truths they reveal about racism's banal ubiquity.

Addressing both the compassionate onlooker and the Black viewer seeking emotional reclamation of the brutalized body, the aesthetic of martyrdom, shaped by a specifically Christian tradition, informs several works created in the 1920s and '30s. They marked a period of advocacy for a series of federal antilynching bills proposed between 1918 and 1934 that were ultimately defeated in both the US Senate and Congress.[7] These works include the solitary, benighted male figures of Hale Woodruff's linocut *By Parties Unknown* (1935, fig. 5.4) and George Bellows's lithograph *The Law Is Too Slow* (1923, fig. 5.5). Both works were included in the 1935 exhibition organized by the NAACP. Woodruff's linocut depicts a modest church, signified by the ornate arches that form its parabolic stained-glass windows and door and by gaps in need of repair along the edifice's wooden siding. At the base of the church, on its steps, is a crumpled human figure, with a man's short hair and tattered clothing. Though his face is concealed, the remnant of a rope visibly dangles from the figure's neck, suggesting that his body was deposited on the steps after being lynched or, perhaps, that the exhausted form has escaped that fate and seeks safe harbor at the doors of the church. Bellows's image, too, traffics in ambivalence and sanctimony, casting the horrifying scene of a man being burned alive into an echo of Christian martyrdom and holy ascension, its subject posed in an ecstatic stance and wreathed in a divine light.

These images are productively contrasted with works that retrospectively engage the heritage of lynching. Kerry James Marshall's revisioning of the lynching souvenir and the holy relic in *Heirlooms and Accessories* (2002, fig. 5.6) literally frames white women within a depiction of precious lockets. Lorna Simpson's *Untitled (Two Necklines)* (1989, fig. 5.7) places the necks of Black women at the center of the image, thereby disrupting many presumptions about the gender and race of those who have suffered from and

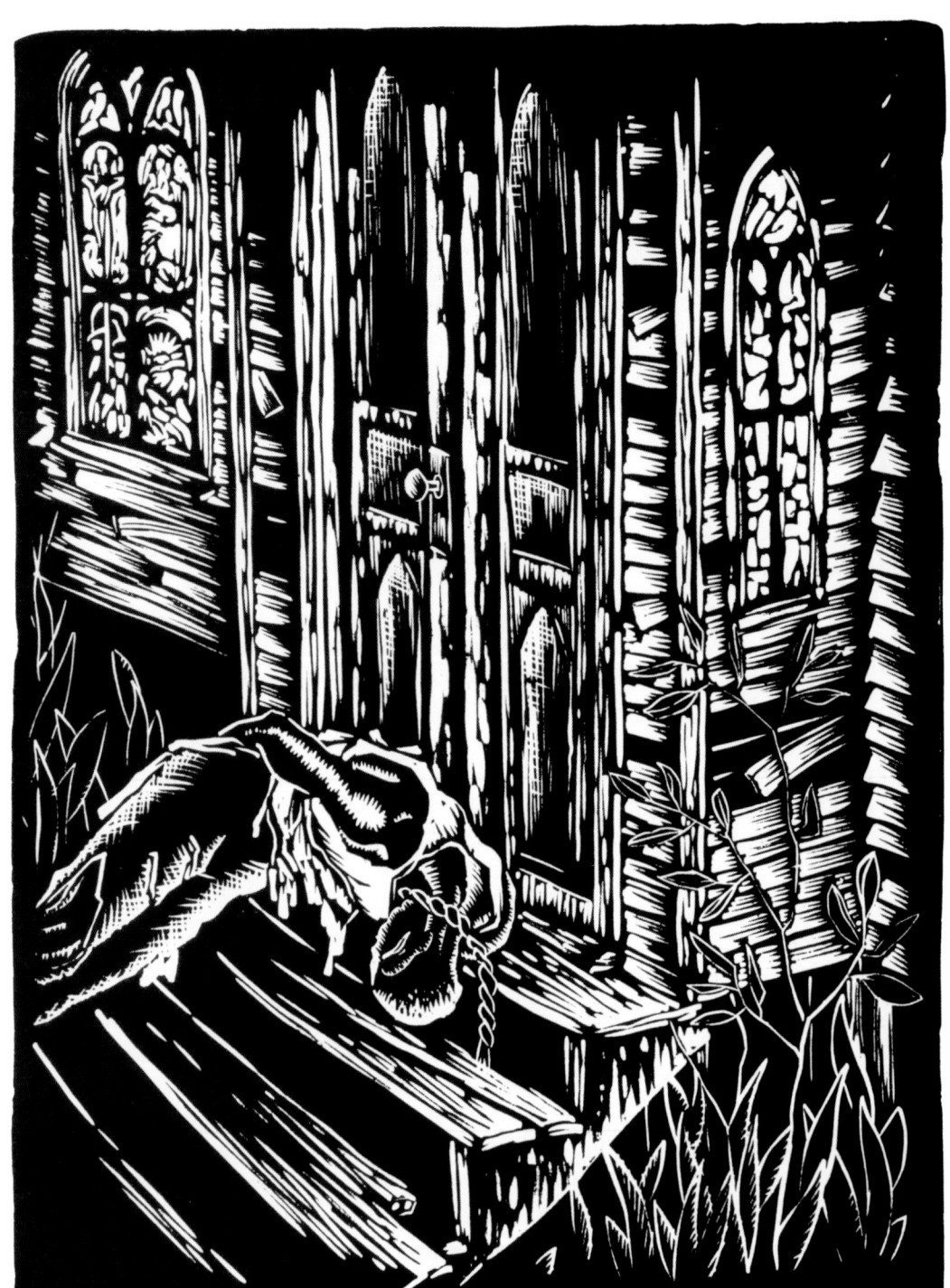

Fig. 5.4 Hale Woodruff, *By Parties Unknown*, 1935, linocut, 12 × 9 inches. Collection of Spelman College, Gift of Kathryn C. and Kenneth I. Chenault, 2001.1.006. © 2021 Estate of Hale Woodruff / Licensed by VAGA at Artists Rights Society (ARS), NY.

Fig. 5.5 George Wesley Bellows, *The Law Is Too Slow*, 1923, lithograph in black on cream Japanese tissue, 17¹⁵⁄₁₆ × 14⁹⁄₁₆ inches (image); 25¹¹⁄₁₆ × 19¹⁄₁₆ inches (sheet). Art Institute of Chicago, George F. Porter Collection, 1925.1567. © Image courtesy of the Art Institute of Chicago / Art Resource, Inc.

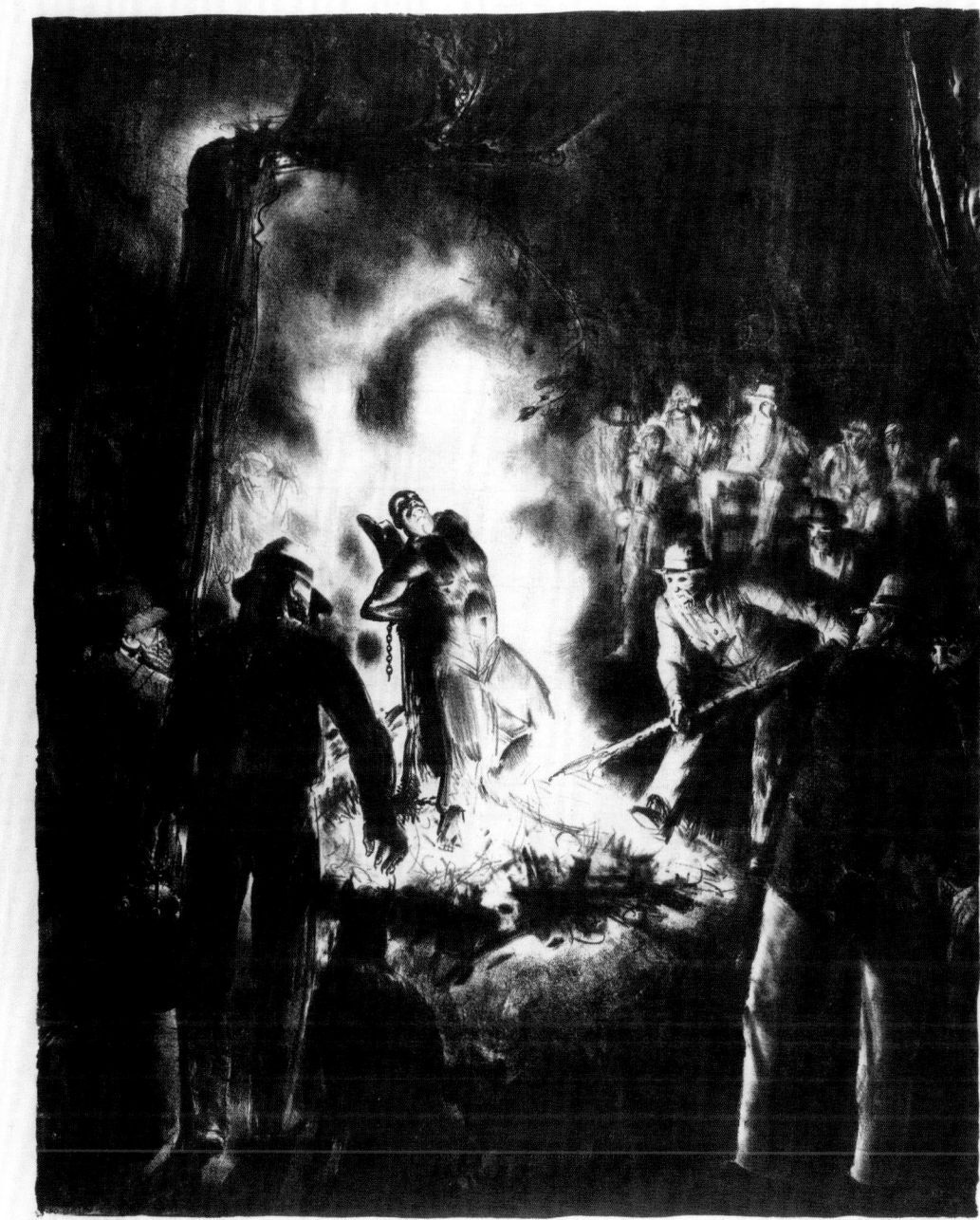

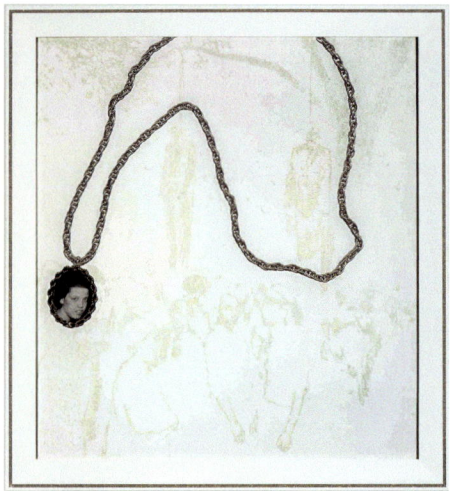 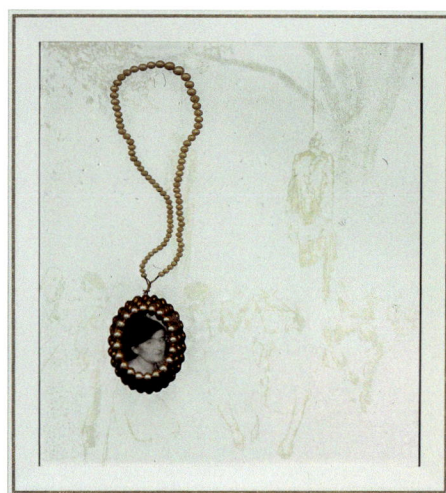 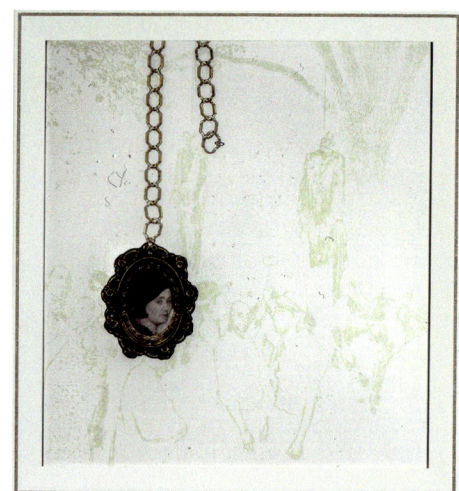

Fig. 5.6 Kerry James Marshall, *Heirlooms and Accessories*, 2002, three inkjet prints on paper in wooden artist's frame with rhinestones, each: 51 × 46 inches (image); 57 × 53 × 3 inches (frame). Smart Museum of Art, University of Chicago, Purchase, Smart Family Fund Foundation for Contemporary Art, and Paul and Miriam Kirkley Fund for Acquisitions, 2004.12a–c. © Kerry James Marshall. Courtesy of Jack Shainman Gallery, New York.

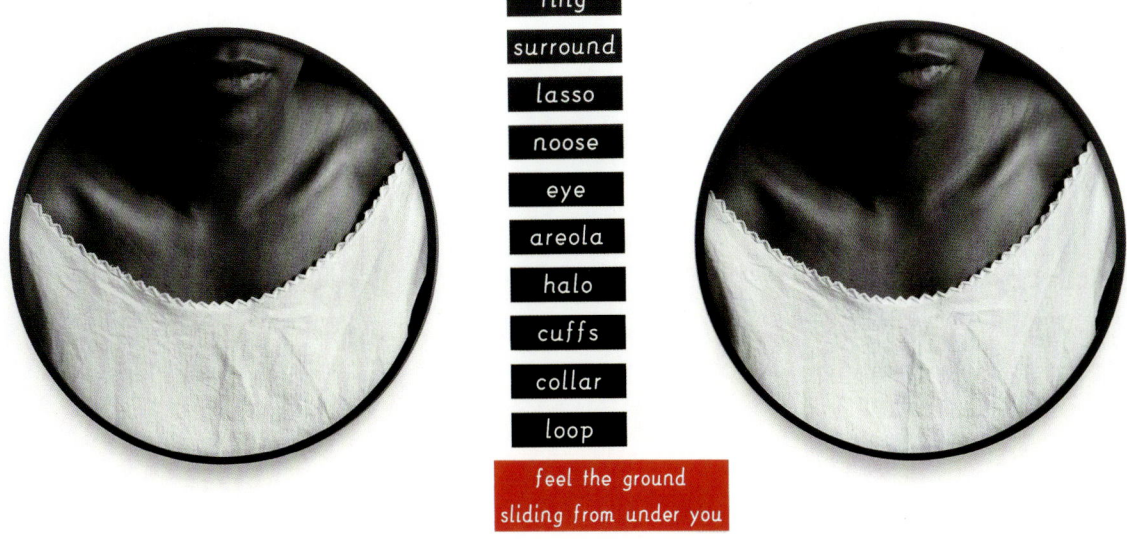

Fig. 5.7   Lorna Simpson, *Untitled (Two Necklines)*, 1989, two gelatin silver prints on paper and eleven plastic plaques, 36 inches (diameter, each print); dimensions variable (plastic plaques). Collection of Carolyn Campagna Kleefeld Contemporary Art Museum of California State University, Long Beach, Purchased with funds from the National Endowment for the Arts, 1990.6a–m. Image © Lorna Simpson. Courtesy of the artist and Hauser & Wirth.

There's SOMETHING going on here... I di[d]
right away. I just saw that he looked so HEL[P]
he didn't look lynched WHAT is that? How l[ong]
to that tree? Can you be black and look at [it]

WHO took
this picture?
Couldn't he just as
easily let the man go? Did he take his cam[era]
and bring back a BLOWTORCH? And wher[e]
with a blowtorch BURN off an ear. Melt an eye[?]
WHO took this picture? HOW can this photogra[ph]
Life answers - Page 141 — no cr[edit]

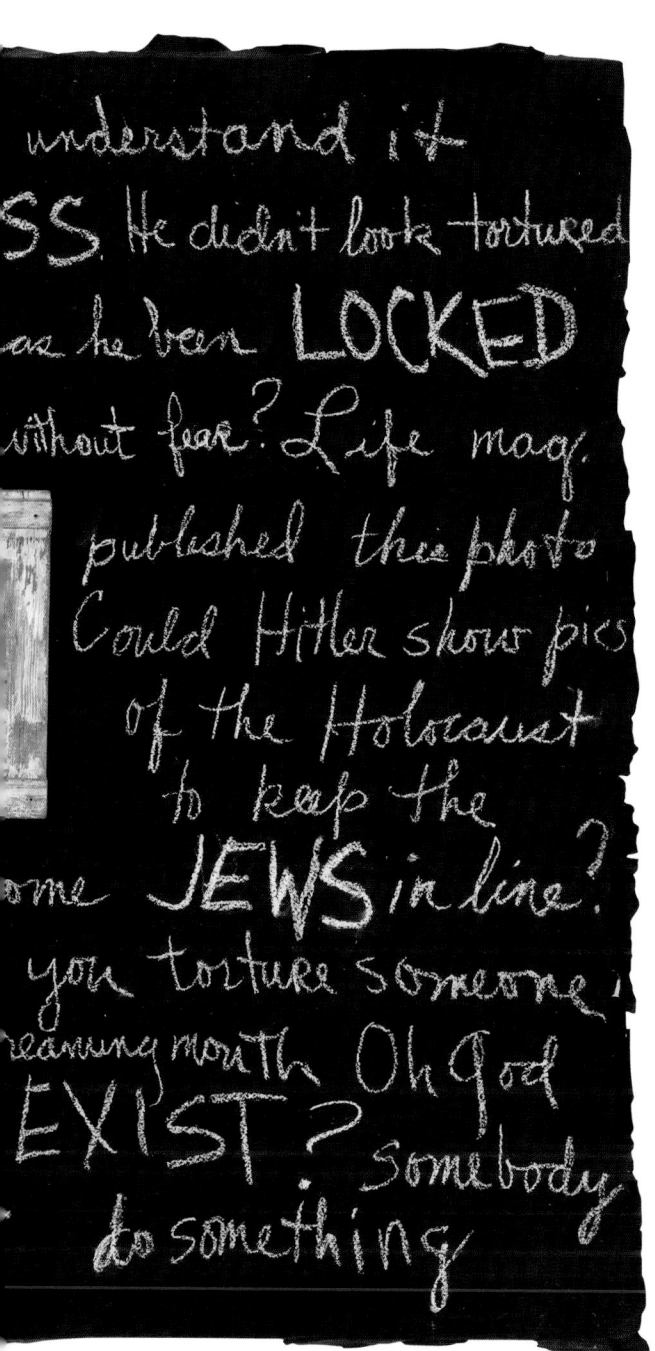

Fig. 5.8   Pat Ward Williams, *Accused/ Blowtorch/Padlock*, 1986, collaged tar paper, oil pastel, found painted wood, found magazine, three gelatin silver prints with printed text on Mylar overlay, and nails and staples, mounted on wood panel, 61¹³⁄₁₆ × 108¼ × 3 inches. Whitney Museum of American Art, New York, Purchase, with funds from the Audrey and Sydney Irmas Charitable Foundation, 93.64. Courtesy of the artist. Digital image © Whitney Museum of American Art, New York / Licensed by Scala / Art Resource, NY.

carried on the legacies of lynching. Unlike in earlier exhibitions centered on anti-Black violence, *A Site of Struggle* represents women both as artists and as the subjects of violence whose names we must say—an acknowledgment that is still sadly belated and necessary.

The vigilante justice typified by lynchings and mirrored in state-sanctioned acts of anti-Black violence such as stop-and-frisk harassment, mass incarceration, and police brutality have been so often repeated that the ritualized gestures associated with those murders and their justification have consolidated into a grotesque array of recognizable motifs. Depictions of the noose and the fire hose, along with depictions of the distorted bodies of Black victims, have come to constitute the defining features of art oriented against anti-Blackness. The rope fashioned into a noose is referenced explicitly across a wide historical range of works. The rope figured in the paintings, etchings, and drawings displayed in the 1935 antilynching show, such as Bellows's *The Law Is Too Slow* and Julius T. Block's *Lynching* (1936), reappears in later condemnations of anti-Black violence, such as Pat Ward Williams's photography- and text-based piece *Accused/Blowtorch/Padlock* (1986, fig. 5.8). An object once collected after lynchings by the mob as a souvenir of their participation in the upholding of Black subjugation, the rope evinces its talismanic yet fragile power in sculptural works by two artists separated by sixty years—Isamu Noguchi's *Death (Lynched Figure)* (1934, see fig. 1.10) and Alison Saar's *Strange Fruit* (1995, fig. 5.9). Each of these artworks centers upon an abstracted human form—more homunculus than clearly human. Both do so in order to draw attention to the precarious tether that leaves the form suspended in midair, earthbound but aloft, literally moving reminders of how this most basic technology—the knot—has been used to sacrifice the lives of individual Black folks (including that of George Hughes, the Sherman, Texas, man whose photographed death-pose inspired Noguchi's work).

These works are not artifacts of mastery over pain and heartbreak. Rather, they may be viewed as discrete, singular reckonings that gesture toward a greater reckoning to come in the overlong modern history of Black subjugation and destruction, toward the ways in which all of us are implicated in the discourse of anti-Black terrorism. Through their unflinching directness, the works use the spectacle of Black degradation against itself, much in the way that self-emancipated abolitionists like

Frederick Douglass presented his scarred body and Mamie Till Mobley, one of the original mothers of the civil rights movement, presented the lynched body of her son, Emmett Till. The reclamation of the image of suffering by artists who are opposed to racial terrorism strives to flip the script and to redistribute righteousness and dignity back to the Black subject. The works are therefore implicated within—not outside of—the logic of lynching, specifically, that insists upon ritual, performance, and public display to cohere a community rooted in anti-Blackness. This is the rub that engenders the productive dis-ease of re-viewing spectacles of Black degradation: to see the condemnation clearly, we must first see what is being condemned. In order for the affective charge to work, viewers must draw upon their knowledge of unredressed racist assaults and murders so that their gaze pierces the surface of the image and finds, in the gestures of the artist, the invitation to be healed.

To regard works such as Noguchi's, or Elizabeth Catlett's *. . . And a special fear for my loved ones* (1946, see fig. 3.1), is to be implicated and embedded in the conditions of image production, circulation, and consumption in which Blackness often enters the visual field through visions of violent anti-Blackness. The subject of these pieces is not authentic Blackness, but rather the very conditions under which Blackness and Black embodiment have come to be known as visible sites of violence by anti-Black regimes (including settler colonialism and enslavement) in the modern world. As Marcus Woods explains of this antiracist visual tradition, "The black figures memorialised in these images are themselves an expression of the visual culture of blackness and possess a valency which we have yet to come to terms with."[8] To behold these works is to conduct the dramatic act of implicating one's self within the primal scene of anti-Blackness. The Blackness that many of us now seek to publicly celebrate and protect drags its legacy of anti-Blackness into the present view, making *us*, the potentially colluding spectators—not just the spectacles of Black death and suffering—the most provocative subjects to be put under examination.

The abstract and the sublime, the non-representational, the synecdochic are aesthetic devices deployed by artists Theaster Gates (see figs. 3.7, 3.8) and Melvin Edwards (see figs. 3.4–6), among others, illustrating that an artistic response to racial terror need not reproduce an indexical or even an iconic figure to denote the horror.[9] These artists remind us through their nonrepresentational practices that what is at stake in the representation of Blackness is not a fidelity to realism or a surface verisimilitude. Instead, they invoke the sublime, the holy, the sacred, the ineffable, and the sheer magnitude of Blackness as a construct.

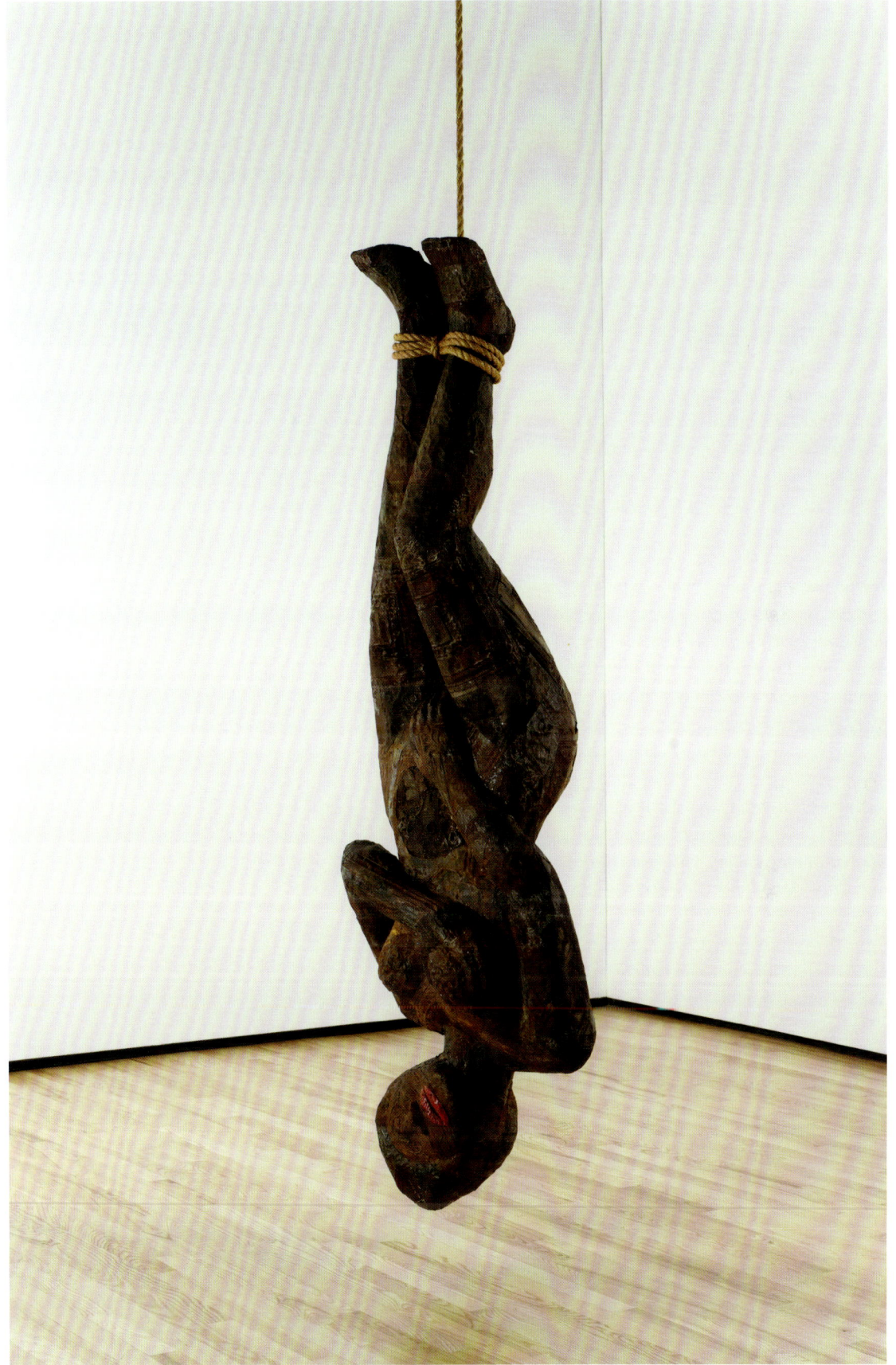

Fig. 5.9   Alison Saar, *Strange Fruit*, 1995, tin alloy, wood, dirt, found objects, rope, and paint, 76 × 21 × 14 inches. Baltimore Museum of Art, 1995.122. © Alison Saar. Courtesy of L.A. Louver, Venice, California.

This vision of Blackness unbound surpasses the conditions of its invention as an index of human inferiority as if by magic. In so doing, the works permit Black abundance to shine and signify beyond the strictures imposed by lynching and by an impoverished racial imagination. These works and artists are in provocative and productive play with the literal and uncritical reference to the real. Like Emory Douglas's cartoons, these pieces present productive counterpoints to the social-documentary photographs that rely upon indexical fidelity for their meaning and argument to be understood.

Crossing the Threshold

In mounting this exhibition, curator Janet Dees and the Block Museum participate in a powerful African diasporic tradition of calling upon and responding to art to acknowledge Black life and, hopefully, inspire drastic improvement in and appreciation for it. The promise of an exhibition is often to draw a clean boundary between the world in which we live and a world in which we are invited to check our embodiment at the door in order to indulge in the voyeurism condoned by the gallery. To the degree that the art institution offers another terrain in which Blackness can be consumed and surveilled without consequence, the museum is an essential site of contestation over the just conditions of acknowledging and respecting Black subjectivity and artistic labor.

As was the case for this show's aforementioned precursors, visitors to *A Site of Struggle* are invited to examine their intentions and their viewing positions. The material thresholds to a view of the works—including the doorway to the gallery space and the covers of the exhibition catalogue—mark the entrance to a space of heavy contemplation but also the promise of potential healing. Consideration of artistic works responding to real-world conditions of injustice and violence need not and, indeed, should not be reduced to an indulgence in or aversion to spectacles of Black suffering. This exhibition is an inquiry into the current and past conditions of our social welfare—the intimate, entangled psychic and physical health of the public commons. The works that appear within the show eschew the sugarcoating that might make this arcing toward justice more palatable. The invitation extended by each work is magnified when presented together as they are in *A Site of Struggle*.

Struggle in the art world—over the just representation of racial terrorism and over justice itself—happens in tandem with struggle in the streets. Here, in the gallery, you are invited to cross the threshold—to pass through the blood-stained gate of institutions historically oriented toward our destruction—and to stand in the light and the sadness. The transgression might be one step toward restoring wholeness to the victims and targets of violence as well as to the very principle of our community. No one, truly, is outside of the regimes of racist terrorism, though there is a difference between those upon whose bodies the terror is enacted and those in whose name the terrorism is conducted.

Here, you are held by the care bestowed by art. Everyone, regardless of their race, is invited to glimpse in these works and in their assembly in the exhibition the beauty that is endowed to all human beings and that the artists represented here attempt to restore. Here is a sort of clearing in which the blessing of Morrison's secular saint, the formerly enslaved matriarch of *Beloved*, the grandmother "Baby Suggs, holy," might inform our looking: "She told them that the only grace they could have was the grace they could imagine. That if they could not see it, they would not have it."[10] It is a grace that can drive us toward wholeness. May that grace borne of the loving but painful tending of the artists, the curator, and your fellow onlookers carry you toward wholeness. So that we all might heal.

Notes

For Maurice Berger, who remembered and is remembered.

Epigraph: Frederick Douglass, *Narrative of the Life of Frederick Douglass* (Boston: Antislavery Office, 1845), 6; Toni Morrison, *Beloved* (New York: Vintage, 1987), 10; Toni Cade Bambara, *The Salt Eaters* (New York: Vintage, 1992), 3, 10.

1   See Courtney R. Baker, *Humane Insight: Looking at Images of African American Suffering and Death*, New Black Studies (Urbana: University of Illinois Pres, 2015).

2   See Nicole R. Fleetwood, *On Racial Icons: Blackness and the Public Imagination* (New Brunswick, NJ: Rutgers University Press, 2015); Leigh Raiford, *Imprisoned in a Luminous Glare: Photography and the African American Freedom Struggle* (Chapel Hill: University of North Carolina Press, 2011); Cheryl Finley, *Committed to Memory: The Art of the Slave Ship Icon* (Princeton, NJ: Princeton University Press, 2018); Bridget R. Cooks, *Exhibiting Blackness: African Americans and the American Art Museum* (Amherst: University of Massachusetts Press, 2011); Sasha Torres, *Black, White, and in Color: Television and Black Civil Rights* (Princeton, NJ: Princeton University Press, 2003); Shawn Michelle Smith, *Photographic Returns: Racial Justice and the Time of Photography* (Durham, NC: Duke University Press, 2020); and Sarah Lewis, *Whitfield Lovell: Kin* (New York, NY: Skira Rizzoli, 2016).

3   Elizabeth Alexander, "'Can You Be Black and Look at This?': Reading the Rodney King Video(s)," *Public Culture* 7, no. 1 (October 1, 1994): 79, http://doi.org/10.1215/08992363-7-1-77.

4   For more on these exhibitions, see Dora Apel and Shawn Michelle Smith, *Lynching Photographs* (Berkeley: University of California Press, 2007); James Allen, ed., *Without Sanctuary: Lynching Photography in America* (Santa Fe, NM: Twin Palms, 2000); Library of Congress, *A Small Nation of People: W. E. B. Du Bois and African American Portraits of Progress* (New York: HarperCollins, 2005); and Shawn Michelle Smith, *Photography on the Color Line: W. E. B. Du Bois, Race, and Visual Culture* (Durham, NC: Duke University Press, 2004).

5   James Baldwin, "Nothing Personal (1964)," *Contributions in Black Studies* 6, no. 1 (2008): 56.

6   Rebecca Wanzo, *Content of Our Caricature: African American Comic Art and Political Belonging* (New York: New York University Press, 2020), 4.

7   The Dyer Antilynching Bill was introduced in 1918 by Congressman Leonidas C. Dyer. The Costigan-Wagner Bill was introduced in 1934 by Senators Edward P. Costigan and Robert Wagner. Both were defeated by organized blocs of representatives from the US South. In 2019, a new bill, titled the Emmett Till Antilynching Act, was passed by Congress on February 26, 2020, and was then sent to the Senate where it awaits consideration at the time of this writing. For more on the antilynching bills, see W. Fitzhugh Brundage, *Under Sentence of Death: Lynching in the South* (Chapel Hill: UNC Press Books, 2017); James Harmon Chadbourn, *Lynching and the Law* (Clark, NJ: Lawbook Exchange, 2008); Daniel Kato, *Liberalizing Lynching: Building a New Racialized State* (New York: Oxford University Press, 2016); Megan M. Francis, *Civil Rights and the Making of the Modern American State* (New York: Cambridge University Press, 2014); and Bobby L. Rush, "H.R.35 - 116th Congress (2019–2020): Emmett Till Antilynching Act," www.congress.gov/bill/116th-congress/house-bill/35/text.

8   Marcus Wood, "Valency and Abjection in the Lynching Postcard: A Test Case in the Reclamation of Black Visual Culture," *Slavery & Abolition* 34, no. 2 (June 2013): 205, http://doi.org/10.1080/0144039X.2013.791173.

9   Sampada Aranke discusses this in more detail in her contribution to this volume, "Functional Abstractions: Sensorial Afterlives of the Black Body."

10   Toni Morrison, *Beloved* (New York: Vintage International, 1987), 103.

Exhibition Checklist

A Red Record: Section A

Laylah Ali (American, b. 1968)
Untitled, 2004
Gouache and pencil on paper
19½ × 28 inches (sight)
Williams College Museum of Art, Museum purchase,
Kathryn Hurd Fund, in honor of Linda Shearer, Director
1989–2004, M.2005.1
Fig. 1.17

Arthur U. Newton Galleries, New York
An Art Commentary on Lynching
Exhibition catalogue, February 15–March 2, 1935
The Newberry Library, Chicago
Fig. 1.9

George Wesley Bellows (American, 1882–1925)
The Law Is Too Slow, 1923
Lithograph in black on cream Japanese tissue
17¹⁵⁄₁₆ × 14⁹⁄₁₆ inches (image); 25¹¹⁄₁₆ × 19¹⁄₁₆ inches (sheet)
Art Institute of Chicago, George F. Porter Collection,
1925.1567
Figs. 1.7, 5.5

George Biddle (American, 1885–1973)
Alabama Code: Our Girls Don't Sleep with Niggers, 1933
Lithograph
13⅜ × 9½ inches (image); 11½ × 15½ inches (sheet)
Mary and Leigh Block Museum of Art, Northwestern
University, 1996.26
Fig. 1.6

Elizabeth Catlett (Mexican, b. United States, 1915–2012)
. . . And a special fear for my loved ones, from the series
The Black Woman, 1946
Linoleum cut
9¼ × 6¾ inches
Mary and Leigh Block Museum of Art, Northwestern
University, 1992.107
Figs. 3.1, 5.11

Ernest Crichlow (American, 1914–2005)
Lovers, 1938/1987
Lithograph on black on wove paper
14¼ × 11⅝ inches (image); 22 × 15 inches (sheet)
National Gallery of Art, Washington, DC, Reba and Dave
Williams Collection, Florian Carr Fund and Gift of the Print
Research Foundation, 2008.115.45
Fig. 1.5

Meta Warrick Fuller (American, 1877–1968)
Mary Tuner: A Silent Protest against Mob Violence, 1919
Photographic reproduction of painted-plaster original
15 × 5¼ × 4½ inches (original)
Image courtesy of Museum of African American History,
Boston and Nantucket
Fig. 1.4

Norman Lewis (American, 1909–1979)
Untitled (Police Beating), 1943
Watercolor, ink, and graphite on paper
20 × 13⅞ inches
Courtesy of the Rodney M. Miller Collection
Fig. 1.1

Isamu Noguchi (American, 1904–1988)
Death (Lynched Figure), 1934
Monel metal, rope
39 × 29¼ × 21 inches
Isamu Noguchi Foundation, New York
Fig. 1.10

Walter Quirt (American, 1902–1968)
The Clinic, 1935
Oil on composition panel
12⁵⁄₁₆ × 15 inches
The Wadsworth Atheneum Museum of Art, The Ella Gallup
Sumner and Mary Catlin Sumner Collection Fund, 1937.208
Page 68

Alison Saar (American, b. 1956)
Strange Fruit, 1995
Tin alloy, wood, dirt, found objects, rope, and paint
76 × 21 × 14 inches
Baltimore Museum of Art, 1995.122
Fig. 5.9

Ida B. Wells (American, 1862–1931)
*A Red Record: Tabulated Statistics and Alleged Causes of
Lynchings in the United States 1892–1893–1894*
Chicago: Donohue and Henneberry, 1895
University of Michigan Library
Cf. fig. 1.3

Charles White (American, 1918–1979)
The Return of the Soldier, 1946
Pen-and-ink drawing on illustration board
24¼ × 18⅞ inches
Library of Congress
Fig. 1.2

Walter F. White (American, 1893–1955)
Rope and Faggot: A Biography of Judge Lynch
New York: Alfred A. Knopf, 1929
Northwestern University Pritzker School of Law Library
Fig. 1.8

Walter F. White (American, 1893–1955)
"The Work of the Mob," in *The Crisis* 16, no. 5
(September 1918)
Charles Deering McCormick Library of Special Collections,
Northwestern University Libraries
Not illustrated

Pat Ward Williams (American, b. 1948)
Accused/Blowtorch/Padlock, 1986
Collaged tar paper, oil pastel, found painted wood, found
magazine, three gelatin silver prints with printed text on
Mylar overlay, and nails and staples, mounted on
wood panel
61¹³⁄₁₆ × 108¼ × 3 inches
Whitney Museum of American Art, New York, Purchase,
with funds from the Audrey and Sydney Irmas Charitable
Foundation, 93.64
Figs. 1.11, 5.8

Hale Woodruff (American, 1900–1980)
By Parties Unknown, 1935
Linocut
12 × 9 inches
Collection of Spelman College, Gift of Kathryn C. and
Kenneth I. Chenault, 2001.1.006
Fig. 5.4

Hale Woodruff (American, 1900–1980)
Giddap!, 1935
Linocut
12 × 9 inches
Collection of Spelman College, Gift of Kathryn C. and
Kenneth I. Chenault, 2001.1.006
Page 69

A Red Record: Section B

The Crisis 42, no. 1 (January 1935)
Featuring Reginald Marsh, *This Is Her First Lynching*, 1934
Charles Deering McCormick Library of Special Collections,
Northwestern University Libraries
Fig. 1.12

Darryl Cowherd (American, b. 1940)
Gage Park Protest, 1967/68
Gelatin silver print
7⁹⁄₁₆ × 11⅛ inches (image); 9⁷⁄₁₆ × 11¹³⁄₁₆ inches (sheet)
Art Institute of Chicago, through prior gifts of the Harold
and Esther Edgerton Family Foundation and D. R. Ryan Jr.,
2017.161
Not Illustrated

Bob Crawford (American, 1938–2015)
Untitled, 1966
Gelatin silver print
5⅞ × 7¹⁵⁄₁₆ inches (image); 7⅞ × 9⅞ inches (sheet)
Art Institute of Chicago, through prior gifts of Emanuel and
Edithann M. Gerard and Hugh Edwards, 2017.173
Fig. 5.1

Ken Gonzales-Day (American, b. 1964)
East First Street (St. James Park), from *Erased Lynching
Series I*, 2000–2013
Archival inkjet on rag paper mounted on cardstock
5 × 3¹³⁄₁₆ inches
Courtesy of the artist and Luis De Jesus, Los Angeles
Fig. 1.16

Ken Gonzales-Day (American, b. 1964)
East First Street #2 (St. James Park), from *Erased Lynching
Series I*, 2000–2013
Archival inkjet print on rag paper mounted on cardstock
5 × 3¹³⁄₁₆ inches
Courtesy of the artist and Luis De Jesus, Los Angeles
Not illustrated

Ken Gonzales-Day (American, b. 1964)
Souvenir, from *Erased Lynching Series I*, 2000–2013
Archival inkjet print on rag paper mounted on cardstock
3¹³⁄₁₆ × 6 inches
Courtesy of the artist and Luis De Jesus, Los Angeles
Not illustrated

Ken Gonzales-Day (American, b. 1964)
Lynching of Jesse Washington, Waco, TX, 1916, 2019, from
Erased Lynching Series II, 2006–20
Inkjet on rag paper mounted on cardstock
6¼ × 3⅞ inches
Courtesy of the artist and Luis De Jesus, Los Angeles
Fig. 1.14

Ken Gonzales-Day (American, b. 1964)
Lynching of Unidentified African American, c. 1925, 2017, from *Erased Lynching Series II*, 2006–20
Inkjet on rag paper mounted on cardstock
6 × 4½ inches
Courtesy of the artist and Luis De Jesus, Los Angeles
Fig. 1.15

Kerry James Marshall (American, b. 1955)
Heirlooms and Accessories, 2002
Three inkjet prints on paper in wooden artist's frame with rhinestones
Each: 51 × 46 inches (image); 57 × 53 × 3 inches (frame)
Smart Museum of Art, University of Chicago, Purchase, Smart Family Fund Foundation for Contemporary Art, and Paul and Miriam Kirkley Fund for Acquisitions, 2004.12a-c
Page 17; figs. 1.13, 5.6

Abstraction and Affect

Laylah Ali (American, b. 1968)
Note drawing, 2008
Ink, colored pencil, ballpoint, and gouache on paper
11 × 8½ inches
Courtesy of the artist
Fig. 1.18

Laylah Ali (American, b. 1968)
Note drawing, 2008
Ink, colored pencil, ballpoint, and gouache on paper
11 × 8½ inches
Courtesy of the artist
Fig. 1.19

Laylah Ali (American, b. 1968)
Note drawing, 2008
Ink, colored pencil, ballpoint, and gouache on paper
11 × 8½ inches
Courtesy of the artist
Fig. 1.20

Laylah Ali (American, b. 1968)
Note drawing, 2008
Ink, colored pencil, ballpoint, and gouache on paper
11 × 8½ inches
Courtesy of the artist
Fig. 1.21

Melvin Edwards (American, b. 1937)
Ida W.B., from the *Lynch Fragments* series, 1990
Welded steel
13 × 14 × 10 inches
Courtesy of the artist and Alexander Gray Associates, New York; Stephen Friedman Gallery, London
Fig. 3.5

Melvin Edwards (American, b. 1937)
Southern Season, from the *Lynch Fragments* series, 1990
Welded steel
14 × 14¾ × 10 inches
Courtesy of the artist and Alexander Gray Associates, New York; Stephen Friedman Gallery, London
Fig. 3.6

Theaster Gates (American, b. 1973)
In Case of Race Riot II, 2011
Wood, pigment, plastic, metal, adhesive
33½ × 26⅝ × 6 inches
Brooklyn Museum of Art, Purchase gift of Jill and Jay Bernstein, 2011.9
Fig. 3.7

Theaster Gates (American, b. 1973)
Minority Majority, 2012
Decommissioned fire hoses and vinyl on plywood
66 × 111½ × 3¾ inches
Whitney Museum of American Art, New York, Gift of Barbara and Michael Gamson, 2016.262
Fig. 3.8

Wilmer Jennings (American, 1910–1990)
At the End of the Rope, 1935
Linocut
8½ × 11 inches
Kenkeleba Gallery, New York
Not illustrated

Christian Marclay (American, b. 1955)
Guitar Drag, 2000
Video projection
14 minutes
Courtesy of the artist and Paula Cooper Gallery, New York
Fig. 1.22

Mendi + Keith Obadike
Number Stations 2 [Red Record], 2015–ongoing
Performance
Courtesy of the artists
Not illustrated

Howardena Pindell (American, b. 1943)
Four Little Girls, 2020
Mixed media on canvas
96 × 108 × 25 inches
Courtesy of the artist and Garth Greenan Gallery
Page 67

Paul Rucker (American, b. 1968)
January 1–September 14, 1919, Red Summer, from the series *Soundless*, 2015
Pine, blowtorch, encaustic, acrylic
16 × 16 × 2 inches
Courtesy of the artist
Page 86

Paul Rucker (American, b. 1968)
June 7, 1998, Jasper, Texas, from the series *Soundless*, 2015
Spruce, purfling, acrylic
48 × 16 × 4 inches
Courtesy of the artist
Fig. 1.23

Paul Rucker (American, b. 1968)
May 15, 1916, Waco, Texas, from the series *Soundless*, 2015
Plywood, blowtorch, encaustic, acrylic
16 × 16 × 2 inches
Courtesy of the artist
Page 87

Paul Rucker (American, b. 1968)
September 15, 1963, Birmingham, Alabama, from the series *Soundless*, 2015
Spruce, purfling, acrylic
16 × 42 × 2 inches
Courtesy of the artist
Fig. 1.24

Molly Jae Vaughan (British, b. 1977) and collaborators
Lateisha "Teish" Green, 400 Block of Seymour Street, Syracuse, from *Project 42*, 2021
Inkjet-printed fabric
Dimensions variable
Courtesy of the artist, commissioned by the Block Museum of Art
Not illustrated

Written on the Body

Elizabeth Catlett (American, 1915–2012)
Civil Rights Congress, 1949
Linocut on cream wove paper
12³⁄₁₆ × 7¹⁄₁₆ inches (image); 8³⁄₁₆ × 12¹³⁄₁₆ inches (sheet)
Art Institute of Chicago, restricted gift of the Leadership Advisory Committee, 2005.143
Page 84

Elizabeth Catlett (American, 1915–2012)
Target Practice, 1970
Bronze, wood, and metal
19½ × 12 × 15¾ inches
Amistad Research Center, Tulane University
Page 85

Darryl Cowherd (American, b. 1940)
Stop White Police from Killing Us—St. Louis, MO, ca. 1966–67
Gelatin silver print
15 × 19 inches (image); 16 × 20 inches (sheet)
Museum of Contemporary Photography, Columbia College, Chicago, 2018.138
Fig. 5.2

David Antonio Cruz (American, b. 1974)
anotherroadblockinourway,butifwegowegotogether, the detroit kids, 2020
Oil and latex on wood panel
72 × 48 inches
Courtesy of the artist and Monique Meloche Gallery, Chicago; Collection of Hill Harper, Detroit
Page 103

Emory Douglas (American, b. 1943)
November 16, 1972, 1972
Photo collage
20 × 14 inches
Richard J. Daley Library, Special Collections and Archives, University of Illinois at Chicago
Page 100

Emory Douglas (American, b. 1943)
May 26, 1973, 1973
Ink wash and graphite pencil
20 × 14 inches
Richard J. Daley Library, Special Collections and Archives, University of Illinois at Chicago
Page 101

Carl and Karen Pope (American, b. 1961)
Palimpsest, 1998–99
Single-channel video, color with sound
6:37 minutes
Courtesy of Carl and Karen Pope
Pages 52–53; fig. 1.27

Lorna Simpson (American, b. 1960)
Necklines, 1989
Gelatin silver prints and engraved Plexiglas plaques
Overall: 68½ × 70 inches
Museum of Contemporary Art, Chicago
Not illustrated

Lorna Simpson (American, b. 1960)
Untitled (Two Necklines), 1989
Two gelatin silver prints on paper and eleven plastic
plaques
36 inches (diameter, each print); dimensions variable
(plastic plaques)
Collection of Carolyn Campagna Kleefeld Contemporary
Art Museum of California State University, Long Beach,
Purchased with funds from the National Endowment for the
Arts, 1990.6a–m
Figs. 1.28, 5.7

Dox Thrash (American, 1893–1965)
After the Lynching, late 1930s
Carborundum mezzotint printed in black ink on wove paper
6¹⁄₁₆ × 8⅞ inches (plate); 8¹⁄₁₆ × 11¹³⁄₁₆ inches (sheet)
Virginia Museum of Fine Arts, Kathleen Boone Samuels
Memorial Fund, 2017.27
Page 66

Carrie Mae Weems (American, b. 1953)
Mirror, Mirror, 1987
Gelatin silver print with text panels
26 × 20¾ × 1½ inches (framed)
Courtesy of the artist and Jack Shainman Gallery, New York
Page 102

Bibliography

Abdur-Rahman, Aliyyah. "'This Horrible Exhibition': Sexuality in Slave Narratives." In *The Oxford Handbook of Slave Narratives*, edited by John Ernest. New York: Oxford University Press, 2014. DOI: 10.1093/oxfordhb /9780199731480.013.009.

Alexander, Elizabeth. "'Can You Be BLACK and Look at This?': Reading the Rodney King Video(s)." In *Black Male: Representations of Masculinity in Contemporary American Art*, edited by Thelma Golden, 90–110. New York: Whitney Museum of American Art, 1994.

Alexander, Elizabeth. "'Can You Be Black and Look at This?': Reading the Rodney King Video(s)." *Public Culture* 7, no. 1 (October 1, 1994): 77–94. http://doi.org/10.1215 /08992363-7-1-77.

Alexander Gray Associates. "Melvin Edwards, *Lynch Fragments*, 1960s–Present." Accessed April 7, 2021, http://www.alexandergray.com/series-projects/melvin -edwards3.

Allen, James, ed. *Without Sanctuary: Lynching Photography in America*. Santa Fe, NM: Twin Palms, 2000.

Anderson, William C. "Against Consuming Images of the Brutalized, Dead and Dying." *Hyperallergic*, June 1, 2018. http://hyperallergic.com/445105/against-consuming -images-of-the-brutalized-dead-and-dying.

Andrews, William L. *To Tell a Free Story: The First Century of Afro-American Autobiography, 1760–1860*. Urbana: University of Illinois, 1986.

Apel, Dora. *Imagery of Lynching: Black Men, White Women, and the Mob*. New Brunswick, NJ: Rutgers University Press, 2004.

Apel, Dora, and Shawn Michelle Smith. *Lynching Photographs*. Berkeley: University of California Press, 2007.

Aranke, Sampada. "Blackouts and Other Visual Escapes." *Art Journal* (Winter 2020): 62–75.

Aranke, Sampada. *Death's Futurity: The Visual Life of Black Power*. Durham, NC: Duke University Press, forthcoming.

Ater, Renée. "Race, Gender, and Nation: Rethinking the Sculpture of Meta Warrick Fuller." PhD diss. University of Maryland, 2000.

Baker, Courtney R. *Humane Insight: Looking at Images of African American Suffering and Death*. New Black Studies. Urbana: University of Illinois Press, 2015.

Baldwin, James. "Nothing Personal (1964)." *Contributions in Black Studies* 6, no. 1 (2008): 56.

Bambara, Toni Cade. *The Salt Eaters*. New York: Vintage, 1992.

Battle-Baptiste, Whitney, and Britt Rusert, eds. *W. E. B. Du Bois's Data Portraits Visualizing Black America: The Color Line at the Turn of the Twentieth Century*. Princeton, NJ: Princeton University Press, 2018.

Beach, Caitlin. "Meta Warrick Fuller's Mary Turner and the Memory of Mob Violence." *NKA: Journal of Contemporary African Art* 36 (May 2015): 16–27.

Beckwith, Naomi, and Valerie Cassel Oliver, eds. *Howardena Pindell: What Remains to Be Seen*. Chicago: Museum of Contemporary Art, 2018.

Bell, Alexandra. "2018 Infinity Award: Applied—Alexandra Bell." International Center of Photography, April 10, 2018. http://www.youtube.com/watch?v=-MHXY6vIoe4.

Bell, Alexandra. "Alexandra Bell's Revelations." *Columbia Journalism Review* (Fall 2018). http://www.cjr.org /special_report/alexandra-bell-new-york-central-park -five.php.

Bell, Alexandra. "Art that Forms New Narratives." Story-tellers Summit 2019, National Geographic Society. http://www.youtube.com/watch?v=wXjkxdRtGe8.

Bell, Alexandra. "An Evening with Alexandra Bell." Spencer Museum of Art, March 6, 2018. http://www.youtube.com /watch?v=1sG54qALVrA.

Bender, Pennee, Joshua Brown, Donna Thompson Ray et al. *Visual Culture of the Civil War* website. http://civilwar .picturinghistory.gc.cuny.edu.

Benzon, Paul, and Sarah Sweeney, eds. "The Aesthetics of Erasure," special issue, *Media-N: Journal of the New Media Caucus* 11, no. 1 (Spring 2015). http://median .newmediacaucus.org/the_aesthetics_of_erasure/.

Bindman, David, Henry Louis Gates, and Karen C. C. Dalton. *The Image of the Black in Western Art*. New ed., Cambridge, MA: Belknap Press of Harvard University Press, 2010–11.

Bourdieu, Pierre. "The Force of Law: Toward a Sociology of the Juridical Field." *The Hastings Law Journal* 38, no. 5 (1987): 805–53.

Brundage, W. Fitzhugh. *Under Sentence of Death: Lynching in the South*. Chapel Hill: UNC Press Books, 2017.

Bunch, Lonnie G., III. *A Fool's Errand: Creating the National Museum of African American History and Culture in the Age of Bush, Obama, and Trump*. Washington, DC: Smithsonian Books, 2019.

Butler, Judith. "Endangered/Endangering: Schematic Racism and White Paranoia." In *Reading Rodney King / Reading Urban Uprising*, edited by Robert Gooding-Williams, 15–22. New York: Routledge, 1993.

Camp, Stephanie M. H., "Early European Views of African Bodies: Beauty." In *Slavery and Sexuality: Reclaiming Intimate Histories in the Americas*, edited by Daina Ramey Berry and Leslie M. Harris, 9–32. Athens: University of Georgia Press, 2019.

Campt, Tina. *Listening to Images*. Durham, NC: Duke University Press, 2018.

Carver, Jordan H. *Spaces of Disappearance: The Architecture of Extraordinary Rendition*. New York: Terreform, 2018.

Cascone, Sarah. "'We Failed': A Cleveland Museum Apologizes for Cancelling an Exhibition on Police Brutality without Consulting the Artist." *Artnet.com*, June 9, 2020. http://news.artnet.com/exhibitions/moca-cleveland -apologizes-cancelling-shaun-leonardo-exhibition -1882671.

Chadbourn, James Harmon. *Lynching and the Law*. Clark, NJ: Lawbook Exchange, 2008.

Cobb, Jasmine Nichole. *Picture Freedom: Remaking Black Visuality in the Early Nineteenth Century*. New York: New York University Press, 2015.

Cooks, Bridget R. *Exhibiting Blackness: African Americans and the American Art Museum*. Amherst: University of Massachusetts Press, 2011.

Copeland, Huey. *Bound to Appear: Art, Slavery, and the Site of Blackness in Multicultural America*. Chicago: University of Chicago Press, 2013.

Copeland, Huey. "Making Black Feminist Art Histories." *American Art* 31, no. 2 (Summer 2017): 27–29.

Copeland, Huey, and Krista Thompson, eds. "New World Slavery and the Matter of the Visual," special issue, *Representations* 113, no. 1 (Winter 2011).

Crenshaw, Kimberlé, and Gary Peller. "Reel Time / Real Justice." In *Reading Rodney King / Reading Urban Uprising*, edited by Robert Gooding-Williams, 56–70. New York: Routledge, 1993.

Davis, Charles T., and Henry Louis Gates Jr., eds. *The Slave's Narrative*. New York: Oxford University Press, 1991.

Dees, Janet. "Rewriting the Body: Carl and Karen Pope's 'Palimpsest.'" Master's thesis. University of Delaware, 2005.

Derrida, Jacques. *Archive Fever: A Freudian Impression*. Chicago: University of Chicago Press, 1998.

Douglass, Frederick. *Narrative of the Life of Frederick Douglass*. Boston: Antislavery Office, 1845.

D'Souza, Aruna. "Act I: Open Casket, Whitney Biennial, 2017." *Whitewalling: Art, Race and Protest in 3 Acts*. New York: Badlands Unlimited, 2018.

Du Bois, W. E. B. "To the Nations of the World" (1900). In *W. E. B. Du Bois: A Reader*, edited by David Levering Lewis, 639. New York: Henry Holt, 1995.

Dunbar, Erica Armstrong. "A Mental and Moral Feast: Reading, Writing, and Sentimentality in Black Philadelphia." *Journal of Women's History* 16, no. 1 (Spring 2004): 78–102.

Edwards, Adrienne. *Blackness in Abstraction*. New York: Pace Gallery, 2016.

Equiano, Olaudah. *The Interesting Narrative of the Life of Olaudah Equiano, Or Gustavus Vassa, the African. Written by Himself*. London: The Author, 1789.

Finley, Cheryl. *Committed to Memory: The Art of the Slave Ship Icon*. Princeton, NJ: Princeton University Press, 2018.

Fleetwood, Nicole R. *Marking Time: Art in the Age of Mass Incarceration*. Cambridge, MA: Harvard University Press, 2020.

Fleetwood, Nicole R. *On Racial Icons: Blackness and the Public Imagination*. New Brunswick, NJ: Rutgers University Press, 2015.

Fleetwood, Nicole R. *Troubling Vision: Performance, Visuality, and Blackness*. Chicago: University of Chicago Press, 2011.

Forensic Architecture, ed. *Forensis: The Architecture of Public Truth*. Berlin: Sternberg Press, 2014.

Fox-Amato, Matthew. *Exposing Slavery: Photography, Human Bondage, and the Birth of Modern Visual Politics in America*. Oxford: Oxford University Press, 2019.

Francis, Megan M. *Civil Rights and the Making of the Modern American State*. New York: Cambridge University Press, 2014.

Gates, Theaster, and Lilly Wei. "Theaster Gates." *Art in America*, December 2011. http://www.artnews.com /art-in-america/features/theaster-gates-62915/.

Gonzalez, Aston. *Visualizing Quality: African American Rights and Visual Culture in the Nineteenth Century*. Chapel Hill: University of North Carolina, 2020, Kindle version.

Gordon, Avery. *Ghostly Matters: Haunting and the Socio-logical Imagination*. Minneapolis: University of Minnesota Press, 1997.

Harper, Phillip Brian. *Abstractionist Aesthetics: Artistic Form and Social Critique in African American Culture*. New York: New York University Press, 2015.

Harris, Leslie M. "From Abolitionist Amalgamators to 'Rulers of the Five Points': The Discourse of Interracial Sex and Reform in Antebellum New York City." In *Sex, Love, Race: Crossing Boundaries in North American History*, edited by Martha Hodes, 191–212. New York: New York University Press, 1999.

Hartman, Saidiya V. *Scenes of Subjection: Terror, Slavery, and Self-Making in Nineteenth-Century America*. New York: Oxford University Press, 1996.

Herzog, Melanie. *Elizabeth Catlett: An American Artist*. Seattle: University of Washington Press, 2005.

Higginbotham, Carmenita. *The Urban Scene: Race, Reginald Marsh and American Art*. University Park: Pennsyl-vania State University Press, 2015.

Jones, Kellie. *South of Pico: African American Artists in Los Angeles in the 1960s and 1970s*. Durham, NC: Duke University Press, 2017.

Jones Royster, Jacqueline, ed. *Southern Horrors and Other Writings: The Anti-Lynching Campaign of Ida B. Wells, 1892–1900*. New York: Bedford Books, 1997.

Kase, Carlos. "'This Guitar Has Seconds to Live': Guitar Drag's Archaeology of Indeterminacy and Violence." *Discourse* 30, no. 3 (Fall 2008): 419–42.

Kato, Daniel. *Liberalizing Lynching: Building a New Racial-ized State*. New York: Oxford University Press, 2016.

Kirschke, Amy. *Art in* Crisis: *W. E. B. Du Bois and the Struggle for African American Identity and Memory*. Bloomington: Indiana University Press, 2007.

Langa, Helen. "Two Antilynching Exhibitions: Politicized Viewpoints, Racial Perspectives, Gendered Constraints." *American Art* 13, no. 1 (Spring 1999): 10–39.

Lapsansky, Emma Jones. "'Since They Got Those Separate Churches': Afro-Americans and Racism in Jacksonian Philadelphia." *American Quarterly* 32, no. 1 (1980): 54–78.

Lapsansky, Phillip. "Graphic Discord: Abolitionist and Antiabolitionist Images." In *The Abolitionist Sisterhood: Women's Political Culture in Antebellum America*, edited by Jean Fagan Yellin and John C. Van Horne, 219–30. Ithaca, NY: Cornell University Press, 1994.

Lewis, Samella. *African American Art and Artists*. Berkeley: University of California Press, 1990.

Lewis, Samella. *Elizabeth Catlett*. Claremont, CA: Hancraft Studios, 1984.

Lewis, Samella, et al. *Elizabeth Catlett: Works on Paper, 1944–1992*. Hampton, VA: Hampton University Museum, 1993.

Lewis, Sarah. *Whitfield Lovell: Kin*. New York: Skira Rizzoli, 2016.

Library of Congress. *A Small Nation of People: W. E. B. Du Bois and African American Portraits of Progress*. New York: HarperCollins, 2005.

Lipsitz, George. *The Possessive Investment in Whiteness: How White People Profit from Identity Politics*. Philadel-phia: Temple University Press, 2006/2018.

Marcus, Greil. "Guitar Drag: 2006/2000." *The History of Rock 'n' Roll in Ten Songs*. New Haven, CT: Yale University Press, 2014.

Marriott, David. *On Black Men*. New York: Columbia University Press, 2000.

Masur, Kate. "'A Rare Phenomenon of Philological Vegeta-tion': The Word 'Contraband' and the Meanings of Emanci-pation in the United States." *Journal of American History* 93, no. 4 (March 2007): 1,050–84.

McInnis, Maurie. "Representing the Slave Trade." In *Slaves Waiting for Sale: Abolitionist Art and the American Slave Trade*. Chicago: University of Chicago Press, 2011.

McNair, Glenn. "The Elijiah Burritt Affair: David Walker's *Appeal* and Partisan Journalism in Antebellum Milledgeville." *Georgia Historical Quarterly* 83, no. 3 (Fall 1999): 448–78.

Mercer, Kobena. *Discrepant Abstraction*. London: Institute of International Visual Arts, 2006.

Morgan, Jennifer L. "'Some Could Suckle over Their Shoulder': Male Travelers, Female Bodies, and the Gendering of Racial Ideology, 1500–1770." *William and Mary Quarterly* 54, no. 1 (1997): 167–92.

Morrison, Toni. *Beloved*. New York: Vintage International, 1987.

Moten, Fred. *In the Break: The Aesthetics of the Black Radical Tradition*. Minneapolis: University of Minnesota Press, 2003.

Mustakeem, Sowande´. *Slavery at Sea: Terror, Sex and Sickness in the Middle Passage*. Urbana: University of Illinois Press, 2016.

Newell, Amanda. "Reginald Dwayne Betts: On Art, Poetry, the Particular Fucked Up Parts of Incarceration, and the Multitudes of I—Interview by Amanda Newell." *Plume*, no. 106 (June 2020). http://plumepoetry.com/reginald-dwayne-betts-on-art-poetry-the-particular-fucked-up-parts-of-incarceration-and-the-multitudes-of-i/.

NXTHVN. "Pleading Freedom: An Exhibition by Titus Kaphar and Reginald Dwayne Betts." Accessed April 23, 2021, http://www.nxthvn.com/calendar/1906/.

Painter, Nell Irvin. "Representing Truth: Sojourner Truth's Knowing and Becoming Known." *Journal of American History* 81, no. 2 (1994): 461–92.

Painter, Nell Irvin. *Sojourner Truth: A Life, A Symbol*. New York: Norton, 1991.

Park, Marlene. "Lynching and Anti-lynching: Art and Politics in the 1930s." *Prospects: Annual of American Cultural Studies* 18 (1993): 311–65.

Philip, M. NourbeSe. *Zong!*. Middletown: Wesleyan University Press, 2008.

Polgar, Paul J. *Standard-Bearers of Equality: America's First Abolition Movement*. Chapel Hill: University of North Carolina Press, 2019. doi:10.5149/9781469653952_polgar.

Potts, Alex. "Melvin Edwards's Sculptural Intensity." In *Melvin Edwards: Five Decades*, edited by Catherine Craft. Dallas: Nasher Sculpture Center, 2015.

Preston, Rohan. "In His Journey from Jail to Yale Law, Felon-Turned Poet 'Writes to Remember Who I Am.'" *Star Tribune*, March 6, 2021. http://www.startribune.com/in-his-journey-from-jail-to-yale-law-felon-turned-poet-writes-to-remember-who-i-am/600030677/?refresh=true.

Raiford, Leigh. *Imprisoned in a Luminous Glare: Photography and the African American Freedom Struggle*. Chapel Hill: University of North Carolina Press, 2011.

Rediker, Marcus. *The Slave Ship: A Human History*. New York: Viking, 2007.

Redmond, Shana L. *Everything Man: The Form and Function of Paul Robeson*. Durham, NC: Duke University Press, 2020.

Robinson, Imani. *Objects Who Testify*. London: PSS, 2019.

Rush, Bobby L. "H.R.35—116th Congress (2019–2020): Emmett Till Antilynching Act." www.congress.gov/bill/116th-congress/house-bill/35/text.

Savage, Kirk. *Standing Soldiers, Kneeling Slaves: Race, War, and Monument in Nineteenth-Century America*. 2nd ed., Princeton, NJ: Princeton University Press, 2018.

Sharpe, Christina. *In the Wake: On Blackness and Being*. Durham, NC: Duke University Press, 2016.

Sinha, Manisha. *The Slave's Cause: A History of Abolition*. New Haven, CT: Yale University Press, 2016.

Slavery Images: A Visual Record of the African Slave Trade and Slave Life in the Early African Diaspora. Accessed December 20, 2020, http://slaveryimages.org/.

Smallwood, Stephanie. *Saltwater Slavery: A Middle Passage from Africa to American Diaspora*. Cambridge, MA: Harvard University Press, 2007.

Smith, Shawn Michelle. *Photographic Returns: Racial Justice and the Time of Photography*. Durham, NC: Duke University Press, 2020.

Smith, Shawn Michelle. *Photography on the Color Line: W. E. B. Du Bois, Race, and Visual Culture*. Durham, NC: Duke University Press, 2004.

Spillers, Hortense. "Mama's Baby, Papa's Maybe: An American Grammar Book." *Diacritics* 17, no. 2 (Summer 1987): 64–81.

St. Felix, Doreen. "How Alexandra Bell Is Disrupting Racism in Journalism." *New Yorker*, May 29, 2018. http://www.newyorker.com/culture/culture-desk/how-alexandra-bell-is-disrupting-racism-in-journalism.

Stauffer, John, Zoe Trodd, and Celeste-Marie Bernier. *Picturing Frederick Douglass: An Illustrated Biography of the Nineteenth Century's Most Photographed Man*. New York: Liveright, 2015.

Thompson, Krista. "The Evidence of Things Not Photographed: Slavery and the Historical Memory in the British West Indies." *Representations* 113 (Winter 2011): 39–71.

Thompson, Krista. *An Eye for the Tropics: Tourism, Photography, and Framing the Caribbean Picturesque*. Durham, NC: Duke University Press, 2006.

Torres, Sasha. *Black, White, and in Color: Television and Black Civil Rights*. Princeton, NJ: Princeton University Press, 2003.

Vendryes, Margaret Rose. "Hanging on Their Walls: An Art Commentary on Lynching, the Forgotten 1935 Art Exhibition." *Race Consciousness: African-American Studies for the New Century*, edited by Judith Fossett and Jeffrey Tucker. New York: New York University Press, 1997.

Walker Howe, Daniel. *What God Hath Wrought: The Transformation of America, 1815–1848*. New York: Oxford University Press, 2007.

Wallace, Maurice O., and Shawn Michelle Smith, eds. *Pictures and Progress: Early Photography and the Making of African American Identity*. Durham, NC: Duke University Press, 2012.

Wallace, Michele. *Dark Designs and Visual Culture*. Durham, NC: Duke University Press, 2004.

Wanzo, Rebecca. *Content of Our Caricature: African American Comic Art and Political Belonging*. New York: New York University Press, 2020.

Weheliye, Alexander. "Diagrammatics as Physiognomy: W. E. B. Du Bois's Graphic Modernities." *CR: The New Centennial Review* 15, no. 2 (2015).

White, Walter F. "The Work of the Mob." *The Crisis* (September 1918): 221–23.

Willis, Deborah. *Picturing Us: African American Identity in Photography*. New York: New Press, 1996.

Willis, Deborah. *Reflections in Black: A History of Black Photographers, 1840 to the Present*. New York: Norton, 2000.

Willis, Deborah, and Barbara Krauthamer. *Envisioning Emancipation: Black Americans and the End of Slavery*. Philadelphia: Temple University Press, 2013.

Wood, Marcus. *Blind Memory: Visual Representations of Slavery in England and America, 1780–1865*. Manchester, UK: Manchester University Press, 2000.

Wood, Marcus. *The Horrible Gift of Freedom: Atlantic Slavery and the Representation of Emancipation*. Athens: University of Georgia Press, 2010.

Wood, Marcus. "Valency and Abjection in the Lynching Postcard: A Test Case in the Reclamation of Black Visual Culture." *Slavery & Abolition* 34, no. 2 (June 2013): 205. http://doi.org/10.1080/0144039X.2013.791173.

Young, Harvey. "Still Standing: Daguerreotypes, Photography, and the Black Body." In *Embodying Black Experience: Stillness, Critical Memory and the Black Body*, 26–75. Ann Arbor: University of Michigan Press, 2010.

Contributor Biographies

Sampada Aranke is an assistant professor of art history, theory, and criticism at the School of the Art Institute of Chicago. Her research interests include performance theories of embodiment, visual culture, and Black cultural and aesthetic theory. Her work has been published in *e-flux*, *Artforum*, *Art Journal*, *ASAP/J*, *October*, and *Trans-Scripts: An Interdisciplinary Online Journal in the Humanities and Social Sciences at UC Irvine*. She has written catalogue essays for Sadie Barnette, Zachary Fabri, Rashid Johnson, Kambui Olujimi, Faith Ringgold, and Sable Elyse Smith. She is currently working on a book manuscript titled *Death's Futurity: The Visual Life of Black Power* (Duke University Press, forthcoming).

Courtney R. Baker is associate professor of English at the University of California, Riverside. She cofounded the program in Black studies at Occidental College in 2018 and served as its inaugural chair. Her book, *Humane Insight: Looking at Images of African American Suffering and Death* (University of Illinois Press, 2015; paperback 2017), explores the long history of African American activists' theorizations and mobilizations of Black bodily precarity. Her research focuses on Blackness, language, and the visual representation of humanist principles. Her scholarship has been published in *Camera Obscura*, the *Journal of American Culture*, *Parallax*, *ASAP/J*, *Avidly*, *Huffington Post: Black Voices*, and *New Black MAN*. Her chapter on African American visual culture in the 1970s was published in *Black Cultural Production after Civil Rights*, edited by Robert Patterson. Her current book manuscript, titled *Tyranny of Realism: Twenty-First Century Blackness and the Ends of Cinema*, examines formalist techniques in recent American and British Black films.

Huey Copeland is Andrew W. Mellon Professor at the Center for Advanced Study in the Visual Arts at the National Gallery of Art, Washington, DC (2020–22), and BFC Presidential Associate Professor of the History of Art at the University of Pennsylvania. His research and teaching focus on modern and contemporary art with an emphasis on articulations of Blackness in the Western visual field from the late eighteenth century to the present. In addition to penning numerous articles, essays, interviews, and reviews, Copeland is an editor of *October* and author of *Bound to Appear: Art, Slavery, and the Site of Blackness in Multicultural America* (University of Chicago Press, 2013).

Janet Dees is the Steven and Lisa Munster Tananbaum Curator of Modern and Contemporary Art at the Block Museum of Art, Northwestern University, where her exhibitions include *Hank Willis Thomas: Unbranded* (2018); *Experiments in Form: Sam Gilliam, Alan Shields, and Frank Stella* (2018); *Carrie Mae Weems: Ritual and Revolution* (2017); *Kader Attia: Reflecting Memory* (2017); and *If You Remember, I'll Remember* (2017). She has also held educational and curatorial positions at SITE Santa Fe, the New York African Burial Ground Project (now the African Burial Ground National Monument), the Metropolitan Museum of Art, the Rosenbach Museum and Library, and the Paul R. Jones Collection of African American Art at the University of Delaware. She is coeditor of and contributor to *If You Remember, I'll Remember* (Block Museum of Art, 2021), *Unsettled Landscapes* (SITE Santa Fe, 2014), and *Linda Mary Montano: You Too Are a Performance Artist* (SITE Santa Fe, 2013).

Leslie M. Harris, professor of history at Northwestern University, is the author of *In the Shadow of Slavery: African Americans in New York City, 1626–1863* (University of Chicago Press, 2003); *Slavery and Sexuality: Reclaiming Intimate Histories in the Americas* (University of Georgia, 2018), with Daina Ramey Berry; and *Slavery and the University: Histories and Legacies* (University of Georgia, 2019), with James T. Campbell and Alfred L. Brophy. She coedited *Slavery in New York* (New Press, 2005), with Ira Berlin; and *Slavery and Freedom in Savannah* (University of Georgia Press, 2014), with Daina Ramey Berry. Harris cofounded and codirected the Transforming Community Project at Emory University, which engaged members of the university community in dialogue, research, and teaching on racial and other forms of human diversity. As the 2020–21 Beatrice Shepherd Blane fellow at the Radcliffe Institute for Advanced Study at Harvard University, she is completing a book titled *Leaving New Orleans: A Personal Urban History*.

LaCharles Ward is a postdoctoral fellow at the University of Pennsylvania in the Annenberg School for Communication. He is a cultural theorist whose research spans the areas of Black visual culture as theory and method, art and aesthetic practices, film and media, history and theories of photography, and law. Ward's current book project, *Black Forensis: Evidence, Visuality, and the Aesthetics of Black Life*, examines the seemingly fixed but mercurial notion of "evidence" as it is brought into relation with anti-Blackness, Black death, and Black life. He received his PhD in rhetoric and public culture from Northwestern University's School of Communication, where he was an affiliate of the Department of African American Studies.

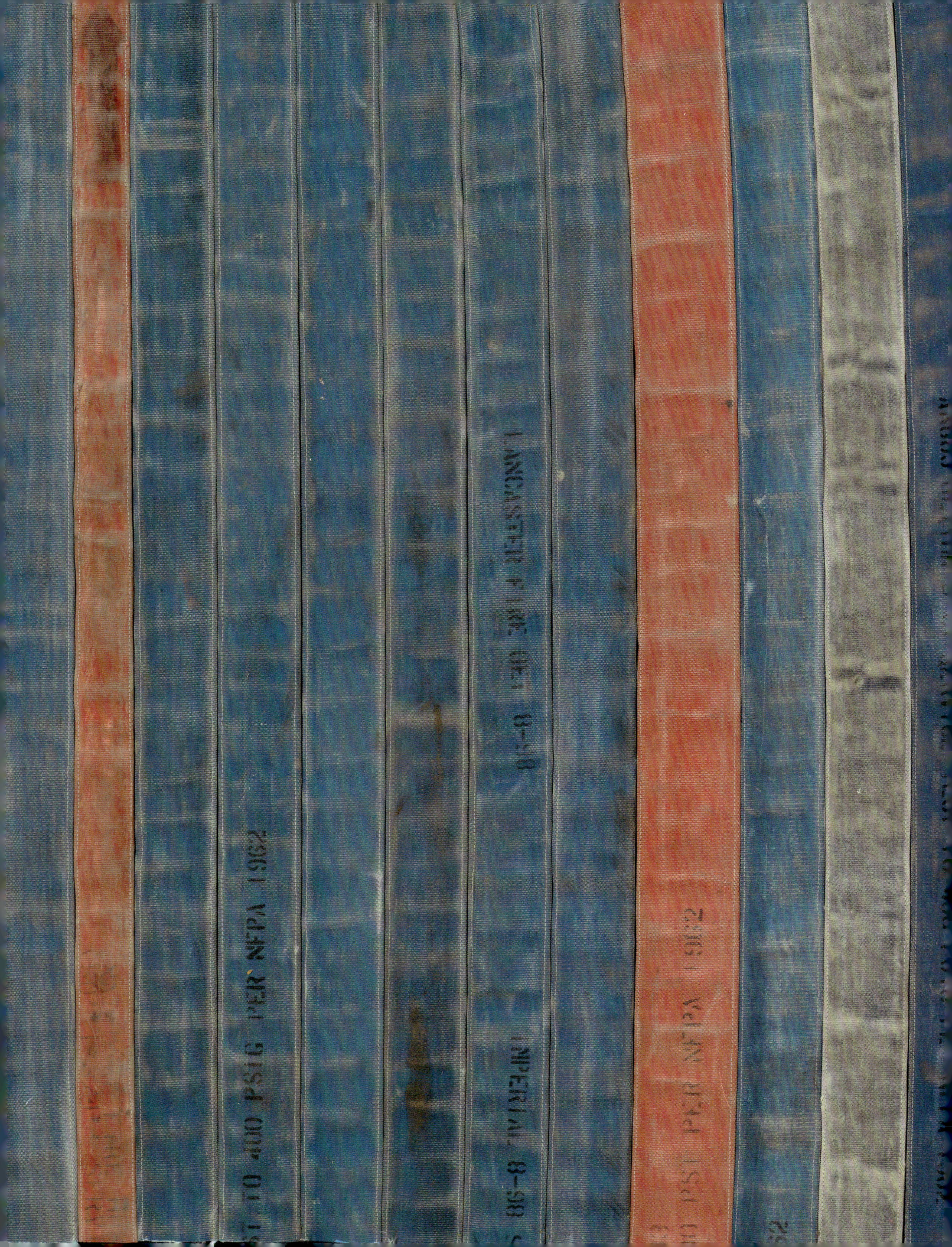

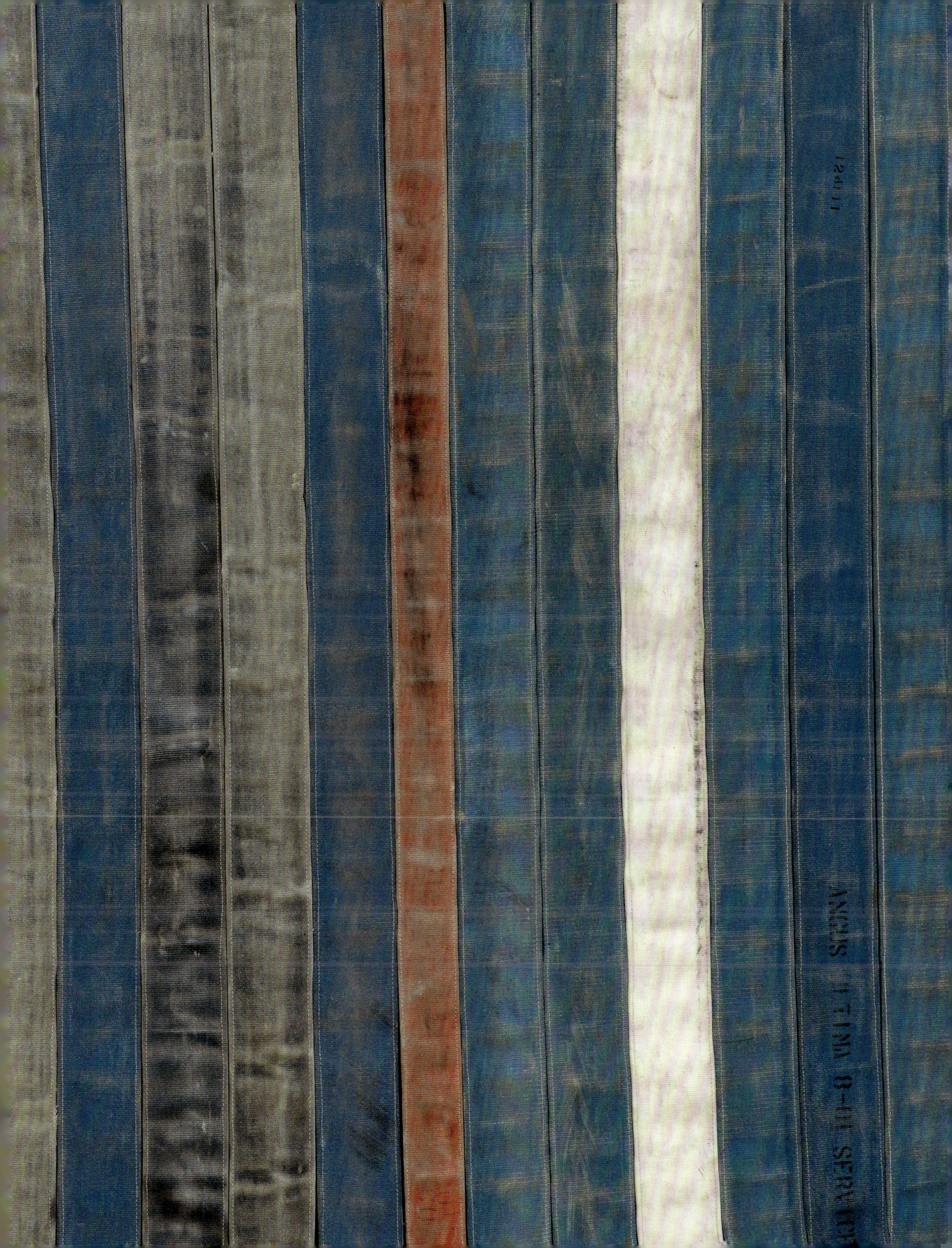

This publication accompanies the exhibition *A Site of Struggle: American Art against Anti-Black Violence*, organized by the Mary and Leigh Block Museum of Art, Northwestern University, on view at the Block January 26–July 10, 2022, and the Montgomery Museum of Fine Arts, August 13–November 6, 2022. The exhibition was curated by Janet Dees, Steven and Lisa Munster Tananbaum Curator of Modern and Contemporary Art at the Block Museum of Art, with the assistance of Alisa Swindell, curatorial research associate.

Lead support for the exhibition is generously provided by the Terra Foundation for American Art. Major support is provided by the Andy Warhol Foundation for the Visual Arts. The project is also supported in part by an award from the National Endowment for the Arts, the Bernstein Family Contemporary Art Fund, the Myers Foundations, the Block DEAI Fund, and the Block Board of Advisors. Generous support is contributed by William Spiegel and Lisa Kadin, the Alumnae of Northwestern University, the David C. and Sarajean Ruttenberg Arts Foundation, the Elizabeth F. Cheney Foundation, and by Lynne Jacobs. The related publication is published by the Block Museum of Art in association with Princeton University Press and is supported by Furthermore: a program of the J. M. Kaplan Fund and the Sandra L. Riggs Publication Fund.

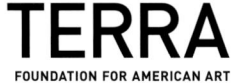

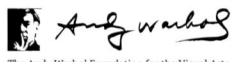

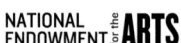

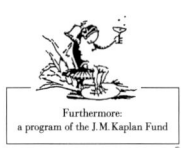

Published by the Mary and Leigh Block Museum of Art
Northwestern University
40 Arts Circle Drive
Evanston, IL 60208
blockmuseum.northwestern.edu

In association with Princeton University Press,
Princeton and Oxford

41 William Street
Princeton, NJ 08540
USA

6 Oxford Street
Woodstock, Oxfordshire OX20 1TR

press.princeton.edu

Produced by Lucia|Marquand, Seattle
luciamarquand.com
Edited by Kristin Swan
Designed by Thomas Eykemans
Typeset by Tina Henderson in Halyard and Freight
Proofread by Brynn Warriner
Printed and bound in Turkey by Ofset Yapimevi

Library of Congress Control Number: 2021947783
ISBN: 978-0-691-20927-2

Frontispiece: Darryl Cowherd, *Stop White Police from Killing Us—St. Louis, MO*, ca. 1966–67 (detail), gelatin silver print, 15 × 19 inches (image); 16 × 20 inches (sheet). Museum of Contemporary Photography, Columbia College, Chicago, 2018.138. Courtesy of Darryl Cowherd.
Pages 52–53: Carl and Karen Pope, *Palimpsest*, 1988–99, still from single-channel video, color with sound, 6:37 minutes. Courtesy of Carl and Karen Pope. Photograph by Clare Britt.
Pages 134–35: Theaster Gates, *Minority Majority*, 2012 (detail), decommissioned fire hoses and vinyl on plywood, 66 × 111½ × 3¾ inches. Whitney Museum of American Art, New York, Gift of Barbara and Michael Gamson, 2016.262.

British Library Cataloging-in-Publication Data is available

10 9 8 7 6 5 4 3 2 1

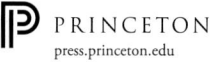

Hemodynamic Monitoring

made Incredibly Easy!

Fifth Edition